Searching
for
Jim

Mark Twain and His Circle Series
Tom Quirk, Editor

Searching for Jim

Slavery in Sam Clemens's World

Terrell Dempsey

University of Missouri Press
Columbia and London

Copyright © 2003 by
The Curators of the University of Missouri
University of Missouri Press, Columbia, Missouri 65201
Printed and bound in the United States of America
First paperback printing, 2005
All rights reserved
5 4 3 2 1   09 08 07 06 05

Library of Congress Cataloging-in-Publication Data

Dempsey, Terrell, 1954–
    Searching for Jim : slavery in Sam Clemens's world / Terrell Dempsey.
        p.   cm. — (Mark Twain and his circle series)
Includes bibliographical references and index.
    ISBN 0-8262-1593-9 (alk. paper)
    1. Twain, Mark, 1835–1910—Political and social views.   2. Twain, Mark, 1835–
1910—Homes and haunts—Missouri—Hannibal.   3. Literature and society—United
States—History—19th century.   4. Antislavery movements—United States—
History—19th century.   5. Slavery—Missouri—Hannibal—History—19th century.
6. Slavery—United States—History—19th century.   7. Authors, American—19th
century—Biography.   8. Twain, Mark, 1835–1910—Family.   9. Hannibal (Mo.)—
Social conditions.   10. Slavery in literature.   11. Racism in literature.   I. Title.
II. Series.
PS1342.S58 D46 2003
818'.409—dc21   2003012787

⊗™   This paper meets the requirements of the
American National Standard for Permanence of Paper
for Printed Library Materials, Z39.48, 1984.

Designer: Jennifer Cropp
Typesetter: BOOKCOMP, Inc.
Printer and binder: Thomson-Shore, Inc.
Typefaces: Palatino, Champers, and Brighton

Frontispiece: Sam Clemens in Hannibal, 1851 or 1852.

For Vicki,
who makes life so
endlessly fascinating.

Contents

Preface

I am an accidental historian. This book began as a quest, which was triggered by a series of events that aroused my curiosity. I have lived and worked in Hannibal, Missouri, since 1987. Just across the river lies Illinois. Today a modern bridge makes passage into that state virtually unnoticeable. My wife and I practice law together. We are licensed in both states and own offices in Hannibal and Quincy, Illinois. Even on days when we don't work in Illinois, we often drive over to the larger town of Quincy for shopping or dinner and a movie. Ours is a seamless bistate world, each side of the river quietly, politely, even blandly midwestern. The two states are, for all practical purposes, indistinguishable. We speak with the same slow flat accent. We are cordial to strangers.

Were it not for Samuel Clemens and his literary alter ego, Mark Twain, few people would have heard of Hannibal, Missouri. The town has consciously sought to exploit the life of its famous resident. It is nearly impossible to count the number of businesses named for Mark Twain or one of his famous characters. Hannibal has adopted "America's Home Town" as its motto. The visitors and convention bureau and the Mark Twain Boyhood Home (never Sam Clemens) have cleaned up local history to match the Norman Rockwell-sanitized version of the town as a childhood paradise. It is a world where little freckle-faced white boys and blonde, pigtailed white girls frolic freely. It is a world of perpetually carefree youth. It is quietly, politely, and blandly wholesome. Its annual Fourth of July celebration is one of the largest in the nation, a three-day extravaganza featuring a jumping frog contest, fence-painting, and fireworks. The centerpiece of that festival is the contest to select Toms and Beckys to represent Hannibal as goodwill ambassadors for the following year.

Hannibal's seventh-graders read *The Adventures of Tom Sawyer* and make a pilgrimage downtown to tour the museum and house where Sam Clemens lived with his mother, sister, and brothers for a short time. The trip is in preparation for the Tom and Becky competition. It is a rite of passage. All students are expected to study Clemens and the local folklore about his life in preparation for the big competition sponsored by the chamber of commerce. Mothers spend hundreds of dollars having costumes sewn for their daughters. Seamstresses who have mastered the calico dresses worn by the Becky contestants are booked far in advance. Acceptable facts are memorized and artifacts collected. Each boy has a slingshot and a fishing pole. Each girl carries a slate chalked "I luv you." All must be able to rattle off the dates relating to "Twain's" life. Of course they must know that Becky Thatcher was really Laura Hawkins. Tom Sawyer was really Mark Twain himself.

It is deadly serious business. For an entire year, the lucky finalists, a dozen boys and girls, get to dress in stylized 1840s costumes and greet the tourists that throng the street around one of the places Sam Clemens lived. The winning pair—the boy and girl who are selected as *the* Tom and Becky—travel around the country as roving ambassadors for Hannibal. The season usually includes a stop at one of the Disney parks, where they are marshals of the daily parade. Some years there may even be a trip abroad.

It was when my oldest daughter reached the seventh grade that it really dawned on me that something was amiss. My daughter was troubled. She is not white. My two daughters are a true American blend of black, Hispanic, and European ancestry—their birth name was Santana. Their birth father was from the Dominican Republic. Their birth mother was a strawberry blonde from Texas. Their mother and I, adoptive parents, are descended from Irish and German immigrants. While there was no written rule that Becky had to be white, there were all those images of her about town. Each year everybody strives to imitate that Norman Rockwell look. Cute curls dangle beneath calico sunbonnets. White gloved hands hold parasols to protect the obligatory fair skin from the sun. It was very clear that the role of Becky was not intended for nonwhites.

This observation drove me to really look at how Hannibal presents the story of Sam Clemens. Besides Tom and Becky, the only other character that draws any mention is Huck Finn. There is a statue of him with Tom downtown at the base of Cardiff Hill, where they roam in perpetual innocence. But Hannibal is careful with Huck. He is just a little rascally for the town to embrace. He is merely the buddy to Tom, the ne'er-do-well childhood friend who will be abandoned in adulthood. He is the supporting cast. There is no mention of any of Clemens's black characters, not even that most famous and controversial of all black characters Clemens created, Jim.

That was not always the case, I knew. I recalled a historical marker—one of several placed about town in the 1930s by the Missouri State Historical Society—that referred to "Niggar Jim." The signs were problematic beyond the obvious misspelling. They referred to fictitious events, not actual history. Then there was the use of the word *Nigger* in the name, which was not only offensive, but wrong in both spelling and usage. The word is not used as part of Jim's name in the novel *Huck Finn.* In Hannibal, however, that's how he was known—because that's how all black people were known until very recently.

The sign actually stood for some time after I arrived in 1987, but in response to complaints, the word *Niggar* was ground off the white painted metal, leaving a very obvious "expletive-deleted" space before the name. After further complaints, the sign was very quietly removed and placed in storage in a city shed. It has since vanished. When the city council agreed to give it to a local history group in 2001, it could not be found. The sign had been one of the few public indications that people of color had ever had anything to do with Hannibal, Sam Clemens, or the creation of the writer Mark Twain.

I reread *Adventures of Huckleberry Finn.* Huckleberry took off from the fictional St. Petersburg with a runaway slave. Modern Hannibal likes to portray itself as Twain's St. Petersburg, but where were the black characters? What had happened to slavery in Hannibal? Where was Jim from *Huckleberry Finn?*

At a friend's suggestion, I read Shelley Fisher Fishkin's *Lighting out for the Territory.* She took the town to task for ignoring its slave history. But what was the story of slavery in Hannibal? I knew that Missouri had been a slave state. On the county courthouse lawn there stands a memorial to rebel soldiers who were executed in 1862.

I started with the bible of local history, the bicentennial history of Hannibal. It was conspicuously quiet about slavery. I spoke with local leaders and was told a variety of what have turned out to be old lies: Yes, there was slavery here, but it was gentler than down south. People weren't beaten or sold. Families weren't split up. It wasn't very common. It wasn't very important—not much to it, really.

Then I began stumbling onto small clues. Rummaging through a bookstall in an antique shop downtown I found a book entitled *A Bible Defence of Slavery.* I had never before encountered the theology of slavery. I would soon learn that churches were the backbone of Missouri's slave culture. The book was touted and sold by a Hannibal newspaper in the 1850s. But looking to books alone was proving to be singularly frustrating.

Then one September Saturday morning I awoke feeling rather discontented. I live just four blocks from the Mississippi River, and my bedroom has a deck. As I sat drinking coffee and looking over the same riverfront where Sam Clemens had played as a boy I thought about *Huckleberry Finn.* How could I find Jim?

The answer came through that most blessed of all phenomena: serendipity. I told Vicki I was going down to the library for a couple of hours—if only I had known the long journey I was beginning. I walked the three blocks to the Hannibal Free Public Library and went to the Missouri Room, the locked haven where books on Twain, Missouri, and Hannibal are kept. There I found it: a metal cabinet filled with spools of microfilm, copies of Hannibal newspapers dating back to the 1840s and from the county seat, Palmyra, from 1839. They included the newspapers where Sam Clemens spent five years as an apprentice.

I took the Hannibal reels and began reading, and there they were: advertisements of slaves for sale or lease, runaway slaves, stories of slave uprisings and acts of violence against whites, countless racist jokes and demeaning stories, and the endless stream of sermons and political speeches attacking abolitionists and defending slavery. I put on a reel from Orion Clemens's newspaper from a time I knew his brother Sam had worked for him. More of the same. I knew that very morning that if I hadn't exactly found Jim, I was on the trail. God bless public libraries.

My wife, Vicki, eagerly joined in the project. She knew when I walked in the door that afternoon that I was on fire, and she became as enthusiastic as I. When I described to her the massive volume of material, she immediately agreed that we should hire students to help with the research. I called a local history professor at Hannibal-LaGrange College and recruited two undergraduate students. They put in hundreds of hours helping us copy every article that referenced slavery. A schoolteacher friend helped over the summer. Friends in the community volunteered to help copy and catalog. We have discovered, photocopied, and indexed thousands of articles.

I found more books through serendipity—one an obscure but fascinating church-published biography of a Methodist minister who lived in Hannibal when Clemens was a boy. I was given access to the session minutes of the Presbyterian church where Clemens's mother and sister were members. I discovered correspondence from people who lived in the area in the 1840s and 1850s and wrote home describing slave culture. I read slave narratives collected in the early part of the twentieth century. Through one of the greatest strokes of luck of all, my friends Frank and Donna Salter went to a sale of surplus city property and purchased long-lost court records of John Marshall Clemens. Those records included the trial of a slave for possession of a knife and sedition.

My seamless Missouri/Illinois world did not exist a century and a half ago. The Mississippi River was not just an unbridged obstacle to commerce, but an iron-curtain-like boundary patrolled by armed men who challenged those who came and went, searched for untended boats, and captured people attempting to flee slavery.

This book is part of the untold story of America's greatest writer and the world that produced him. Surprisingly, Sam Clemens and his family played a role in protecting and perpetuating slavery. In the end, Sam himself helped obscure the history of this world. It was a world in turmoil and conflict. It was a world of faith, not science—where people saw the social order, including slavery, as ordained by God. It was a world of constant vigilance against the internal threat of slave thefts, violence and revolts—and against the ever-growing threat of abolitionism just across the river to the east in Illinois and to the north in Iowa. It was a world where the child who many would claim was the model for Becky Thatcher owned her own slave as a girl. It was a world where human beings were assets and constituted the greatest holding of wealth outside of land in the county. It was a world where itinerant preachers, traveling salesmen, and immigrants were suspected of being abolition agents sent to steal slaves. It was a strange and alien place, a slave culture unlike the more familiar slavery of the cotton plantations in the Deep South, sugarcane plantations of Texas and Louisiana, or the rice plantations of the Gullah region of South Carolina.

This book is the story of the real world where Sam Clemens grew up. His was no Tom Sawyer childhood. This is the true story of his role and experiences with slavery that I discovered while searching for Jim. Here, in the story of Hannibal slavery, lie the very roots of Mark Twain.

Acknowledgments

While I take full responsibility for this book's shortcomings, credit for its strengths must be shared with the many outstanding individuals who did so much to make this work possible. I have discovered that Mark Twain scholars are some of the most delightful, inquisitive people one could ever meet. Prominent professors shared research with me, read my manuscript, guided me, and treated me as a colleague.

I have been fortunate to work with Barb Schmidt, an outstanding researcher, who maintains a fantastic Mark Twain website. If an article by or about Sam Clemens/Mark Twain has been catalogued, she can find it. She has my undying gratitude. I have also been fortunate to have Dave Thomson as a friend and a confidant. I have greatly benefited from his depth of knowledge of Sam Clemens and Hannibal and from his help with materials and illustrations. Dave first took me to old Baptist Cemetery and showed me Agness Flautleroy's grave—a rare and beautiful moment.

Vic Doyno of the State University of New York at Buffalo knows Huckleberry Finn better than anyone on this planet. I had the good fortune to meet Vic at a conference in Elmira, New York, in 2001. He guided me through writing the book, and he has been a wonderful friend, mentor, and teacher.

Tom Quirk is editor for the University of Missouri's Mark Twain and His Circle series, and I thank him for including my book in the series. I also want to thank the dedicated and creative staff at the University of Missouri Press. Robert Sattelmeyer, Ed Branch, and Ron Powers all read the manuscript and offered suggestions. Robert deserves full credit for his discovery of Sam Clemens and the Boston Vigilance Committee. Ed has spent his career studying Twain, yet retains a boyish enthusiasm. I value our friendship. And as for Ron, while it is intimidating to have your prose read by a friend who has both a Pulitzer Prize and a Emmy Award, he, too, has been a mentor.

I want to thank my good friends Frank and Donna Salter for entrusting the court records of John Marshall Clemens to me after they found them at a Hannibal surplus property auction. Donna, Hannibal's most overqualified high school teacher—with a bachelor's degree from Stanford and a Ph.D. in biochemistry from the University of Texas—also assisted with research.

I was greatly assisted by Bob Hirst and Vic Fischer of the Mark Twain Project at the University of California, Berkeley. Kent Rasmussen, Shelley Fisher Fishkin, Lou Budd, and Martin Zehr all were helpful, as were Gretchen Sharlow, Jane McCone, and Mark Woodhouse of the Center for Mark Twain Studies at Elmira College.

My research assistants from Hannibal-LaGrange College, all recommended by Professor Sam Swisher, were particularly helpful. Lindsey O'Donnell worked with me throughout the project. She is presently a graduate student in history at the University of Missouri–Columbia, and she will be a meticulous historian. She was assisted by Melinda Sheffler and Kelly Hobson.

The staff of the Hannibal Free Public Library also provided invaluable assistance. Ann Sundermeyer, Toni Rose, Donna Caldwell, Sharon Lamberson, Hilary Mossell, Sheila Dennehy, Cindy Haun, and Peggy Northcraft exceeded all reasonable expectations: They located books through interlibrary loan. They searched on their own for sources that might be of use.

The *Hannibal Courier-Post*, successor to the paper where Sam Clemens began his writing career, has become a second home to me. Early versions of some chapters first appeared as articles in the newspaper. Jack Whitaker, Mary Lou Montgomery, and Bev Darr have been friends and colleagues, and they have encouraged me when many people in Hannibal would just as soon forget that slavery ever existed.

My thanks to John Huffman, at Mark Twain's birthplace in Florida, Missouri, and Roger Boyd, at the Battle of Athens State Historic Site, both outstanding historians.

Roberta Hagood and her late husband, Hurley, Marsha Mayfield, Connie Morrison, Annie Dixon, Charles Anton and his late wife, Ruth, Frank and Sara North, James Joplin, Candace and John Klemann, Henry Sweets, Lew Gordon, Patricia Minter, Guy and Sandy Callison, Sam Akers, Holly and John Wealer, David Huck, and Ron Brown all provided valuable assistance.

The following groups and institutions were also of incalculable help: Friends of Historic Hannibal, the New-York Historical Society, the State

Historical Society of Missouri, the Mark Twain Forum, the Mark Twain Project at the University of California, Berkeley, and the Center for Mark Twain Studies at Elmira College.

Finally, I thank my wife, Vicki Dempsey. We have been together since we were nineteen years old—thirty years now. We practice law together. Her background as an English teacher has been invaluable. She has read every word of this book and participated at each stage of its writing. To her I can honestly say that I did not realize when I went down to the library that Saturday morning four years ago "to see if there is anything about slavery in Hannibal" that it would turn into this maneater. I thank God she is so understanding.

Searching
for
Jim

He held himself responsible for the wrong which the white race had done the black race in slavery.

William Dean Howells, *My Mark Twain*

Chapter 1

A Performance

Spring 1891—Hartford, Connecticut

Now, in your interview, you have certainly been most accurate; you have set down the sentences I uttered as I said them. But you have not a word of explanation; what my manner was at several points is not indicated. Therefore, no reader can possibly know where I was in earnest and where I was joking; or whether I was joking altogether or in earnest altogether.

Mark Twain to Edward W. Bok, circa 1888

Samuel Clemens waited for his appointment to arrive. He whiled the time away at his billiard table. His trademark cigar smoldered in his mouth as one had nearly every day since he took up smoking in earnest forty-four years earlier, at age twelve, in the offices of Hannibal's *Missouri Courier*. The visitor was an important one: Raymond Blathwait was coming to interview Mark Twain for the *Pall Mall Gazette* of London.[1]

Clemens no doubt appreciated the importance of the moment. The *Pall Mall Gazette* was a major newspaper in a time when there was no radio and no television. Outside the lecture hall circuit, a forum Mark Twain had mastered years before, the only way to address the public was through newspapers or magazines. This interview was particularly important because American audiences would not be seeing Twain on stage for several years. Clemens and his family were going to live in Europe. The article would be reprinted in the *New York World* on May 31, 1891.

Blathwait would interview Mark Twain, not Sam Clemens. That name, Mark Twain, was more than a nom de plume. Mark Twain was a public

1. Blathwait is also spelled Blathwayt in some sources.

persona, a master of native humor and slow-drawled hyperbole. There were expectations of Twain that Clemens did not have to bear. Twain could be wry and barbed. He could exaggerate. He would be witty, and the truth . . . well, the precise truth wasn't as important as the entertainment.

When the reporter was ushered into the billiard room, Clemens shook his hand and inquired about a mutual friend. Then he seated his guest and gave him an excellent cigar. Clemens made Blathwait comfortable and puffed him with a compliment that raised the journalist to his own level, telling him, "A good interviewer has in him the making of a perfect novelist." Downplaying his own importance, Clemens told Blathwait that he must bear the lion's share of the interview.

Then the performance began. Asked to give his opinion on the comparative merits of American and British humor, Clemens ran his hand through his hair and slipped with ease into the Mark Twain persona. With his famous slow drawl he answered, "That is a question I am particularly and specially unqualified to answer. I might go out into the road there," he pointed out the window, "and with a brickbat I would knock down three or four men in an hour who would know more than I about humor and its merits and its varieties."

This was the Twain America loved: the self-deprecating wit; the absolute master of American humor claiming he knew nothing of humor. Blathwait lapped it up. Twain went on dramatically, explaining how he never read humor; in broad Twain overstatement he enumerated all the things he would read before turning to humor—biography, history, diaries, personal memoirs, and then the dictionaries and encyclopedias. "Then, if still alive, I should read what humorous books might be there. That is an absolutely perfect test and proof that I have no great taste for humor."

After Twain had continued on for a while longer exaggerating his ignorance on humor, Blathwait complimented him, "The gaiety of nations, Mr. Twain, will be eclipsed when your humor ceases." Twain literally bowed to his audience of one in the billiard room.

The interview continued through lunch. Twain paced the room blowing billows of smoke, tossing his hair, and punctuating his remarks by wagging a finger. He took a verbal swipe at Bret Harte. All the while Blathwait sat writing furiously, prodding the performance with the occasional question. After lunch Blathwait broached the subject. He told Twain that *Adventures of Huckleberry Finn* was his favorite book and complimented the author on "the wonderful knowledge of dialect" displayed in the book.

Twain's response would help distort history for more than a century: It would protect Clemens's parents, mask the town of Hannibal, and obscure Clemens's own training as a writer. These may not have been Clemens's intentions. He was merely being Mark Twain, the entertainer.

> I was born in one of those States and I lived a great deal of my boyhood on a plantation of my uncle's, where forty or fifty Negroes lived belonging to him, and who had been drawn from two or three States and so I gradually absorbed their different dialects which they had brought with them. It must be exceedingly difficult to acquire a dialect by study and observation. In the vast majority of cases it probably can be done as in my case, only by absorption. So a child might pick up the differences in dialect by means of that unconscious absorption when a practiced writer could not do it twenty years later by closest observation.[2]

Twain took another swipe at Bret Harte and the *New York World.* Harte had tried to write a Pike County, Missouri, dialect, Twain drawled, but he had only been in Pike County in "budding manhood. . . . The *World* called him the Prince of dialecticians, but there is not a dialect sentence of his that will stand examination."

Having thus insulted his rival, Twain complimented his friend Joel Chandler Harris on his use of dialect in the Uncle Remus tales. In this interview he did not mention his own Uncle Dan'l, the Uncle Remus device to which he would refer in other interviews. He did not include that refinement to the story with Blathwait.

Twain capped the interview by showing Blathwait the check for $450,000, which he had paid to Ulysses S. Grant's estate when he had acted as publisher of Grant's *Personal Memoirs.* The amount was the most ever paid to the author of a book at that time. Twain had the check framed and hung on the wall.

As Twain was escorting Blathwait to the door, he paused in front of a splendid bust of Henry Ward Beecher, the famous abolitionist. Twain had paid the artist's way to study art in Europe. Twain said the sculptor had repaid him with the bust. He commented, "We are well rewarded by that bust, which is the best one ever done of the great American preacher." And so the performance ended with a salute to Grant, the savior of the Union, and Beecher, an abolitionist.

Blathwait wrote the interview, and for the next century scholars very properly cited it as proof that Mark Twain had learned about dialect on his

2. Raymond Blathwait, "Mark Twain on Humor . . . T. B. Aldrich the Wittiest Man," 26.

Uncle John Quarles's "plantation" among his forty to fifty slaves. No fact checker at the *Gazette* or *World* bothered to discover that "the plantation" has actually been a 240-acre farm and that no one in Missouri had ever referred to it as a "plantation." John Quarles had owned six slaves in 1840 and eleven in 1850, many of them too old or too young to have been of much use on the farm.[3] Sam Clemens had not mentioned a word about his daily interactions with the slaves that belonged to his own parents. He did not talk about his daily interactions with the slaves in Hannibal or mention that he had eaten his meals alongside slaves when he began his newspaper apprenticeship. He didn't discuss the racist stories (containing dialect) that were a staple of Hannibal newspapers that he had not only read, but also set into type between 1848 and sometime in 1853. While admiring the bust of Henry Ward Beecher, Clemens did not mention the direct actions that he and his family took against the abolitionists.

It's a fascinating story, and it begins in 1839.

3. Manuscript Census Schedules: Slaves, Monroe County, Missouri, 1840, 1850.

Chapter 2

1839

It is curious—the space-annihilating power of thought. For just one second, all that goes to make the me in me was in a Missourian village.

Mark Twain, *Following the Equator*

The year 1839 was an important one for Hannibal, Missouri. The state legislature chartered the community as a town that spring, and in April, the town board of trustees began writing local ordinances. In the autumn, though no one could have suspected it at the time, a far more auspicious event occurred. John Marshall Clemens moved his family, including little redheaded Sam, to town. Sam was just a few weeks shy of his fourth birthday.

Hannibal was a muddy place. The streets were dirt, and the town was situated in a milewide valley between a picturesque bluff called Lover's Leap to the south and Holliday's Hill to the north. Mark Twain would make the latter famous as Cardiff Hill in *The Adventures of Tom Sawyer*, playground for the imaginary Tom and Huck. Through the valley ran Bear Creek, a meager stream that emptied into the Mississippi River to the east. When low, Bear Creek was too shallow for even a johnboat or canoe. The valley would be a key to Hannibal's development. The valley led west to the unhindered prairie of northern Missouri. In time the first railroad to cross the state would make the gentle climb up Bear Creek Valley, span the prairie, and end at the Missouri River at St. Joseph. But the railroad was still two decades away, merely a dream in the minds of eastern speculators and local boosters.

Rivers were the highways of the western United States in 1839. The state of Missouri was only eighteen years old and had the good fortune to be river rich. The Mississippi formed the state's eastern boundary, and the Missouri River ran like a belt across the state's middle before turning northward at what is now Kansas City. After a minor adjustment to the original boundaries with the addition of the Platte Purchase, the Missouri River became the western boundary of northern Missouri. Being easy to reach, Missouri was a valuable piece of property.

Farmers and merchants floated flatboats and keelboats loaded with produce and other products down the Mississippi to New Orleans. Immigrants took steamboats down the Ohio River to the junction with the Mississippi at Cairo, Illinois, then took the Mississippi north or south. Some traveled to St. Louis then followed the Missouri River to the prime lands in the western part of the state. Others continued north to northeast Missouri, Illinois, Iowa, Minnesota, and Wisconsin. Towns and settlements naturally occurred at river junctions and bends in the river or where natural valleys allowed easy access to inland areas. Steamboats needed wood for their boilers, and passengers needed food and supplies.

Early speculators realized Hannibal was a natural site for a town. A group of investors purchased land and carved it into lots to be sold to buyers back East sight unseen. Even before a railroad was constructed, farmers working the rich soils to the west in the Salt River and Grand River Valleys could bring their products to market in Hannibal. Manufactured products from the East could be transported on the same Ohio River–Mississippi River path as the immigrants. Goods could also be "coasted" down the Atlantic shore and around Florida from New England or sailed from Europe to New Orleans and carried as cargo on the decks of the large steamboats that plied the Mississippi.

Settlers clustered along the rivers not only for ease of transportation but also because of farming practices. Most of northern Missouri had been planed flat during the last ice age. It was a fertile prairie, but in the 1830s immigrants did not yet possess the plow that would enable them to bust it. Early guidebooks, such as L. R. Bek's *Gazetteer of Missouri* (1823), emphasized the importance of farming in cleared forests in Missouri; prairie soil was considered less fertile than forest soil.[1] In northeast Missouri, woodlands were found along the rivers.

Hannibal was little more than a village of one thousand souls in the fall

1. Franklin Howard Bennett, *The Hannibal and St. Joseph Railroad and the Development of Northern Missouri, 1847–1870: A Study of Land and Colonization Policies*, 10.

of 1839, but it was growing. Coal smoke from the shops of three black-smiths curled up into the cool air over the valley. There was plenty of work fitting horseshoes, repairing plows, and forging the wagon jacks, tools, nails, and hinges for the little community. Three sawmills, at least one of which was steam powered, sawed logs into uniform lumber for sturdy permanent houses to replace the early log houses. The wood of log structures contracted, allowing wind through, and rotted quickly if not enclosed in clapboard. Stone was quarried for foundations, and brick was fired from clay deposits.

The November day the Clemenses arrived, the sweet smoke of oak and hickory fires from residents' hearths hung in the air. And carried on the wind was the pungent scent of hogs. Then, as today, pork was the principal meat produced in the area. Farmers allowed their pigs to run loose about the town and roam the oak forests, churning the already muddy streets and fattening themselves on acorns and other edibles rooted up among the trees. When the hogs were large enough, farmers would finish them on corn before slaughtering them. The pork industry had moved beyond subsistence slaughtering. There were two pork-packing plants in Hannibal. The squeals of hogs punctuated the air as animals were slaughtered, processed, and packed in wooden barrels.

Adding to the odor was a tanyard where pigskins and cowhides were turned into leather for harnesses, saddles, and yokes. A factory produced rope from the hemp plants cultivated by local farmers. Another factory transformed the local tobacco crop into cigars and chewing tobacco. Along the riverfront were four general stores, two log hotels, and three saloons where men would meet to drink and talk. There were two churches and two schools, one public and the other private. But the public school would close in a few years for lack of interest.[2]

Hannibal could be a very attractive place. The hills to the north and south along the river were of little use to farmers and were left in their natural state. They were wooded then, as today, with oak and hickory. Black walnut trees were also abundant. Giant cottonwoods grew in the moist soil of the bottoms. Wildlife was plentiful, and game was common on the dinner table.

Because Bear Creek Valley runs west to east, it produces one very beautiful phenomenon. At sunset on rainy or misty days, rays of light form a rainbow that appears to start at the base of Lover's Leap to the south and disappear into the Illinois bottoms across the river. On such a day how peaceful Hannibal looks, how full of promise. How deceptive.

2. J. Hurley Hagood and Roberta Roland Hagood, *The Story of Hannibal*, 29.

Over the next twenty-five years, trouble would torment this little town. Because of a bizarre combination of geography and politics, this world, the world of Sam Clemens's youth, would know little peace. The problem was slavery.

Just twelve miles to the north of Hannibal, and across the river, was the town of Quincy, Illinois. Illinois had been a state since 1818. It had been formed from the old Northwest Territory, which included Ohio, Indiana, Michigan, and Wisconsin. The Northwest Ordinance of 1787 had forever forbidden slavery in the Territory or in the states to be formed from it. Illinois had experienced slavery under the French and British, but the institution was dying out, though it continued on, thinly disguised, until nearly 1840 under the guise of "indentured servitude."[3] By 1839, hardworking artisans and farmers who did not practice slavery had been settled on the prairies of Illinois for thirty years. Slavery was frowned upon; free people worked for wages. Settlers came from all parts of the United States and Europe to live in Illinois.

But Missouri was carved from the Louisiana Purchase, which Thomas Jefferson had acquired from France. In the centuries under French and Spanish rule, slavery had been allowed throughout the Territory. When Missouri petitioned Congress for admission as a state in 1817, it sought to come in as a slave state. This preference triggered a national debate, for conflict between the slave states and the free states was already evident. The admission of another slave state would alter the balance of power. After much debate the Missouri Compromise was reached. The first part of the compromise was easy. To balance the admission of Missouri, the northern portion of Massachusetts was carved off and admitted as the free state of Maine, thus assuring a balance in the U.S. Senate.

The second part of the Missouri Compromise would guarantee Missouri trouble until the Civil War finally decided the issue of slavery. Missouri was admitted as a slave state, but no other territory north of the latitudinal line thirty-six degrees, thirty minutes would be so admitted. Only Missouri's "bootheel," which protrudes into Arkansas, lay south of the line. Not only was Missouri to share an eastern border with a free state, but the territory to the north and west would always be free as well. By design, Missouri was a peninsula of slavery in free territory.[4]

This geographic fact seemed of little consequence at the time. The territory to the west, which would become Kansas and Nebraska, was marked

3. Stephen Middleton, *The Black Laws in the Old Northwest*, 271–74.
4. Duane Meyer, *The Heritage of Missouri: A History*, 154–57.

on most available maps as the Great American Desert. The steel plow, which John Deere would invent to bust the sod of the plains, was not yet envisioned. Other than lonely fur trappers, few people had even crossed the plains. Lewis and Clark had traversed them by hugging the Missouri River. Zebulon Pike had braved them with a party of explorers. In the year 1820, Missouri was the West.[5]

After admission as a slave state, Missouri became a magnet for emigrants from other slave states. They came for a variety of reasons. Second and third sons left the states of Virginia, North and South Carolina, Tennessee, and Kentucky because of the practice of primogeniture, the practice of leaving the land to firstborn sons in order to keep holdings intact. Younger sons were expected to make it on their own. As lands filled up back East, these men sought land in the West. Sons of slave owners were attracted to Missouri because they could bring their slaves and acquire others.

Missouri also attracted southern whites who sought a fresh start in the West. They came to Missouri with slaves in tow and settled first the lands along the Missouri and Mississippi Rivers. By 1840, Missouri had a population of 383,702, including 323,888 whites and 58,240 slaves. In Marion County, where Hannibal was the largest town, there were 7,239 whites and 2,342 slaves. The number of free blacks, primarily slaves whose owners had allowed them to purchase their freedom or manumitted them in wills, was small. In Missouri there were only 1,574, and in Marion County, only 42. Free blacks were free mainly in name. They lived a precarious existence in a world of hate, fear, and intolerance. They were required to post a bond and register with the city or county where they resided. They were barred from holding most jobs.

Southerners established a slave culture in Missouri that flourished in the river valleys and adjacent rich lands. This culture was more than an economic system, although like stocks in a modern portfolio, slaves were an important asset to many families. Slaves were bought and sold. Results of slave sales were monitored regularly in the newspapers so people could calculate their wealth. Slaves were passed from generation to generation by inheritance. They were used as collateral for loans. Slaves were seized and sold to satisfy court judgments. In short, they were human livestock.

5. As late as 1849, when gold was discovered in California, most people who went to the goldfields took ships around South America or to the Isthmus of Panama, where they crossed to the Pacific and boarded other ships for the journey north to San Francisco. Most of those who left Missouri went downriver to New Orleans, where they boarded new ships.

But slavery was far more—it formed the very heart of the society and touched every aspect of community life.

Ownership of slaves was a mark of social status in young Hannibal. Slaves were an indication of importance. There was a stratification of labor, and there were many types of work white people did not do. In fact, it was better for a white person to let the work go undone than to embarrass himself by doing "nigger" work. Slaves labored on the riverfront loading and unloading boats. The dirty work in the tanyard and hog lots of Hannibal was done by slaves. About the house, the proper white wife supervised a domestic slave, who built the fire, did the laundry, and cooked. Often the slave was a child.

Slavery was only the lowest rung of the class system of slave culture. As Sam Clemens observed years later,

> there were grades of society—people of good family, people of unclassified family, people of no family. Everybody knew everybody, and was affable to everybody, and nobody put on any visible airs; yet the class lines were quite clearly drawn and the familiar social life of each class was restricted to that class. It was a little democracy which was full of liberty, equality, and Fourth of July, and sincerely so, too; yet you perceived that the aristocratic taint was there. It was there, and nobody found fault with the fact, or ever stopped to reflect that its presence was an inconsistency.[6]

It was not just the wealthy people of Hannibal who enjoyed the fruits of slave labor. For those white people who could not afford the purchase price of a slave, there was an alternative that allowed them to avoid the embarrassment of performing menial work. People of relatively modest means could easily lease slaves by the year to work as cooks, washerwomen, and maids. Farmers and businessmen hired slaves to do the hard physical work that needed doing in this early stage of the machine age. The lease system provided cheap labor to the housewives, industries, and storekeepers of Hannibal and easy income to slaveholders.

Religion played a crucial role in Hannibal's slave culture. Churches were instrumental in maintaining the institution. Slave owners were comforted from the pulpit and told slavery was the will of God. Slaves were brought to church, where they were told that God wanted them to obey their masters. A popular New Testament lesson told how the Apostle Paul had instructed a runaway Christian servant to go home and be a good

6. Charles Neider, ed., *The Autobiography of Mark Twain*, 28.

slave. Dissent was not tolerated. In the Hannibal of Sam Clemens's youth, people who opposed slavery opposed the will of God.

Slave cultures never rest easy, and Hannibal in 1839 was no exception. The whip and shackle were essential tools of physical coercion. This naturally bred resentment in slaves, and therein lay the unknown, unknowable danger. Fear of slave revolt always lurked in the background. Tales of families being poisoned by slaves were reported frequently in the newspaper and sent chills down spines of wary masters and caused suspicious glances to be cast toward the servants. Control of slaves was extremely important. It was vital to keep slaves both ignorant and isolated from one another as much as possible. The fear was not unfounded. The memory of Nat Turner's revolt in 1831 was still fresh. That Virginia slave had risen up, and blood had flowed before he and his followers were captured. Fifty-five whites had been killed in the rebellion, and in retaliation, the Commonwealth of Virginia had executed fifty-five slaves. The event had sent a wave of fear through the slave states.[7]

One of the first acts of business of the board of trustees of the newly organized Town of Hannibal was to adopt "An Ordinance Respecting Slaves, Free Negroes, and Mulattoes." The first meeting of the board took place on April 4, 1839, and the ordinance was approved on April 23. The ordinance tightly controlled the slaves of Hannibal and provided for enforcement by the justice of the peace and the town constable.[8]

The Hannibal slave code regulated the conduct of not just slaves, but of free blacks and mulattoes as well. (A mulatto was defined in Missouri as any person who had one grandparent who was a Negro.) To prevent insurrection, the ordinance contained several provisions that governed concerted conduct. Any slave or free black or mulatto who participated in a riot or unlawful assembly could receive up to thirty-nine lashes, at the discretion of the justice of the peace, to be administered by the town constable. The ordinance strictly defined unlawful assembly. Under Hannibal's slave law, not more than five slaves or free Negroes or mulattoes could assemble at any one place at the same time within the Town of Hannibal, except in discharge of their duties to their masters, owners, or overseers. The only exception was for a worship service with a white minister or a Negro minister who had obtained permission from the town trustees to hold a religious meeting. Only a highly trusted minister would be

7. Louis P. Masur, *1831, Year of Eclipse*, 11–21.

8. Minute Book of Board of Trustees, City of Hannibal, 1839–1849, collection 1115, manuscript division, State Historical Society of Missouri, Columbia. See appendix for slave ordinance.

granted such permission. An unfettered meeting was a dangerous threat to Hannibal's slave culture.

Liquor was considered a danger in the hands of slaves or free Negroes and mulattoes. Though it was not codified in law, there was a general prohibition against work being done on Sundays. Except for domestic servants, neither whites nor slaves worked on Sunday. Reflecting a general fear that liquor would unleash the coiled passions of slaves, the Hannibal slave ordinance made giving or selling liquor to a slave or a free Negro or mulatto on a Sunday an offense punishable by a twenty-five-dollar fine.

The slave ordinance went beyond protecting Hannibal against insurrection and drunkenness. The law sought to ensure the submission of all African Americans. Up to thirty-nine lashes could be given African Americans for assault or battery or for using insulting language or gestures to any white person within the town. To make certain that African Americans would not get the idea they were on equal footing with the white people of Hannibal, and undoubtedly to protect white labor, free Negroes and mulattoes and slaves were denied the right to hire their own time or enter into contracts for labor. If prosecuted, they faced a stiff fine of from ten to one hundred dollars. Nor could slaves live in Hannibal, except in the household of an owner or a master with the white person present. This further hindered a skilled slave from hiring his time to someone in Hannibal.

Perhaps the most bizarre, yet most telling, provision of the Hannibal slave code was the section that provided for ten to twenty lashes on the bare back for any slave or free Negro or mulatto who "shall wantonly canter or gallop any horse, mare or gelding, or jack-ass or mule, within the town of Hannibal." This provision, like the provision banning insulting white people, was aimed at ensuring submissive behavior on the part of the enslaved population. It is hard to imagine a culture so insecure that it could not tolerate a slave cantering a horse through town. The slave code was certainly not original to Hannibal. Towns across the South adopted similar codes; Hannibal's, like many of Missouri's slave laws, tended to follow the state of Virginia. Punishment was limited to thirty-nine lashes because forty lashes may have been considered lethal. Thirty-nine or fewer would generally not kill the recipient and deprive the slave's owner or master of a valuable piece of property. Moreover, thirty-nine was thought by many to be the number of lashes Jesus Christ received at the order of Pontius Pilot.

The ordinance referred to owners and masters because the two were not the same. An owner held title to a slave and might hire that slave to someone else, who was then a master. Under Hannibal's slave ordinance both people held the same power over the life of a slave. The slave ordinance is significant in the story of the development of Sam Clemens because in a few short years his father would be the justice of the peace and charged with enforcement of the law.

The fear of slave revolt and the threat of runaways framed the politics of Hannibal until the Civil War. In addition to city ordinances, the state legislature in Jefferson City churned out a series of laws. A rigid system of patrols to monitor the border and watch the movements of slaves and free blacks was established. Teaching reading to slaves was banned. White citizens were authorized to stop, interrogate, arrest, and beat suspected runaways. They were allowed to stop, interrogate, and arrest suspected abolition agents. The situation spun wildly out of control over the next two decades.

In 1839, this slave culture was a very familiar, safe, and comfortable world to the Clemens family. The future seemed bright for them and for Hannibal that year. New economic prospects loomed on the horizon for John Marshall Clemens in the little river town. As the temperature dropped that November, the Clemens family unpacked their furniture from the wagon and carried it upstairs to their apartment above the little store on Main Street. No one could have seen that a most important event for Hannibal and American literature was unfolding: the arrival of the little four-year-old, ginger-haired boy who would become Mark Twain on the banks of the Mississippi River.

Chapter 3

Slavery and the Clemens Family

She brought him two or three negroes, but nothing else I think.

The Autobiography of Mark Twain

The Clemens family was accustomed to having slaves. John Marshall Clemens, born in Campbell County, Virginia, in 1798, was proud to be from an old Virginia family and claimed distant relation to royalty. Like many nineteenth-century Virginians, he was hidebound by tradition. Owning slaves was a family tradition. Slaves were passed from generation to generation, frequently constituting a major portion of each generation's inheritance. Records show that Sam Clemens's great-grandmother Rachel Moorman received one Negro girl, Jude, as part of her inheritance from her father. All of Sam Clemens's grandparents were slave owners. When John Marshall Clemens's father died, his estate included ten slaves. John Marshall's share consisted of three: a Negro woman named Mariah, a girl, Louisa, and a boy named Green.[1]

Slavery was a way of life for John Marshall Clemens. As an adult, he practiced law and was licensed in Kentucky. The first record of him in his chosen profession is an indenture for a slave belonging to his sister, which he signed "John Marshall Clemens, Atty."

On May 6, 1823, John Marshall Clemens married Jane Lampton. She brought three slaves to the marriage, giving the couple an even half dozen.[2] Like John Marshall, Jane had inherited her slaves. The young couple and the six slaves set up housekeeping in Columbia, Kentucky.

1. Dixon Wecter, *Sam Clemens of Hannibal*, 13.
2. Ibid., 28.

But they didn't live there long. After a year they relocated to Jackson County, Tennessee. John Marshall Clemens was one of those thousands of restless Americans who couldn't stand to stay in one place too long. He was a poor businessman and spent his lifetime stumbling from one failed venture to another. A proud man, educated and bordering on arrogant, he would fold his tent after a disappointment in one place, pack up the family, and move on. As he encountered financial difficulty, he sold the slaves he and Jane had inherited.

In the summer of 1825 the family moved to Jamestown, Tennessee, where John Marshall Clemens became county commissioner and was chosen first circuit clerk of Fentress County, Tennessee. He also occasionally served as acting state attorney general. This was the high-water mark of John Marshall Clemens's business life. He built a house and began purchasing land. He was convinced that he could become wealthy in land speculation. He purchased land grants totaling as much as seventy thousand acres, then sat back to wait for the land to increase in value. It never did during his lifetime. The soil was forested with yellow pine and too poor to grow anything else.

When the legal business slowed down, he opened a general store—a perennial error in his life. Of the four stores he operated in his lifetime, all failed. His family was growing. A son, Orion, was born on July 17, 1825, followed by a daughter, Pamela, on September 13, 1827. In 1828, another son, Pleasant Hannibal Clemens, was born, but he lived only three months. On May 31, 1830, another daughter, Margaret, was born. The business in Jamestown was not successful, and in 1831 John Marshall Clemens gave up and moved nine miles to Three Forks of Wolf River, Tennessee. There he bought two hundred acres and built a two-story log house. He opened another store in nearby Pall Mall, Tennessee, on the north side of the river, where he also served as the local postmaster from 1832 until 1835. Still, success and happiness eluded him. By 1835 he and Jane had only one slave left, a woman named Jennie.

The Clemenses Come to Missouri

Jane's sister Patsy had married an amiable and successful fellow named John Quarles in 1831 and moved to Florida, Missouri. The Quarleses found the success that had eluded the Clemenses. John Quarles had a popular general store in Florida, a little hamlet on the Salt River. Missouri was the frontier, and the population was growing. The Quarleses wrote to the Clemenses with tales of the great potential in Missouri. As their

Tennessee prospects withered, it is not hard to imagine John Marshall and Jane Clemens reading the letters by the fireside and dreaming of the possibilities in this new state. John Marshall Clemens came to believe that his future lay in Missouri. In 1835, the family packed up and made the long voyage down the Ohio to the Mississippi, which they then took up to St. Louis. They traveled to Florida by wagon and on foot. The slave Jennie, last of the half dozen human beings inherited by John Marshall and Jane Clemens, went with the family. She had no choice.

When they arrived in Florida, Missouri, they lived with the Quarles family. But after a short time, they moved into a two-room clapboard house. John Marshall Clemens bought one hundred twenty acres east of town and two other tracts, eighty acres near the Ralls County line and another forty acres north of town. On November 30, 1835, Samuel Clemens was born—the first Missourian in the family.

Despite opportunities in the new land, John Marshall Clemens followed the familiar route to failure. He first worked in his brother-in-law's store, but in an act of marked ingratitude, he then set up a competing store in the same hamlet. He was active in community life. Florida was on the Salt River. The Salt was a minor tributary of the Mississippi. Steamboats could navigate only a few miles up the Salt. However, there was a scheme to build a series of dams so that steamboats could come as far as Florida. John Marshall Clemens was one of sixteen commissioners appointed by the Missouri Legislature to the Salt River Navigation Company. It failed. In February 1837, he headed a commission to incorporate the Florida and Paris Railroad to build a line from little Florida to the county seat in Paris, Missouri. It failed.

His store failed.

In 1837 he became a county judge in Monroe County. The position of county judge was like that of a county commissioner today. The county court was both the legislative and executive body of the county, and it also dealt with probate matters. The judgeship was a part-time position. While their financial fortunes dwindled, the Clemens family continued to grow. On July 13, 1838, another son, Henry, was born. Then tragedy again touched the Clemens family when their daughter Margaret died on August 17, 1839. She was just nine years old.

After the death of Margaret and the failures he experienced in Florida, John Marshall Clemens followed the familiar pattern and looked for a different place to try his luck. His eye turned to the northeast, where the little town of Hannibal didn't have to worry about building dams to be a river port. The next year, in what would turn out to be another of his snake-bitten business deals, John Marshall Clemens sold his Monroe

County land to Ira Stout and from Stout bought a quarter of a city block in Hannibal for seven thousand dollars. He opened a general store in the Virginia House Hotel on the corner of Hill and Main Streets. The family lived above the store. John Marshall Clemens borrowed money to stock the general store and put fifteen-year-old Orion to work as the store clerk. That store, too, would fail.

Clemens had paid too much for the property. If anything was true about the man, it was this: he was an abysmal businessman. In Hannibal he would follow the same failing mixture of business and political office. Although financial success would elude him, John Marshall Clemens stumbled into an important role as a defender of slave culture. The Missouri to which he had moved was already under attack from a new breed of critic that sought to destroy slavery.

The Honey Tree War

Shortly after the Clemens family arrived in Hannibal, the Honey Tree War took place. The conflict took its name from an incident in which a Missourian followed lines of honey bees into disputed territory and chopped down the hollow trees containing their hives. While the event is almost laughingly dismissed by local historians, it can be seen, in retrospect, as an ill omen. In its first two decades of statehood, Missouri had little conflict with neighboring states and territories. The abolition movement had begun but was mainly limited to the distribution of newspapers and sermons. There was little animosity between Missouri and either Illinois or Iowa. But in 1839 a boundary dispute broke out between Iowa and Missouri; it began just forty-five miles north of Hannibal.

When the U.S. Congress authorized Missouri to organize as a state, it left the eastern end of the northern boundary ambiguous. The legislation described it as the "parallel of latitude which passes through the rapids of the river Des Moines, Making said line to correspond with the Indian boundary line."[3]

People began to move into the area, and in 1836 the Missouri Legislature passed a law requiring that the boundary be surveyed. The Missouri surveyors went to work and, although they had great difficulty identifying "the rapids of the river Des Moines," they did establish a boundary line that was officially approved by the state legislature in February 1839. The region to the north of Missouri had been part of the Territory

3. Meyer, *Heritage of Missouri*, 182.

of Michigan from 1834 to 1835, and in late 1835 had been declared part of the Territory of Wisconsin. In 1838 the Territory of Iowa was formed. As the boundary of the southeast corner of the proposed state, the Iowa legislature identified a line approximately ten miles south of the line the Missouri government recognized. There were few settlers in the region and only one settlement, today's Farmington, Iowa, but if the territory was free soil, southerners could not settle there with slaves.

Congress sought to resolve the dispute but only made matters worse. The federal surveyor was unable to reach a definite conclusion. From the ambiguous language describing the boundary he was able to lay out four different lines, any one of which could be legitimately considered the boundary. Naturally, Missouri favored the northernmost line; Iowa, the southernmost.

Trouble broke out in the summer of 1839. The governors of Missouri and Iowa Territory publicly declared their unwillingness to compromise. Both men issued proclamations warning the officers of the other's government not to extend their jurisdiction over the area in dispute. When, in August 1839, Sheriff Uriah Gregory of Clark County, Missouri, attempted to collect taxes in the area, he received a hostile reception from a group of settlers at a house-raising near Farmington. The settlers produced weapons, and the sheriff retreated hastily.

Three months later Sheriff Gregory made another attempt to extend Missouri jurisdiction over the area and was arrested by the sheriff of Van Buren County, Iowa. The Missouri sheriff was charged with usurpation of authority and jailed in Muscatine, Iowa. This set the wheels in motion: Governor Lilburn Boggs called up the Missouri state militia to protect the territory of Missouri. Governor Robert Lucas of Iowa responded with a compromise proposal. Lucas asked that Congress pick one of the four lines, but the conciliatory gesture was rejected by Boggs. Lucas then ordered out the Iowa militia.

Some 2,200 Missouri militiamen, including John Marshall Clemens, were called to arms. However, when the units assembled in Lewis, Clark, and Knox Counties, there were only 600 to 800 men present. Many, like Clemens, did not respond to the call. The Iowans mustered 1,200 men in the disputed area. Iowa and Missouri stood musket barrel to musket barrel over the real estate near the confluence of the Des Moines and the Mississippi Rivers. Battle seemed inevitable.

However, the soldiers on both sides lacked the will to shoot one another. Committees from the militias negotiated a truce. The citizen soldiers decided both states had been poorly led by their politicians and instead of combat, turned on their leaders. The soldiers hanged both governors in effigy. In frontier style, they cut a deer carcass in two. On one half they put a sign saying "Governor Lucas of Iowa"; on the other half they put a sign that read "Governor Boggs of Missouri." With mock ceremony the two halves of the deer carcass were duly executed. Then the effigies of the politicians were solemnly taken down and buried with great pomp, and the two sides withdrew. The boundary issue was ultimately decided by the United States Supreme Court in 1849: the disputed area was divided almost exactly down the middle. Thus, the first dispute between free soil and slave ended in comedy. No blood was shed, and people still laugh about the encounter. But it was a harbinger of things to come.

Twenty-two years later, on August 5, 1861, similar forces would meet just a few miles away at the little community of Athens, Missouri, on the Des Moines River. There four hundred Iowans and pro-Union Missourians met twelve hundred Missouri State Guard troops under Martin Green. This time no committees met. The muskets roared, and the Union troops chased the Missouri troops from the field. Fifty-four men died in one of the first and northernmost battles of the Civil War fought just twenty miles west of Keokuk, Iowa. In that war the slave culture of Sam Clemens's youth would be destroyed.[4]

4. George McCrary, *Sketches of War History, 1861–1865*, vol. 1, *War Papers and Personal Reminiscences, 1861–1865;* Perry McCandless, *A History of Missouri, Volume 2: 1820 to 1860*, 111–16.

Chapter 4

The Abolition Movement across the River

All of a sudden he proclaimed himself an abolitionist—straight out and publicly! He said that negro slavery was a crime, an infamy. For a moment the town was paralyzed with astonishment; then it broke into a fury of rage.

Mark Twain, "A Scrap of Curious History"

Hannibal was still at peace with the people across the river in 1839, but change was rapidly approaching. A movement was growing in Illinois that would soon radically alter the very nature of society in its western neighbor. This radicalization had begun six years earlier on the East Coast and rapidly spread west. By 1835, the abolition movement had reached Quincy, Illinois, and while it was young and untried, it would soon have an impact.

The American abolition movement had existed before 1833, but with the founding of the American Anti-Slavery Society that year by William Lloyd Garrison it took on new life. The organization began flooding the nation with radical tracts. Under Garrison's leadership, the abolitionists began attacking not only slavery, but also the morality of the slaveholder and the culture of slavery itself. At the same time, a groundswell of religious feeling was starting. The three decades preceding the Civil War were a great period of religious revivals known as the Second Awakening. In slave culture, these meetings, and the organizations supporting them, were primarily directed toward personal morality, focused on saving the individual from damnation. But in many parts of the nation, especially outside areas dominated by slave culture, revivals frequently focused on institutional reform. Converts thought society would be perfected when everyone was filled with the Holy Spirit. From these revivals, primarily in the Northeast, sprang the prison reform, the public school, and the temperance movements. Eastern revivalists hoped that by removing insufferable social conditions, they could bring sinners to God. In this environment, the antislavery movement found a place to grow. Revivalists like Theodore Weld and Albert Barnes began to preach against slavery. If slavery could be abolished, they argued, master and slave could be brought to God. This religious abolitionist movement caught fire, and churches became bases for rapid expansion. As converts joined forces with other abolitionists, however, abolition moved out of the churches and became an end in itself. Religious conversion became secondary to emancipation of slaves, even among religious abolitionists.[1]

The Adams County Anti-Slavery Society was organized under the leadership of Henry Snow and Richard Eells. Eells and his wife, Jane Bestor Eells, had come to Quincy from Connecticut in 1833. Eells established a medical practice in Quincy. The Eellses had had two daughters but both had died by 1834; thus, the childless couple devoted their time to, and perhaps channeled their grief into, the abolition movement and the Underground Railroad. The Eellses are credited with aiding several hundred slaves escape via the Underground Railroad.[2]

The Adams County abolitionists set forth their goal in their organization's constitution:

> Whereas we the undersigned citizens of Adams County in the State of Illinois feeling deeply impressed with the sense of the awful sin of slavery as sanctioned by the laws and unblushingly practiced by many in these United States and feeling conscious as we do that it is in direct violation of the Laws of God and of the first principles of our republican institutions; that the continuance of it is highly dangerous to our civil and religious Liberties; and that we cannot conscientiously discharge our duty to our God and to our fellow men without giving our Public and united testimony against it.[3]

1. Thomas Peterson, "The Myth of Ham among White, Antebellum Southerners," 42.
2. Eells is generally given all the credit for the family's Underground Railroad activity, but his wife must have participated since slaves were known to come to the house.
3. *Constitution of the Adams County Anti-Slavery Society*, Historical Society of Quincy and Adams County, Illinois.

This radical statement opened a wide fissure between slaveholders and nonslaveholders. Prior to this time, slavery had been attacked in an abstract way by emancipation and colonization societies. Emancipationists had a fairly broad range of views. Some argued that slavery was bad for society, not because of any wrong done to slaves, but because of the effect it had on white people. They believed slavery undermined the work ethic. Almost all emancipationists and colonizationists were concerned about free blacks, whom they considered potential criminals and a bad example for slaves. Other emancipationists were simply racists who sought to rid society of all blacks. Emancipationists could be found in all portions of the country, in slave states as well as in free.

These new abolitionists attacked slaveholders outright, viewing them as sinners violating the laws of God. The loyalty of slaveholders was called into question by the abolition movement. Slavery was seen as a threat to the republic and the liberties of the people. This was a radical departure from the old emancipation movements that had been acceptable in slave culture. Abolitionists sought not emancipation or freeing of some slaves, but the complete abolishment of the institution of slavery.

The new movement was considered extremely provocative in Missouri. The abolitionists spoke of obedience to the law, but there could be no mistaking their belief that they answered to a higher authority.

> The object of this Society shall be to endeavor by all means sanctioned by Law, *Humanity and Religion,* to effect the entire abolition of slavery in these United States. That is shall be our duty, to convince all our fellow citizens by arguments addressed to their understandings and consciences that Slave-holding is a heinous Sin in the sight of God, and that duty, safety and the best interests of all concerned require its immediate abandonment.[4]

The biggest threat to slave culture came from the social aim of the abolition movement. "The Society shall endeavor to elevate the character and condition of the People of colour by encouraging their the intellectual, religious and moral improvement, and by doing away Public Prejudice against them."[5] This was a threat against the established order of slave culture. However, Anti-Slavery Society doctrine at this date was opposed to the use of violence. The Adams County chapter renounced the use of force to end slavery.

4. Ibid.
5. Ibid.

In Missouri and other slave states there was an immediate reaction to the creation of abolition societies. White people, whether slaveholders or not, reexamined slavery, and they affirmed its fundamental importance to the culture and economy.[6] In 1852 William Gilmore Simms, one of the foremost men of letters in the antebellum South, commented on the radical shift in southern thinking that followed the development of the abolition movement in an essay entitled "Morals of Slavery":

> Twenty years ago, few persons in the South undertook to justify Negro Slavery, except on the score of necessity. Now, very few persons in the same region question their perfect right to the labor of their slaves,—and more,—their moral obligation to keep them still subject, as slaves, and to compel their labor, so long as they remain the inferior beings which we find them now, and which they seem to have been from the beginning. This is a great good, the fruit wholly of the hostile pressure. It has forced us to examine into the sources of the truth.[7]

A theology in support of slavery grew in the slave culture of northeast Missouri. Eventually it would force out any nonconformists. Nationally, Protestant churches divided into slave and free. An ideological earthquake shook and divided the nation along the fault line of slavery. When the seismic shifts of ideology took place, Sam Clemens's Hannibal found itself at the epicenter of the quake.

David Nelson

David Nelson, the founder of Hannibal's First Presbyterian Church, personified the changes occurring across slave culture. Like John Marshall Clemens and other settlers of northeast Missouri, Nelson was a southerner. He was born September 24, 1793, near Jonesboro, Tennessee, to a family of Presbyterian ministers. He was well educated for the time. Nelson broke with family tradition and studied medicine. He attended Washington College then apprenticed himself to a physician in Danville, Kentucky. After further training in Philadelphia, he became a surgeon in the War of 1812. He served with an expeditionary force that invaded Canada

6. Peterson, "Myth of Ham," 29.
7. William Gilmore Simms, *The Morals of Slavery,* 179; Peterson, "Myth of Ham," 16.

and later served under Andrew Jackson in Alabama and Florida. Unlike John Marshall Clemens, Nelson was financially successful. After the war, he returned to Jonesboro and built up a lucrative medical practice.

During this time he was intrigued by the naturalistic doctrines popular among the scientific community. In the spirit of Jeffersonian inquiry, he turned his back on his family's austere Calvinism and, in his own words, was "an honest, unreflecting deist." Deists believed in the existence of God on purely rational grounds and dispensed with reliance on revelation or authority. In their view, after God created the world and natural laws, He then took no further part in its functioning. Needless to say, this philosophy distressed Nelson's conservative religious family in Jonesboro. He further distressed his family by drinking and playing cards.

At age twenty-two, he eloped. His wife was a staunchly religious Presbyterian woman, and she gradually brought him back to Calvinism and the Presbyterian Church. With the rediscovery of his family's faith came a rediscovery of the old family vocation. In April 1825 he was licensed to preach by the Abingdon Presbytery in Virginia. Within six months he had quit the practice of medicine altogether and became an evangelist. Again, he found success. He published an account of his return from deism to Calvinism, *The Cause and Cure of Infidelity.* More than 100,000 copies were distributed by the American Tract Society in the 1830s—making it a solid best-seller for the times.

In his freethinking days he had already emancipated his own slaves. At the time, he was an emancipationist of the Jeffersonian colonization school, not an abolitionist. That was yet to come. His evangelical duties soon took him west to Missouri. In 1831, Nelson settled in Marion County, where he founded and became president of Marion College, a Presbyterian school for the training of "pious young men." It had two campuses in Marion County, a preparatory school at West Ely, a few miles west of Hannibal, and a college campus at Philadelphia, Missouri, to the north. He spent the next few years evangelizing around the area.

In 1832, Nelson met with ten Hannibal Presbyterians in the home of Abner O. Nash to organize a Presbyterian church in Hannibal. Nash, a slaveholder, would be a prominent member of city government and the Presbyterian church for years to come, and he would help pass Hannibal's first slave code in 1839. For the first year the church was in existence, only whites joined. Then in September 1833, the first slaves were admitted into membership. Members forty-one and forty-two were recorded as Ester and Elin, described in the church's session minutes as colored women. They were followed by Elizabeth, Daniel, Sukey, and Phillis, also in September. York, "a colored man," was added in February 1834 along with Ralph, another slave. In May 1834, James, "a colored man," belonging to a Mr. Grant became the seventy-fifth member of the growing congregation. William, Mary, Siwir, and Caroline also joined in this early period. In the register of church members, slaves were indicated by first names followed with the notation "col w" or "col m."[8] Nelson frequently filled the pulpit as visiting minister. There is nothing to indicate he ever spoke against slavery in Marion County at this time. Slaveholding members felt comfortable in the church. They brought their slaves into the fold confident the servants would be instructed on their duty of obedience.

However, in 1835 David Nelson underwent a conversion as profound as his earlier return to Calvinism. He heard abolitionist theologican Theodore Weld at the Presbyterian General Assembly that year in Pittsburgh, Pennsylvania, and together with more than a quarter of those present, he "pledged himself openly to the Cause" of abolition.[9]

Nelson returned to Marion College after the assembly with fire in his belly. He became an agent of the American Anti-Slavery Society, and in 1836 he turned on the slaveholders of Marion county. In May of that year, two men arrived in Hannibal with antislavery tracts and pamphlets. A mob formed after word of the abolitionists' presence spread. A search began, and the men were captured about thirty miles north of Hannibal at Philadelphia, Missouri, in northern Marion County. The abolitionist materials were found hidden in an outbuilding. The materials were destroyed and the men given the choice of being hanged or leaving the county. They chose to leave.

With tensions running high in Marion County, Nelson attended a revival meeting in Palmyra in May 1836. From the pulpit Nelson called upon slaveholders to repent of their sins and free their slaves. A layperson, William Muldrow, handed Nelson an announcement asking for contributions that would be used to buy slaves and send them to Africa. None of this sat well with the members, who were very content with their slaveholding. Some in the congregation took great offense. John Bosley was one. He drew a pistol and attempted to shoot Muldrow, but the gun misfired. Muldrow, not taking kindly to the attempted murder, then stabbed Bosley with a knife. A melee broke out in the church, and fighters even tumbled out into the churchyard. At least twenty men participated in the Presbyterian brawl.

Nelson and Muldrow, seeing that the situation was out of control, fled. Bosley was found and jailed, but Nelson eluded the good citizens of

8. Session minutes, First Presbyterian Church, Hannibal, Missouri.
9. *Emancipator*, June 16, 1835.

Marion County and made his way to safety in Quincy, Illinois. The crowd then turned its attention to Marion College. Faced with eviction from the county, the college trustees quickly issued a statement designed to calm the people of Marion County: "The faculty of Marion College utterly disapprove as unchristian and illegal, the circulation of all books calculated to make the slave population of this state discontented." Faculty and students were instructed not to preach emancipation or abolition or to teach reading to slaves. The college was spared and more important, the leading educational and religious institution in the county had branded abolition "unchristian." The *Marion Journal*, a county newspaper, blamed the incident on Nelson and warned other abolitionists, "our citizens will not, under any circumstances, permit them, with impunity, to disturb the repose of society."[10]

The founder of the First Presbyterian Church of Hannibal, where young Sam Clemens attended Sunday school, found himself exiled to Illinois for his antislavery views. He started a new school called the Mission Institute in Adams County, Illinois, just across the river from Marion County. In Illinois, Nelson scarcely bothered to conceal his abolitionist activities. There was little need. The Adams County Anti-Slavery Society was thriving. Zealous men and women, determined to see slavery brought to an end, were already helping any runaway slaves lucky enough to make it across the Mississippi River on their way to Chicago, Detroit, and Canada. But they relied on slaves getting to Quincy on their own. Soon they would begin exploring ways to actively liberate slaves in Missouri.

10. George R. Lee, *Slavery North of St. Louis*, 125; *Marion Journal*, May 28, 1836; Lee, *Slavery North of St. Louis*, 126.

Chapter 5

The Contest Begins

In that day, for a man to speak out openly and proclaim himself
an enemy of negro slavery was simply to proclaim himself a
madman. For he was blaspheming against the holiest thing
known to a Missourian, and could not be in his right mind.

Mark Twain, "A Scrap of Curious History"

David Nelson was lucky to have escaped Missouri with his life. In St.
Louis, Missouri, another Presbyterian was running afoul of Missouri's
slave culture. In 1833, the Reverend Elijah P. Lovejoy established the *St.
Louis Observer*, a newspaper that covered religious issues from a strongly
anti-Catholic position.

A friend and colleague of Nelson's, Lovejoy also found himself swept
up in the abolition movement, but he made a gradual transition from
emancipationist/colonizer to abolitionist. His editorials on the institution
of slavery were fairly tame and conciliatory in the beginning. But in 1836,
an event occurred that radicalized Lovejoy.

On April 28, 1836, a free mulatto steamboat steward named Francis
McIntosh was arrested by police officers William Mull and George Hammond for fighting on the riverfront.[1] As the officers were escorting McIntosh to the city jail, the prisoner asked what his punishment would be.
Hammond, maliciously and jokingly, told him he would probably be
hanged.

There was no reason for McIntosh to disbelieve Hammond. Free blacks
lived a precarious existence in Missouri, and arbitrary justice was all too

---

1. Janet S. Hermann, "The McIntosh Affair," 123.

common. The steward believed he was on his way to be hanged. In an attempt to escape, he pulled a knife, stabbed Mull in the stomach, and slashed Hammond's neck, severing his jugular vein. A group of men observed what happened and chased McIntosh through the city streets, eventually trapping him in a building. The men dragged McIntosh to the city jail.

A mob of more than five hundred men, many of them armed, soon gathered outside the St. Louis jail and began demanding the surrender of McIntosh. Many were from respected St. Louis families. When the jailer refused to turn over his prisoner, the mob used sledgehammers to break into the jail. They dragged McIntosh into the street. His fate was decided when someone in the crowd cried out to burn him. The mob dragged McIntosh to an oak tree and chained him to the trunk. Men then began piling wood around him. As the pyre was constructed, McIntosh begged to be shot. A fourteen-year-old boy said to be Hammond's son brought some shavings and kindling and was given the "honor" of starting the fire.

As the fire grew, McIntosh's agony increased. Some people in the crowd asked that he be shot in the name of mercy, but others threatened to shoot anyone who put McIntosh out of his misery. It took ten or fifteen minutes for the hapless McIntosh to die. The crowd stood silently watching the man slowly burn to death then roast beyond recognition in the cruel blaze. Then the mob quietly dispersed, leaving McIntosh's gruesome remains against the charred oak. The next morning neighborhood boys made a game of throwing stones at the black and disfigured corpse, still chained to the tree. The object was to see who should first succeed in breaking the skull.[2]

Residents of St. Louis, and of towns throughout Missouri, took the news of the lynching very calmly. Many prominent citizens had participated, and others took it in stride—one couldn't have free Negroes killing police officers. But laws appeared to have been broken: The sheriff had been disobeyed, the jailhouse broken into, and a free black man killed without due process of law. A grand jury was called upon to review the matter. The grand jury was conducted by a curiously named St. Louis judge: Luke E. Lawless. While the grand jury was to determine if sufficient evidence existed to issue indictments, Lawless's job was to instruct them on the law as it applied to the case. Lawless took a very curious position in regard to the lynching. He instructed the grand jury that if they found the lynching

2. Joseph Lovejoy and Owen Lovejoy, eds., *Memoir of the Rev. Elijah P. Lovejoy*, 171.

to be the act of a multitude, it would not be punishable by common law. Thus charged, the grand jury had no choice but to return no indictments. St. Louis breathed a sigh of relief and went on about its business.

In the free states, moderate and abolitionist papers expressed outrage at the judicial endorsement of lynch law. In sermons and in recruiting abolitionist Theodore Weld used the McIntosh lynching as an example of the tyranny and injustice of slave culture. He included a chapter on the lynching in his important antislavery book *American Slavery as It Is.*

> Lest this demonstration of "public opinion" should be regarded as a sudden impulse merely, not an index of the settled tone of feeling in that community, it is important to add, that the Hon. Luke E. Lawless, Judge of the Circuit Court of Missouri, at a session of that Court in the City of St. Louis, some months after the burning of this man, decided officially that since the burning of McIntosh was the act, either directly or by the countenance of a majority of the citizens, it is "a case which transcends the jurisdiction" of the Grand Jury! Thus the state of Missouri has proclaimed to the world, that the wretches who perpetrated that unspeakably diabolical murder, and the thousands that stood by consenting to it, were her representatives and the Bench sanctifies it with the solemnity of a judicial decision.[3]

The lynching and its aftermath were fodder for the abolitionist press nationwide, but Elijah Lovejoy wrote particularly vehement editorials in the *St. Louis Observer.* He attacked mob rule, the grand jury, and Judge Lawless. A series of articles increasingly critical of slavery incited threats and attacks upon him and the paper. He received letters warning him to cease publishing and leave Missouri or face dire consequences. Then rocks were thrown at his office. Finally, his office was ransacked and most of his furniture thrown into the Mississippi River.

For his own safety, Lovejoy moved his newspaper across the Mississippi River to the little town of Alton, Illinois, in September 1836, but he did not tone down his editorials. Instead he became increasingly vocal, advocating immediate emancipation without compensation to slaveholders—and he sent his newspaper into Missouri at every opportunity.

The Missouri Legislature took note of the *Observer* and the seizure of the antislavery literature in Marion County. On February 1, 1837, it passed an "act to prohibit the publication, circulation, or promulgation of the abolition doctrine." The new law made it a felony to publish, circulate, write,

---

3. Theodore Dwight Weld, *American Slavery as It Is: Testimony of a Thousand Witnesses,* 157.

speak, or print any facts, arguments, reasoning, or opinions that might excite slaves or other persons of color to rebellion, sedition, mutiny, insurrection, or murder. It was a very broad law and carried stiff penalties: A first offence was punishable by a fine of up to one thousand dollars and two years in jail, a second offense, twenty years, a third, life![4]

The message could not have been clearer. Elijah Lovejoy was an outlaw in Missouri. Sending his abolitionist paper into the state was a crime. Following Judge Lawless's logic, a mob would be fully justified in bringing this criminal to justice. The city of Alton, though in Illinois, had a number of citizens with southern roots and strong Missouri connections. The town was tied economically to the burgeoning markets of St. Louis and other towns in Missouri. Mob justice was not just a Missouri phenomenon. With the encouragement of—and no doubt the participation of—Missourians, three presses belonging to Lovejoy were destroyed in the next fifteen months. Instead of intimidating Lovejoy, the attacks emboldened him while elevating him in the abolition movement. Here was a man who would stand up to the mobs and slaveholders. Outside support enabled him to keep replacing the presses.

On November 7, 1837, the fourth press arrived in Alton. It was delivered to a warehouse, and a small company of armed guards, including Lovejoy, his brother Owen, and several friends, was organized to stand watch over it. That evening, twenty armed men called on the owner of the warehouse and demanded the press. When they were refused, the men attacked. In the violence that ensued, one of the attackers was shot and killed. Then, as Elijah Lovejoy was climbing down a ladder from the building, someone shot and killed him.

Following Lovejoy's death, the guards surrendered the press to the attackers, who, unfazed by the violence, went quietly and methodically about the business of dismantling the press. After it was knocked apart and thrown into the river, they left.

Elijah Lovejoy only grew more powerful in death; he served as the movement's first white martyr. In Missouri and Alton, communities remained calmly approving of the mob action, but nationally, Lovejoy's death galvanized radicals and breathed new life into the antislavery crusade. Pulpits across the North rang with sermons eulogizing Elijah Lovejoy. Pamphleteers chronicled his life and death. In Quincy, David Nelson and the Adams County Anti-Slavery Society took note of the death of

4. *Laws of the State of Missouri*, 2d ed. (St. Louis, Mo.: Chambers & Knapp, 1841), 3. See appendix.

Lovejoy and determined to intensify their attacks on slavery. They gazed across the Mississippi River into Marion County and plotted.

Slave Thieves

Nelson had two campuses for his little Presbyterian Mission Institute. The first, on 185 acres outside Quincy, was called Mission Institute Number 1. There Nelson built his home, which he called Oakland, as well as a red barn, a chapel, and twenty log houses for students. The other campus was located in Quincy. It consisted of a two-story classroom building, a chapel, and more log houses for students. Nelson claimed the purpose of the school was to train missionaries for service in foreign lands and among the Native Americans.[5] In reality, the institute was a hotbed of abolition activity and was a well-used stop on the young Underground Railroad. Slaves who made it to the institute could count on help from the faculty, students, and staff.

Nelson was joined at the institute by Richard Eells, who taught medicine and science. They lectured openly in Quincy and surrounding Illinois towns on abolition and slavery, recruiting new members for the abolition movement and stirring resentment in Missouri. The increasing level of abolitionist propaganda in Illinois and other free states antagonized slaveholders. On February 12, 1839, the Missouri Legislature adopted a resolution calling on governors in free states to quiet abolitionists. The legislature, in language that clearly anticipated the Civil War, declared:

> That whereas, the institution of domestic slavery, as it now exists in many of the States of this confederacy, whether or not a moral or political evil, was entailed on us by our ancestors, recognized by the constitution of the United States—the paramount law of the land,—and, by that same instrument, forming the solemn compact which binds these States together, entirely and alone left to be regulated by the domestic policy of the several States: and whereas the interference with that institution on the part of the citizens of other portions of the Union, among whom it may not be tolerated, is unconstitutional; a gross violation of the solemn compact subsisting between the States of the confederacy; officious, derogating from the dignity of the slave-holding States, and insulting to their sovereignty; well calculated to disturb their domestic

5. Lee, *Slavery North of St. Louis*, 128.

peace, light up the torch, and plunge them amid the horrors of servile insurrection and war; disturb the friendly feeling and intercourse, which should ever subsist between the several States of the confederacy, and ultimately destroy their union, peace and happiness.[6]

Interestingly, the resolution expresses ambivalence about the morality of slavery. At this early stage of the battle over abolition, Missouri's slave culture could still acknowledge that slavery might be "a moral or political evil." In the decades to come, it would be political suicide for a politician to utter that sentiment—even as a conciliatory gesture to nonslaveholders. The legislature continued to warn about the danger abolitionists posed:

and whereas we have long viewed with feelings of deep regret the disposition continually fostered and promoted by the citizens of many of the States of this Union, wantonly to intermeddle with such institution, as manifested by numerous disorganizaing [sic] and insurrectionary movements; and have as fondly anticipated that the evil tendency of such a course of policy must long ere this have been seen and desisted from; but in these reasonable expectations, and calculations upon the sober sense and patriotism of our eastern brethren; we have been very disagreeably disappointed; Therefore, the southern and southwestern States, in these numerous and continued acts of insult to their sovereignty, are admonished in language too plain to be misunderstood, that the dreadful crisis is actually approaching, when each of them must look out means adequate to its own protection, poise itself upon its reserved rights, and prepare for defending its domestic institutions from wanton invasion, whether from foreign or domestic enemies, "peaceably if they can, forcibly, if they must."

Missouri was throwing down the gauntlet. The talk of force here is significant. Not only had Lovejoy been killed, but Missouri was warning Illinois, in particular, that it would not tolerate incursions onto its soil and that hot pursuit of slaves would take place. The legislature then adopted six resolutions and directed the Missouri governor to circulate them to other governors. The resolutions declared that the power to regulate slavery was expressly reserved to each state. Interference by citizens of one state with institutions of another was "grossly insulting to their sovereignty and ultimately tending to destroy the union, peace and happiness of these confederated States." The legislature applauded U.S.

6. *Laws of Missouri*, 337.

representatives and senators from slaveholding states for standing firm for slavery and denounced abolitionists as envying southern prosperity and seeking to destroy the domestic peace. They called for an end to the "invasion."

The restless abolitionists at the Presbyterian Mission Institute knew that agitating in Illinois for an end to slavery would accomplish little. Slavery did not exist there. The enemy was across the river in Missouri, where abolitionists were not only unwelcome but faced the very real prospect of death or imprisonment. The antislavery message could not get far in Missouri. The 1837 law banning such agitation was sufficiently broad that any abolitionist speech could be construed as a crime. So the men and women of the Adams County Anti-Slavery Society and those at the institute waited, watched for runaways to come to them in Illinois, and talked. Their efforts weren't wasted. Free blacks in Quincy knew to direct runaway slaves to the institute or Eells's two-story brick house. Institute students would spend weekend nights on the riverfront looking for runaways to aid. But the waiting was hard for the abolitionists, and they grew increasingly frustrated as they sat month after month in free territory, knowing that just across the river were thousands of people toiling in bondage. In July 1841 two students and an enthusiastic mechanic employed at the institute grew tired of waiting and took a step that shook the abolitionist movement and turned a national spotlight on Marion County.

Thompson, Work, and Burr

Thompson, Work, and Burr were a funny-looking lot. James Burr, a native of New York, was a young man, six feet, four inches tall, lanky and lean. Twenty-five-year-old George Thompson, also a New Yorker, stood only five feet tall and looked like a midget next to Burr. Alanson Work was a mechanic, or maintenance man. Originally from Middletown, Connecticut, Work was forty years old and had a wife and four children living at the institute. The three, along with all the faculty, students, and staff at the Presbyterian Mission Institute, hated slavery. They, like other young northern Presbyterians in the New School abolition movement led by Theodore Weld and his disciples David Nelson and Richard Eells, felt it was their religious duty to actively aid the slaves in Missouri in gaining their freedom. Tired of waiting for slaves to come to them, they wanted to act. They prayed for God's counsel and consulted with other students and with one another. Driven by their growing passion to end slavery, they determined to go into Missouri and attempt to entice slaves back across the Mississippi and put them on the track to Canada. There is no evidence that they sought Nelson's permission.[7]

Their plan was simple. They would walk up to slaves and invite them to run off with them. It was a terribly flawed idea. Little is known about their activities before July 11, 1841, but it appears that Burr and one other fellow had gone out scouting around the end of June. The other fellow was probably Alanson Work, but witnesses at the trial could only remember the towering Burr with certainty. Work would certainly have been less memorable. They rowed across the river and pretended to be travelers. They inquired of white people they encountered whether anyone in the neighborhood was looking for laborers, and they asked for directions. When they encountered slaves, they were direct. They assumed slaves would take them at face value. They introduced themselves and invited the slaves to run off with them. Witnesses testified that Burr was seen speaking with some Negroes on the farm of Mordicai Boulware in Marion County and was seen coming from Richard Woolfolk's place. Woolfolk owned a number of slaves and had leased several to his neighbor William Brown. On that scouting trip Burr met a slave named Anthony at the Woolfolk farm. Burr told Anthony that if he wished to go to freedom, Burr and his friend would take him. The slave refused.

It is hard today to imagine how strange and alien Work and Burr must have seemed to Anthony. White people in Missouri did not speak to slaves as equals. Slaves were property like horses, pigs, and chickens and were very aware of their monetary value to their masters. Slaves did not get to travel and were uneducated. They didn't generally have access to newspapers and couldn't have read them in any case. Even if Anthony could have read, he couldn't have gotten an abolition newspaper in Marion County—distributing them was a felony. In all likelihood, he didn't realize such a thing as an abolitionist existed. Anthony, like most slaves, did not trust white people.

On July 11, 1841, Burr again crossed the Mississippi River, this time with Work and Thompson. With more faith than caution the three men marched into Marion County determined to liberate some slaves.[8] Banking the boat near the Fabius River, Burr and Work went inland until they came upon the house belonging to Richard Woolfolk two and a half miles from the Mississippi. Woolfolk was not at home, and they took the opportunity to speak with the slave woman who kept the house. They told

7. George Thompson, *Prison Life and Reflections;* Circuit Court records of Marion County, Missouri.
8. *Liberator,* October 8, 1841.

her they were there to take her to freedom the next day if she wanted to go. They told her to be at a willow thicket near the river the next night to begin her trip to Canada.

Next, the two abolitionists went into the fields and spoke with a group of slaves hauling lumber without white supervision. Work and Burr again made their pitch. The slaves were Paris, Allen, Prince, John, and Anthony, the slave whom Burr had approached two weeks earlier. Paris was owned by William P. Brown; Allen, Prince, and John were leased to Brown for the year. The slaves were bewildered when the two white men approached them and spoke to them. As on Burr's earlier trip, the slaves seemed uncertain of the men from Illinois. Burr and Work must have been confused by the failure of the slaves to jump at the chance to get their freedom. They talked to the slaves and quoted the Bible—which must have sounded equally strange to slaves accustomed to hearing only those verses that supported slavery.

Unable to convince the slaves on the spot, Work and Burr told them they would meet them the next night at the willow thicket and would talk to them more then. The two abolitionists agreed to explain to the slaves the details of the trek to Canada and their chance for freedom—and if the slaves wanted to go, the men would row them across the Mississippi and start them on their way the next night. To the abolitionists' delight, the slaves agreed to meet them in the thicket. Work and Burr went back to the river, and Thompson rowed them back across the Mississippi. They were happy with the thought that the next night, with a little more explanation, they could bring a fresh batch of slaves to the red barn of the institute. They were terribly naive.

After the abolitionists left, the confused slaves talked among themselves. No white man had ever shown an interest in their well-being. This talk of freedom seemed fantastic. They were incapable of taking Work and Burr at face value and instead concluded, logically, that the abolitionists were slave thieves trying to decoy them from their masters and take them down the river and sell them to cotton or sugar planters. The thought of someone stealing from their masters was not particularly disturbing, but being sold downriver was a thing they dreaded worse than death. They had heard from their masters how miserable things were on the cotton and sugar plantations—the masters used the threat of sale to keep them in line. "Misbehave and master has no choice but to sell you down the river," they had been told. With Anthony as their leader, the men decided the prudent course was to report the abolitionists to William P. Brown.[9]

9. *Palmyra Missouri Whig* (hereinafter *PMW*), July 17, 1841; Circuit Court records of Marion County, Missouri.

Brown knew exactly what to do when Anthony came to him. He set a trap for Thompson, Work, and Burr. Though he was undoubtedly better informed about abolitionists—every slaveholder in the county knew about Nelson, Eells, and the Presbyterian Mission Institute across the river—he agreed with Anthony on one thing: Thompson, Work, and Burr were thieves. He was determined to catch them and see them in jail.

To ensure the cooperation of the slaves, Brown promised each of them five dollars for telling him about the plot and helping him catch the men. Five dollars was then a princely sum. Brown was savvy enough to know he needed more evidence if Thompson, Work, and Burr were to be prosecuted. So far they had only discussed their plan with the slaves themselves. This presented a problem because, under Missouri law, slaves could not testify in court. Even when the defendant was someone so low as an abolitionist, it was unthinkable and illegal in slave culture for a black man to testify against a white man. It was essential that the slaves get the three men to talk about the plot where white men could overhear them. Brown had Anthony rehearse questions he was to ask the abolitionists in the willow thicket. Since Work and Burr had agreed to explain more at the next meeting, it would be relatively easy.

Then Brown rode from neighbor to neighbor to raise the alarm and arrange for men to gather the next night with their shotguns and squirrel rifles near the rendezvous point. Five men answered the call: Samuel D. Wiseman, Mordicai Boulware, David Alton, John E. Shepherd, and George Heath. Hiding in the bush would be easy for these men. Hunting was a popular hobby in the Mississippi River bottoms. Everyone supplemented the larder with wild turkey, rabbit, squirrel, and deer. All knew how to handle a rifle or shotgun.

The next night Thompson, Work, and Burr kept the appointment. Fog lay on the river that July evening. It was near midnight when Thompson rowed the skiff to the bank and dropped off Work and Burr. Thompson then disappeared with the skiff back into the fog to await their return. Work and Burr pushed through the dark tangle of cottonwoods and vines on the riverbank and moved toward the willow thicket. Brown and the posse had been waiting in the brush since ten P.M.

When the abolitionists arrived, they gave a prearranged signal. Anthony answered with the countersign, and Work and Burr walked out of the brush. Brown and the posse lay concealed nearby. They strained to hear the voices of the two white men and five slaves over the sounds of the tree frogs and crickets. Anthony dutifully asked the two students the memorized questions, and the abolitionists soon began making incriminating statements. They trusted the slaves completely. Burr and Work told the slaves they had experience in liberating slaves—they had helped four slaves escape, and the last one had left the college just four weeks ago. They assured the slaves the passage was safe. In answer to Anthony's questions, Burr and Work said the runaways would travel by night and be hidden by friends during the day until they came to a great lake where they would be taken by steamboat to freedom. In true Judas style, Anthony said, "We will be governed by your directions." Excited, Burr answered that if they would do that and be faithful they would all get free. Burr grabbed the arm of Paris and began walking toward the river, where Thompson waited for the short ride to Illinois. Work followed with Allen and Prince. The abolitionists were undoubtedly rejoicing. Their happiness was short-lived.

They had taken only a few steps when Brown appeared with his gun pointed squarely at Burr's chest. On his order the other Marion County men rose and the ominous clicks of the cocking of a half dozen firearms were heard. Burr sprang forward, but Brown ordered him to stop or he would "blow him through." The tall youth surrendered. Burr and Work were stunned when the slaves they so recently had planned to lead to freedom tied them up at their master's direction.

To the credit of Brown and the Marion County men, they did not beat or lynch the two shocked abolitionists. They marched them instead to Boulware's place. Brown questioned Work and Burr and told them that he knew they were not alone. At first they denied having an accomplice, but Work finally admitted that a third man, Thompson, was waiting with a skiff on the Mississippi near the mouth of the Fabius River.

Leaving the others to guard Burr and Work, Brown and Wiseman took the slaves Paris, Allen, and Prince and headed to the river to capture Thompson. As before, Brown intended to hide and have the slaves question the abolitionist so he and Wiseman could testify against him in court. Brown ordered Paris, Allen, and Prince to go ahead in case Thompson was on the riverbank; he and Wiseman followed with their guns. When they got to the river, Thompson was nowhere to be found. On Brown's instruction, Paris rapped his knuckles against a fence rail, and in response came the splashing of oars as Thompson rowed out of the fog and guided the boat to the bank. The two white men ducked back into the brush.

When the skiff reached the bank, the three slaves dutifully secured it. Brown and Wiseman strained to hear the men over the slapping water and night noises of the woods. Frustrated, Brown shouted for the slaves to haul Thompson out of the boat or get hold of the skiff and hold on. He bounded out of the brush with his shotgun in hand.

Thompson, not realizing he had been betrayed, grabbed the oars and shouted for the slaves to push off and jump in the boat, but they held the skiff firm. The confused Thompson pleaded with them to get in so they could get away. When Brown reached the boat, he leveled his gun at Thompson and ordered him to surrender. Thompson gave up easily. Flushed with pride over his victory, Brown asked Thompson why he was trying to decoy away his Negroes. Thompson replied that he felt it was his duty to do what he could for his fellow man and quoted scripture to Brown, but the slaveholder was unmoved. He could not comprehend, nor could the slaves themselves, why a white man would steal a slave for no monetary gain. Brown did a good job of getting Thompson to incriminate himself: Thompson admitted he intended to take them across the river. Keeping his shotgun aimed at Thompson's chest, Brown had the slaves pull the abolitionist from the boat, tie him, and march him to William Boulware's house to join Work and Burr.

There the three men were held overnight. They were not mistreated. The next morning they were marched, still under armed guard, to the Marion County Jail at Palmyra. Word of their capture had spread, and a curious thing happened. As the men crossed the countryside, they were joined by a throng of people who jeered and swore at the bewildered abolitionists. They arrived in Palmyra at the head of a victorious parade like captives in Rome. At the local jail, the men were shackled and bound to large wooden chairs. Men, women, and children came to the window of the jail to stare at these oddities and to taunt them. Firebrands in the community called for their hanging.

Chapter 6

The Trial of Thompson, Work, and Burr

The most ingenious and infallible agency for defeating justice that human wisdom could contrive.

Mark Twain, *Roughing It*

Word spread throughout Marion County, and larger crowds gathered in Palmyra. Thompson, Work, and Burr were proof of the shaveholders' worst fears: Abolitionist radicals from across the river would not be content to "agitate" about slavery; they were ready to invade Missouri and steal slaves. A lynch mob formed, but the county responded by posting armed guards at the jail and at the courthouse. Faced with firm opposition and assurances the men would be tried and convicted, the mob allowed the judicial process to work, and it moved very quickly, especially by today's standards. On July 13, 1841, the same day they marched into Palmyra, William Brown and Samuel Wiseman appeared before the circuit court and filed affidavits stating what had happened the night before. The abolitionists were ordered held without bond until the grand jury convened in September.

Meanwhile, the people of Marion County began eyeing strangers suspiciously. Although there had been antislavery activity in Marion County, never before had white men been caught trying to free slaves. The editor of the *Palmyra Missouri Whig* warned the public: "[I]t becomes our duty to notify the people of the means which may be employed to beguile, betray, and even decoy away our slaves from our very doors, to the end that all may be upon the watch—that if there are Abolitionists among us who would employ such artifice for the purpose of effecting their infamous purposes, that they may be detected and brought to merited punishment."[1]

From the very beginning, the people of Marion County had interpreted the slaves' reporting of the abolitionists as an act of loyalty. Whites regarded it as proof that slaves were happy with their position in life. The newspaper issued a warning to abolitionists:

> We have another object in view also, in publishing the manner of the capture of those men—it is, that all Abolitionists everywhere may be notified of the condition of our slaves and the estimation in which they hold them and their doctrines—that Abolitionists everywhere may learn from the conduct of those slaves in the capture of those men, that they need none of their aid, and are ready to refuse their ill-timed assistance—that slaves as they are, they know too much of the effects of Abolition doctrines upon the condition of slaves elsewhere, to favor their plans or aid their schemes—that they have no confidence in men who advise a violation of all law, human and divine—who disseminate far and wide a system whereby the bonds of slavery, which, before the introduction of their wicked schemes, were worn without oppression, are drawn closer and closer, and which will be rendered more and more intolerable to the slave, in proportion as the doctrines of Abolition shall more or less prevail. Let the Abolitionist, with all his boasted love of Virtue and Philanthropy, learn from the lessons of fidelity, patriotism and honesty evinced in the conduct of those slaves.[2]

The circuit attorney, James R. Abernethy, prepared charges against the three. He described Thompson, Work, and Burr as "evil disposed persons . . . wickedly devising and intending to defraud and prejudice" the slaveholders. The abolitionists, he claimed, "did among themselves, conspire, combine, agree and confederate together wickedly and feloniously to steal take and carry away" the slaves.[3]

The case quickly drew national attention, and, like the case of Elijah Lovejoy, polarized the country. The three men were seen either as new martyrs to the abolitionists' cause or as proof of the increasing radicalism and recklessness of antislavery zealots. Though Thompson, Work, and Burr were not lynched, they were denied bond, and that aspect of the case did not play well even with the moderate, nonabolitionist press in free states. A man charged with murder in Marion County had recently

1. *PMW*, July 17, 1841.
2. Ibid.
3. Circuit Court records of Marion County, Missouri.

been granted bond, and it was easy for radicals to argue that in slave-holding Missouri abolitionists were regarded as more threatening than murderers.

The men were kept in leg irons attached to a long chain anchored to the wall of the jail. Curious crowds continued to gather each day outside the jail and gaze through the windows of the cell. Those lucky enough to know a guard were allowed to come to the door for a closer look. Some mocked the prisoners; others just stared at the misguided fanatics.

After a week, the men were allowed a Bible, and then friends from the Presbyterian Mission Institute braved the crowds to bring other books to them. Thompson, Work, and Burr passed the time in Bible study, prayer, and singing. They also wrote letters to friends, family, and newspapers. Though they had to come to Missouri with the modest goal of freeing slaves a few at a time, Thompson, Work, and Burr discovered their true role in the dark confines of the Palmyra jail. They were to prove themselves excellent propagandists. Just a week after their capture, they wrote to William Lloyd Garrison's abolitionist newspaper:

> We are comfortably situated, much more so than was Peter, or Paul and Silas, and the ancient Christians. We can read, sing and pray. We have enough to eat and drink. We are only fastened by one leg to a chain, and have blankets to lay upon. We can look out, and see people and things and have plenty of company. Our food and fresh water is brought to us three times a day. The walls of our house are four feet thick, with two inner doors, each having three rows of iron grates. But we have no desire to get out. "Let them come and bring us out." We have no desire to be set at Liberty, unless it can be done by law, and God will be glorified by it. If it is the will of our Father that we should lie here six weeks, we shall try and be contented, cheerful and happy, and profit by it.
>
> If then He sees it will be best for us, and for His glory, that we should go to Jefferson [the state prison] seven, ten, or fifteen years, we will still rejoice, and trust in the Lord feeling that He will do only that for us which will be best for us and His cause.[4]

The abolitionist press adored these brave new martyrs who suffered like early Christians in the "dungeon" of Marion County, Missouri. The three abolitionists asked not for insurrection, jailbreak, or even legal assistance—only for prayers from their brethren in the cause. It all made brilliant propaganda. Straight razors could not be entrusted to prisoners, and the Marion County sheriff shaved inmates only one day a week.

4. *Liberator*, August 27, 1841.

Unfortunately, he elected to do this on Sunday. Thompson, Work, and Burr considered this to be a violation of the Sabbath. They protested. When Work refused to come down for his shave one morning, he was forcibly taken from his cell, and half of his head was shaved. When he refused again, he was stripped to the waist and given ten lashes by the jailor. When his ordeal was finished, Work forgave the man who had whipped him. In a letter to the outside world, Thompson noted that Work had suffered under the same whip as the slaves.

Missourians remained unmoved by the men's zeal and proceeded steadfastly toward their trial. The grand jury met in September and returned indictments. Sheriff John Jordan Montgomery, a slave owner himself, was instructed to gather a jury to hear the case, which, in 1841, meant handpicking twelve men. Now, great care is taken that a jury is randomly drawn from the community, but then, the sheriff might just walk down the street or go into a saloon where a ready pool of men could be found and draft them for jury duty. For important cases, he would impanel what was known as a "blue ribbon" jury, for which he would pick prominent men from the community. *Missouri v. Burr, Work, and Thompson* was the most important case yet heard in Marion County and required responsible, important men. John Marshall Clemens was selected for the jury.

By the fall of 1841, the store he had opened in Hannibal had predictably failed, but Clemens had clearly nurtured some political connections and was considered respectable and reliable by the Whig sheriff. This is not surprising. Although he would never be admitted to the bar to practice law in Missouri, he had been an attorney in Tennessee. He had also been moderately successful in government, having been a postmaster and an attorney general in Tennessee and a county judge in Monroe County, Missouri. He was an outspoken conservative Whig. Perhaps most important of all for this jury, he was a slave owner—though by this time he had only a single slave, Jennie. John Marshall Clemens was part of and understood slave culture. He could be counted on to do the right thing with the abolitionists.

Most of the other jurors were prominent men. Daniel Hendricks had been elected a judge of the Marion County Court in 1827 and had served as an election judge for twenty years. In 1836, Hendricks had been appointed one of three commissioners to adjudicate a land dispute between Hannibal founders Moses D. Bates and Stephen Glascock. Franklin Whaley, also a Whig, was the county surveyor and a captain in the local militia. William Jones was the founder of the village of Houston. Milton Jones had been an early settler in the county, and his house in Round Grove Township was used as a polling place. Joseph Thompson owned a Palmyra hog-packing plant, and he was a captain in the local militia. Z. G. Draper was the postmaster of Hannibal. One of the first fifty residents of the town, he had signed the petition for incorporation of Hannibal and had served with Franklin Whaley on the commission to divide the Bates and Glascock land. The other jurors were: Johnathon Cluff, J. W. Jeffries, H. T. Bowles, John Shumate, and David Hornecan. At least six of the jurors had been listed as slave owners in the 1840 census. Milton Jones, Clemens, and Jeffries owned one slave each; Cluff, six; William Jones, seven; and H. T. Bowles lived with his father, who owned ten slaves.

The judge in the case was Priestly H. McBride. McBride was politically astute. He had been secretary of state for Missouri in 1829 and 1830. He became the circuit judge for Marion County in 1830. Within four years of the case of *Missouri v. Burr, Work, and Thompson* he would be appointed to the Missouri Supreme Court.

At trial, each side was represented by three attorneys. Because of the high-profile nature of the case, Marion County citizens raised money to bring a special prosecuting attorney, J. B. Crocket, from St. Louis to act as lead counsel. The local prosecuting attorney, James R. Abernethy, a Whig who had run unopposed in the election of 1840, and Thomas L. Anderson, a rising political star in Marion County, assisted Crocket. Anderson, who owned eleven slaves, had volunteered to help the prosecution, and he served without pay.

The lead counsel for the abolitionists was a local Marion County attorney named Samuel T. Glover. He was retained by Alanson Work, who paid with a note for $250. Glover, like many early Marion County settlers, was a Virginian by birth. He had settled in Palmyra, Missouri, in 1837 and was the leader of the local bar and active in Whig politics. He would play a prominent role in many of Marion County's major cases. Assisting him were Uriel Wright, a graduate of West Point, a captain in the local militia, and an active Whig; and C. A. Warren, a Quincy, Illinois, man, who was sympathetic to the abolitionists.

Defendants Thompson, Work, and Burr were charged with larceny—simple theft of property. The trial lasted for three days and drew the largest crowd ever to attend a trial in Marion County. Spectators filled the windows, hallway, and stairs leading to the courtroom and poured out onto the lawn. They were a boisterous group, and they made certain that everyone knew they were there for more than mere entertainment. If the result did not please them, they were prepared to take action.

Respectable citizens said that if the court didn't punish the abolitionists, the mob would. Less-respectable citizens went so far as to threaten Thompson, Work, and Burr directly, saying that if they were acquitted they would never leave Missouri alive. A neutral reporter for a St. Louis newspaper observed, "I am of opinion that it would be much better for the prisoners to be sent to the penitentiary, than to be turned loose here, for there is no telling what scenes might be enacted."[5]

Armed guards had already been posted at the jail and in the courtroom, and additional precautions were taken. In the courtroom special gates were erected at the ends of the bar separating the spectators' seats from the attorneys and judge in order to keep the crowds from rushing the prisoners. Despite the threatening talk, the trial was conducted without incident. Many trial observers came from Quincy, including students from the hated Presbyterian Mission Institute. They were treated courteously and even rented rooms. Mrs. Alanson Work and several ladies of the institute were put up as guests by the Muldrow family in Palmyra.[6] It must have been a particularly trying time for Mrs. Work. While her husband was incarcerated, the youngest of her four children, a two-year-old daughter, died.

In a move that disappointed abolitionists across the country, who wanted to see slavery itself put on trial, the attorneys representing Thompson, Work, and Burr relied on a technical defense. Since they were charged with theft, their attorneys maintained their innocence on the theory that they never had control of the slaves. It was a losing proposition. As had Judge Lawless, regarding Elijah Lovejoy, the judge decided what applicable law the jury was to consider. The jury decided the facts. Judge McBride was not going to let the abolitionists off easily.

The trial was an exceedingly simple affair: The white men who had captured the three abolitionists testified about the events of July 12, 1841; there were no witnesses for the defense, nor was there a lofty battle of ideas to amuse readers in the salons of Boston. The attorneys for the abolitionists did not offer a shred of evidence concerning the immorality of slavery or their doctrine of abolition. They produced no character witnesses. They relied instead on their cross-examination of the state's witnesses to show that the three men charged never took possession of the slaves. Their tactic is summed up in the instructions the attorneys for Thompson, Work, and Burr proposed that the court give the jury.

Glover, Wright, and Warren knew that in Missouri it was not illegal to entice a slave to run away. Thompson, Work, and Burr would have faced the same charges if they had stolen any piece of property. The defense at-

5. *PMW*, September 25, 1841.

6. Adams County Anti-Slavery Society, *Narrative of Facts Respecting Alanson Work, Jas. E. Burr and Geo. Thompson*, 19.

torneys relied on a very precise and technical tactic. They asked McBride to instruct the jury that the law required that before the jury could find the defendants guilty of stealing, they first must find that the abolitionists had possessed the slaves and placed them under their "control, dominion, or authority."

Moreover, they asked that if the jury did find that the three men had "possessed" the slaves, the jury would have to believe that the abolition- ists intended to take the slaves for themselves. Finally, the defense asked the judge to state that it was not sufficient just to show that Thompson, Work, and Burr were willing to give aid and assistance to the slaves in crossing the Mississippi River and in getting away to Canada, but that the three abolitionists had to have intended to sell or hire the slaves or keep them for themselves.[7]

The attorneys for the defense were taking a calculated risk. It was a valid defense in that the instructions were technically correct. The defense was gambling that the judge would find that the state had charged the men with the wrong crime. Perhaps Thompson, Work, and Burr had vi- olated the 1837 law against promulgating abolitionist ideas and seeking to incite rebellion in the slaves by asking them to run away, but the three abolitionists were not thieves. The danger was that the judge would not go along with their interpretation of the law.

He didn't. Like Lawless in the McIntosh case, McBride had a great deal of discretion in instructing the jury, and his decision should not be sur- prising. To say that the abolitionists were not guilty of theft was to give the doctrine of abolition credence. The Missouri Legislature had already declared the doctrine illegal in the state of Missouri. Furthermore, slaves were property. To take another's property was theft—even if this was not a conventional case of theft. Undoubtedly his thoughts were mirrored by the editor of the *Palmyra Missouri Whig*: "Suppose for instance, that those men had been cleared; could not every man in this community have done the same thing with impunity?"[8]

McBride did not give the jury the instructions prepared by the attorneys for Thompson, Work, and Burr. Instead he submitted the instructions pre- pared by the state's attorneys, which left the jury very little to deliberate: the three men were guilty if they had taken and carried the slaves away. The judge broadly defined "taking and carrying." He told the jury that if the abolitionists had caused the slaves to move "one step," then they had

7. Circuit Court records of Marion County, Missouri. See appendix for the instructions tendered by the defense.
8. *PMW*, September 25, 1841.

stolen the slaves. Under the prosecution's instructions, as given by the judge, it did not matter if the "taking" had been by "physical" or "moral" force. In a particularly bizarre instruction, the judge told the jury that if the defendants had intended to defraud the owners and deprive them of their slaves to give ownership of the slaves to the slaves themselves, they were guilty of theft. It was a twisted but logical idea—property could own itself. A runaway slave was stealing from his master to give himself to himself.[9]

The jury handed down a harsh sentence: twelve years for each man in the Missouri State Penitentiary. McBride gladly imposed the jury's sentence. He wanted to clearly warn abolitionists—implement your ideas in Missouri, and you go to prison. In the abolition camp, other lessons were learned from the case.

Thompson, Work, and Burr were transported to the penitentiary in Jefferson City by stagecoach. A posse of a half dozen men on horseback armed with pistols and knives escorted the stage on the three-day trip. A rumor had reached Marion County that armed abolitionists planned to free the three abolitionists. It was merely a rumor. Sheriff Montgomery rode in the stage with the prisoners. Montgomery was a member of the Presbyterian church in Palmyra. While the abolitionists had been in his jail, Montgomery had refused to speak to them. Even in the cramped quarters of the stage he spoke with them very little. Thompson finally induced the sheriff to talk about slavery and religion, and Montgomery told the prisoners that he considered their mentor, David Nelson, a very bad man who was "not fit to live."[10] He told them he thought their behavior in trying to set the slaves free was unchristian.

Thompson, Work, and Burr made some favorable impression on the people of Marion County. Both McBride and the jailer at Palmyra wrote letters to the warden on their behalf. Their own attorney, Samuel T. Glover, wrote to the warden as well. His letter was similar to the judge's and jailer's. Glover wrote: "I am of the opinion that they are conscientious men, and mean to do right according to their views of right. I think, sir, they would be incapable of stealing, in the common acceptation of that term—and what they have done, has been induced by mistaken opinions of duty in regard to the subject of slavery—they being practically and emphatically ABOLITIONISTS."[11]

9. Circuit Court records of Marion County, Missouri. See appendix for the instructions tendered by the state.
10. Thompson, *Prison Life and Reflections,* 113.
11. Ibid., 110.

The case of Thompson, Work, and Burr triggered a vicious backlash against strangers in Missouri. Suspicion replaced hospitality toward outsiders. No traveling peddler, itinerant preacher, or emigrant would ever again be welcomed in Missouri's slave culture without careful questioning and examination. Feelings hardened toward anyone from Illinois or Iowa, and over the coming two decades these feelings would grow increasingly bitter.

Missouri's slave culture learned another lesson from the case—and inadvertently helped make the work of the Underground Railroad easier in northeast Missouri. Rather than analyzing why Anthony and his fellow slaves had betrayed their would-be rescuers, slaveholders clung to the notion that the slaves had acted out of loyalty to their masters. "True to their masters & own interests, true also to the laws of their country—instead of being duped by the specious promises of those men," was how the Marion county press described them.[12] This presumption of loyalty allowed slaves and free blacks to organize more easily. The idea of the loyal slave would last right up until the Civil War, when some locals would still believe that no slave could be made to fight against his master.

The Martyrs

Thompson, Work, and Burr became more committed abolitionists in prison. If the judge and jury had intended to break the three men, they failed miserably. The prisoners churned out a series of letters and books that sparked bonfires of conscience across the free states.

The Friend of Man, an abolition newspaper, wrote, "If the Prince of Darkness should offer a premium for the vilest judicial act of the 19th century, this act of the Court of Missouri would receive it."[13] On October 4, 1841, an antislavery concert for prayer was held in Quincy, Illinois. A resolution was passed denouncing the trial, verdict, and sentence. It protested that Thompson, Work, and Burr had been convicted not for any felony, but for the idea of abolition. The *Hartford Observer* called the three men "Victims of Slavery."[14]

Constantly comparing himself and his friends to the early Christian martyrs, Thompson churned out letters that portrayed the three as vic-

---

12. *PMW,* July 17, 1841.
13. *Liberator,* December 10, 1841.
14. Ibid., October 8, 1841.

tims. "Doubtless you have heard the cause of my being in this place," he wrote on September 15, 1841,

> for stretching out my hand to help the poor—for following the Samari-
> tan's example—for loving my neighbor as myself—for doing to others,
> as I would have them do to me—for acting out the principles of the
> Bible, and the spirit of the gospel—or, plainly, for attempting to help
> across the river, one who wished and requested the assistance; being in
> trouble, and desiring to escape from the iron despotism of slavery. Such,
> brother is my offense.[15]

Of course, Thompson was stretching the truth. He had gone into Missouri seeking to bring slaves to freedom, not responding to a request for aid. Had the slaves trusted white people enough to request help, Work and Burr would probably not have been betrayed and caught. Cool heads in the abolition camp reflected on what happened to Thompson, Work, and Burr and realized that if slaves were to be brought out of Missouri and other slave states, it would be necessary to involve people that the slaves trusted. They realized that a small pool of such people was already present in Marion County—the few free blacks that scratched a living on the margins of society. They would be the key to reaching slaves with the message of freedom. They would serve as conductors and offer way stations on the Underground Railroad on the slave side of the river. Whites would help on the Illinois and Iowa sides. It would be a slow process, but over the next two decades the Underground Railroad would grow, and more blacks would find freedom by making their way across the Mississippi and then north to Canada through Chicago or Detroit.

The real winner in the trial of Thompson, Work, and Burr was John Marshall Clemens. Sam Clemens's father was lucky to have had a role in the biggest criminal case in Marion County. He had proven his loyalty to his community and slavery. He and the other jurors were treated as local heroes for convicting the men and imposing long prison sentences. It was the only good luck John Marshall Clemens would have in 1841.

15. Ibid., November 5, 1841.

Chapter 7

Judge John Marshall Clemens

The case was at last submitted, and duly finished by the judge with an absurd decision and a ridiculous sentence.

Mark Twain, *The Innocents Abroad*

Just a month after the big trial, on October 13, 1841, John and Jane Clemens lost all of their real estate in Hannibal. The property was transferred for the benefit of their creditors to James Kerr, a dry goods merchant in St. Louis, who held the majority of the debt. A year to the day later, the property was auctioned, but it failed to bring an adequate price.[1] The winter of 1842 was a hard one for the Clemens family.

Desperate for money, Clemens determined to travel to Mississippi, where he planned to collect on a twenty-year-old debt that was due him from a man named Lester. He planned to go on to Tennessee and try to sell his land holdings there.

The trip was a disaster. Clemens located the deadbeat near Vicksburg, but consistent with his lifetime of poor business deals, Clemens was out-negotiated. He inexplicably traded a note worth $470 for another in the amount of $250, payable the next spring. In Tennessee, he was unable to find a buyer for his land. Although vast, the property was rocky, with poor soil, and unattractive to farmers. Clemens returned to Hannibal in March 1842, poorer than when he had left—his trip had cost $200.

John Marshall Clemens returned to a slave culture increasingly under siege. Abolitionists were gaining strength in Illinois and Iowa; slaves were running away. Clemens now harvested the political seed he had sowed in

1. Wecter, *Sam Clemens of Hannibal*, 70.

the trial of Thomson, Work, and Burr. Hannibal voters elected him justice of the peace in the fall of 1842. It was a part-time job and paid very little, but it did pay. It was a welcome source of revenue in hard times. (The position is now that of municipal judge, requires hearing two hour-long sessions of court a week, and pays an annual salary of $6000.) Clemens collected different fees for various services. In 1845, the first year for which full records are available, Clemens collected $144 in fees. As an added benefit, Clemens was once again allowed to use the title "judge."

The court of the justice of the peace convened every few months for a few days, or as needed. Most of Clemens's docket consisted of small collection cases in which creditors sought to obtain judgment on notes they had taken from debtors. He also heard minor criminal cases and performed marriages. The job was not considered important; it was the lowest rung on the judicial totem pole. When he died in 1847, his obituary in the *Hannibal Gazette* referred to him as Judge Clemens but did not mention his service as justice of the peace; it did mention his contribution to Hannibal as one of the founders of the Hannibal Library.

While the income from the new position was welcome, it was not sufficient to maintain the family. Clemens was forced to take a job as a clerk in a wholesale grocery and dry goods business. On May 5, 1845, he wrote to his daughter Pamela, who was visiting friends in Florida, Missouri, "I have removed my office of Justice to Messrs McCune & Holliday's counting room where I have taken Mr. Dame's place as clerk—I did not succeed in making such arrangements as would enable me to go into business advantageously on my own acct—and thought it best therefore not to attempt it at present."[2]

John Marshall Clemens may have known the Holliday family of Monroe County from his time in Florida, Missouri. Clemens had served on the Monroe County Court before moving to Hannibal in 1839. Holliday and McCune was a commission merchant firm. The company purchased groceries and dry goods in St. Louis and shipped them by steamboat up the Mississippi to Hannibal. There the goods were warehoused before being transported by wagon to Monroe County, where they were sold.

The patriarch of the Holliday family was Joseph Holliday. His wife's family were the McCunes. Holliday's son John James lived in Hannibal. The Holliday family is important in American history for more than merely providing a job to John Marshall Clemens. While in Hannibal, John James had a daughter who became the great-grandmother of Presi-

2. John Marshall Clemens to Pamela Clemens, May 5, 1845, Mark Twain Papers and Project, University of California, Berkley.

dent George H. W. Bush (and great-great-grandmother of President George W. Bush.) In one of history's little ironies, John James's inheritance from his father Joseph Holliday was a slave named Walker. The Holliday and McCune Company allowed Clemens to hold court in their office as the need arose.

Despite his very modest financial situation, and despite the fact that he was not a practicing attorney in Missouri, the proud John Marshall Clemens took his position very seriously—too seriously for some. He became the object of public ridicule on at least one occasion. In 1846, Abraham Hathaway was accused of embezzlement and was brought before Judge Clemens. The meaning of embezzlement has changed a bit over the years. Hathaway was accused of hiding two horses that belonged to Ambrose D. Baker with the intent of stealing them. Clemens, together with another Marion County justice of the peace, Richard Holliday, examined Baker and the witnesses on March 25 and 26, 1846. On March 27, Clemens stated that there was not enough evidence to hold Hathaway: "it appears from the evidence before us that there is no probable cause for charging the prisoner with said offence and the said Abraham Hathaway, the prisoner, is therefore discharged—and it is ordered and adjudged that the state pay the costs of the prosecution."[3] For his services in the two-day case, Clemens charged $11.10—a large fee for one of his cases.

The next day Ambrose Baker appeared in Clemens's court with some new evidence. Clemens issued another warrant and had Hathaway arrested again.[4] Hathaway's attorney went immediately to the Hannibal Court of Common Pleas and filed a writ of habeas corpus challenging the arrest. Judge Van Swearingen, the circuit judge, held an immediate hearing and threw out the charges. He issued an order releasing Hathaway from custody. Van Swearingen decided that an individual who had been once arrested, examined by a magistrate about a criminal offense, and discharged could not lawfully be reexamined about the same offence. The first decision bars further arrest and examination for the same offense. Of course, this is the familiar principle of double jeopardy.

Clemens was so incensed at the action of his superior judge that he did a very unusual thing. He wrote a legal opinion for the April 30, 1846, *Hannibal Journal* in which he defended his action. While the original *Journal* story was destroyed in a fire in the late 1840s, the *Palmyra Missouri Whig* reported the incident. Jacob Sosey, the editor, found Clemens's spunk amusing.

3. Court records of John Marshall Clemens, 324.
4. Ibid., 326.

Mr. Clemens admits the judge has the power over him; but insists that he can out-argue the Judge. We do not profess to know anything about law matters; but we do not remember to have seen before an inferior tribunal reviewing the opinion of a higher court. The age we live in is an age of improvement however, and for aught [sic] we know, we may live to see the day when the Supreme Court of the land may be the tribunal of the first resort, and causes of importance will be appealed downwards from that body to a grand inquest of Justices of the Peace gathered up from all the townships in the State.[5]

Despite this public rebuke, Clemens could not restrain himself from writing another opinion, which was published in the Hannibal newspaper the following week. While it too has been lost, we have the following observation from the *Palmyra Missouri Whig:* "Mr. Justice Clemens is out again this week in another long article on his Honor Judge Van Swearingen. This Justice Clemens must be a pretty obstinate fellow thus to maul and hammer his betters. We suppose the Judge begins to think as was said of another once: 'had I known he was so cunning of fence, I would have seen him d-d ere I had fought him.'" Hannibal must be an unruly city. Our little Justices in the little town of Palmyra don't do so."[6]

Clemens had another important job as justice of the peace: He enforced the slave ordinance of Hannibal. The records for the first two years have been lost, but the fall docket for 1844 contains a case of a slave tried for sedition and possession of a knife. His name was Henry. He had no last name; he was simply Henry, as is reflected in the court record: *The State v. Henry, a slave.*[7]

On September 14, 1844, Henry was brought before Judge Clemens. Henry undoubtedly knew the law and the outcome of the case before he entered the Hannibal courtroom. Slaves were well drilled in the deference to be given whites. Custom and a lifetime of physical punishment for transgressions, real or imagined, had given most blacks an advanced education in feigning subservience. In Missouri, all blacks were presumed to be slaves unless they could prove otherwise. Any white citizen had the authority under state law to administer a whipping to any slave if he or she thought it warranted. Pastors hammered home the message of subservience in sermon after sermon—*Servants obey your masters! Slavery is the will of God.*

5. *PMW,* May 7, 1846.
6. Ibid., May 14, 1846.
7. Court records of John Marshall Clemens, 17.

The city slave ordinance set forth the manner in which slaves were to conduct themselves in Hannibal. Henry surely knew the treatment he could expect if he crossed the line. "Uppity" behavior could get a slave in serious trouble. Henry had been arrested for possession of an unlawful weapon and for seditious speech, and he would have known that the Hannibal ordinance provided for whipping a slave who merely cantered a horse, so he was sure to be whipped for making threats. Whippings were a public matter in Marion County. On farms where there were groups of slaves, if a slave was whipped, other slaves were made to watch. A whipping for violating the Hannibal slave ordinance was administered on the street.

He was tried under the second section of the ordinance that governed the conduct of slaves, free Negroes, and mulattoes toward whites. The ordinance provided for the punishment for those who "shall menace, or abuse, or insult any white person, or shall use any insulting language or gestures." Violators were subject to be brought before the justice of the peace in said town and "receive on his or her bare back any number of lashes not exceeding thirty-nine, at the discretion of said Justice, to be well laid on by the Town Constable." Slaves had to be very careful not to say anything that could be construed as threatening to a white person.[8]

The weapon charge was also very serious. State statute prohibited slaves from having weapons. The knife was characterized as "offensive"—"to wit a large Butchers or Bowie Knife." Hannibal's slave culture had been jumpy since the arrest and trial of Thompson, Work, and Burr, and any threat was taken seriously. The complaining witness was a Henry W. Collins.

The justice of the peace was a powerful person to the slaves of Hannibal. Hannibal was a small place, and Henry surely knew the attitudes of John Marshall Clemens toward slaves. He may have known Clemens had sold Jennie to a local slave trader, who shipped her downriver. He might have known that just three years earlier Clemens had served on the jury in the well-publicized trial of the abolitionists who had slipped over the Mississippi from free-state Illinois to help slaves escape. Henry might have known the young Illinois idealists were convicted and sentenced to twelve years in the Missouri State Penitentiary. The justice of the peace and the community did not take lightly threats to Missouri human property nor did they tolerate troublemaking slaves.

At Henry's trial, one witness, James Caldwell, was subpoenaed for the state. Two witnesses were subpoenaed on Henry's behalf: John Kitts

8. Minute Book of Hannibal, 1839–1849.

and a man named Ritchie. The court reporter didn't record Ritchie's first name. We don't know what the witnesses actually said. The record of the proceeding is just one page. We'll never know what prompted Henry to make threatening remarks. Perhaps he had been drinking and let down his guard, the defenses that were essential to a slave's survival. Perhaps he had merely taken all he could take living in such an oppressive society and boiled over.

We do know the verdict John Marshall Clemens entered. He recorded, "Whereupon, it appearing from the testimony of the witnesses aforesaid that said accused did commit the offences charged in the warrant against him, etc the said slave Henry is convicted thereof, and ordered to receive twenty lashes at the hands of the constable."[9] Henry was undoubtedly taken from the courtroom and whipped in public. We don't know who gathered around to watch as Henry took his twenty lashes "well laid on," but the crowd might have included the sons of the justice of the peace. Nine-year-old Sam liked to play about Hannibal on pretty fall days. A public whipping would have been high entertainment in 1844 Hannibal.

9. Court records of John Marshall Clemens, 18.

Chapter 8

Slavery and the Churches of Hannibal

The wise and the good and the holy were unanimous in the conviction that slavery was right, righteous, sacred, the peculiar pet of the Deity and a condition which the slave himself ought to be daily and nightly thankful for.

The Autobiography of Mark Twain

The Clemens women joined the First Presbyterian Church of Hannibal in early 1841. Sam's sister Pamela became a member on February 7, 1841, and was joined by mother Jane on February 18. Jane was baptized four days later. There is no record that John Marshall Clemens or his sons ever joined the church. The church, founded by David Nelson, was then only nine years old. No sermons advocating abolition had been heard in Hannibal since the exiling of Nelson in 1836 for antislavery activity and the Missouri Legislature's outlawing of abolitionist speech and literature the following year.[1]

Nelson was hardly alone in triggering backlash responses with his abolitionist message. During the Second Great Awakening, northern revivalists increasingly became involved in the antislavery campaign. Southern clergymen responded by disavowing the religious enthusiasm that threatened the foundations of their society. Before 1837 in the General Assemblies of the Presbyterian Church, the "old school" clergy, who objected to revivalism on theological grounds, were in a distinct minority to the "new school," who supported the Second Awakening. This schism deepened,

1. Session minutes, First Presbyterian Church, Hannibal, Missouri, February 22, 1841; *Laws of Missouri*, 3.

and the Presbyterians soon broke into two separate groups. Southerners, for the most part, had not been deeply involved in this theological controversy; however, the attacks on slavery made them suspicious of the excesses of revivalism in the North. Many members of slave culture were attracted to the old school of theology. Conservative by nature, they appreciated structured church services without highly emotional revivals and the resulting excitement, agitation, and reform movements.

Slavery split the Presbyterian Church, but the dispute was couched in terms of religious doctrine. The church held annual national conventions called assemblies. At the 1837 assembly, church members from slaveholding regions united with some northern old school clergy to expel the new school clergy. The old school group formed a new General Assembly and retained the name Presbyterian. The old Presbyterian assembly, which predated the schism, was called new school. The schism thundered through the church. The Hannibal congregation first voted on the issue in 1840. The church was affiliated with the St. Charles Presbytery. Nine of fourteen churches in the local Presbytery voted in favor of associating with the old school group. The Hannibal church affiliated itself with the new school St. Louis Presbytery in the Missouri synod.

The new school itself soon divided into two camps. While still allowing, even encouraging, revivals, churches in slaveholding states focused on personal improvement and redemption as opposed to societal reform. This kept new school preachers from tinkering with slavery but permitted church members to enjoy the energizing benefits of revival meetings. This was the path taken by the Hannibal church.

The abortive raid of Thompson, Work, and Burr was proof enough of the danger of new school theology to many Missouri Presbyterians. David Nelson and thousands of other new schoolers lived just across the Mississippi River and preached abolition at revivals, teaching the doctrine to impressionable young men. To the old school proponents, continuing with volatile revivals was a dangerous course—unleashing the genie of the camp meeting could lead people astray and possibly to the unchristian doctrine of abolition. Hannibal's new school proponents accepted revivals so long as they focused on safe subjects, such as refraining from dancing, drinking, tobacco, and cards. Feelings ran high within the congregation and triggered a split in the Hannibal church.

On January 16, 1842, one elder and twenty-four members of the First Presbyterian Church withdrew from the congregation. They organized the Second Presbyterian Church and joined the Palmyra Presbytery, which was affiliated with the old school. With this split came a very interesting change in the practices of the First Presbyterian Church. Prior to 1842, slaves had been freely admitted as members of the church. But after 1842, no slaves were admitted. Slaves may have attended First Presbyterian, but they were no longer admitted as members. The Second Presbyterian Church (old school) continued the practice of admitting slaves. Jane and Pamela Clemens stayed with the newly segregated First Presbyterian Church.

The difference between old and new school Presbyterians is not as clear-cut as the splits that would divide the Methodists and Baptists, but in May of 1845, at their respective general assemblies, the Presbyterian groups articulated their positions on slavery. The old school adopted the following resolution in Philadelphia:

> That the institution of slavery, existing in these United States, is not sinful on the part of civil society.
>
> 1. That slavery, as it exists in these United States, is not a sinful offence.
>
> 2. That civil government is not bound to abolish slavery in these United States.
>
> 3. That it is not agreeable to the word of God for any person intentionally to induce those held in slavery to rebel against their masters.[2]

The old school's clear support of slavery gave the institution a strong boost in slave states. However, the new school assembly, meeting in Cincinnati, articulated a compromise position on slavery.

The new school performed a very delicate balancing act, trying to remain a national church despite being the birthplace of the religious abolition movement. In Cincinnati, petitions, called memorials, were presented by three different groups. The first was from a group of moderates who wished for the assembly to take some middle ground. With their thinking closely mirroring that of the American Colonization Society, they sought to have the General Assembly of the new school declare that slavery as it existed in the United States was a social evil. They did not wish to eliminate slavery immediately, however. They wished the General Assembly to adopt measures for the "amelioration of the condition of the slaves." The second group of petitioners did not seek any modification of slavery as an institution but wanted to call upon members of the church to work in states like Missouri to repeal laws that forbade the teaching of slaves to read. They argued that slaves should be taught reading so they would be able to read the Bible. A third group, the abolitionists, called upon the assembly to declare slavery a moral evil: "a heinous sin in the sight of God." This group called for administering "church discipline" upon anyone in the church who owned slaves. As a practical matter, this

2. *PMW*, June 4, 1845.

would have meant that slaveholders would have been kicked out of the church. These memorials were all turned over to a committee on the subject of slavery. The new school assembly refused to adopt the abolitionist position. A report that the assembly adopted by a vote of 164 to 12 stated:

> slavery existed in the days of Christ and his apostles. . . . That they did not denounce the relation itself as sinful, as inconsistent with Christianity; that slaveholders were admitted to membership in the churches organized by the apostles; that whilst they were required to treat their slaves with kindness, and as rational, accountable, immortal beings, and if Christians, as brethren in the Lord, they were not commanded to emancipate them; that slaves were required to be "obedient to their masters according to the flesh, with fear and trembling, with singleness of heart as unto Christ," are facts which meet the eye of every reader of the New Testament.[3]

While the assembly refused to denounce slavery as evil, it did acknowledge that there was "evil" connected with slavery, and it repudiated the traffic of slaves for gain, the separation of families for the sake of "filthy lucre" or convenience of the master, or cruel treatment of slaves in any respect. The report called upon members to seek laws to protect slaves from "cruel treatment by wicked men," but it stopped short of calling members to teach slaves to read. Instead, it said, slaves should have "the right to receive religious instruction." The church took the position that however desirable it was to "ameliorate" the condition of the slave in the South and Southwest, these objects "can never be secured by ecclesiastical legislation."[4] The only improvement the new school church could offer to the slave was teaching "the glorious doctrines of the Gospel." The assembly concluded that to adopt the abolitionist position would be to separate the northern and southern portions of the church.

Thus the new school Presbyterians limped along. The First Presbyterian Church in Hannibal could safely stay affiliated with the group. As the years passed, the abolitionists' numbers continued to grow in the northern new school congregations. In Hannibal's First Presbyterian Church, slavery remained a nonissue. Local church leaders busied themselves with the personal lives of congregation members. Session minutes of the 1840s are full of reports about the moral wanderings of the flock. Committees were dispatched to counsel church members who had been seen

3. Ibid.
4. Ibid.

dancing at a public ball. A member appeared before the session and confessed that he had gambled at cards. Another member who had been repeatedly drunk and involved in fights had not attended church in six months. The session tried to call him to a hearing, but a visiting committee could never find him sober enough to appear![5]

Sam Clemens's boyhood venture into abstinence from tobacco and alcohol with the Cadets of Temperance would have been consistent with his mother's church views. Reform the individual, but leave social change to government. Revivals continued to be important, and the annual camp meeting was greatly anticipated. The First Presbyterian Church held a yearly encampment on grounds three miles west of Hannibal.[6]

Slavery was never condemned from the pulpit. When addressed, it was celebrated. While no copies of sermons delivered at First Presbyterian Church survive, public reaction to the conversion of the Reverend Joseph L. Bennett to abolitionism in 1856 sheds light on the subject. On July 17, respectable members of Hannibal society, and in particular the members of the First Presbyterian Church, were shocked by an article in the *Hannibal Weekly Messenger*. A trusted friend who had baptized their babies, married young couples, and buried their dead had betrayed them. A contributor to the newspaper monitored the abolitionist press and had detected the turncoat and dispatched an article to the editor.

"I observe in the *Boston Daily Atlas*," wrote the man known only as "M.," "an abstract of a sermon preached in Cambridge, Mass., by the Rev. J. L. Bennett, former Pastor of the First Presbyterian Church in this city [Hannibal]. The *Boston Atlas* is a rabid political paper, intensely abolition, urging, by all sorts of falsehood and slander, the election of Fremont and Dayton."[7]

Fremont and Dayton were the openly antislavery candidates of the new Republican Party. Their candidacy was doomed to fail, but they were paving the way for Lincoln's successful run in 1860, which, in turn, would trigger the Civil War. Reviled throughout the slave states, Fremont was particularly disliked in Hannibal because he was the son-in-law of a former United States senator from Missouri, Thomas Hart Benton, and viewed as a traitor. "As Mr. Bennett's sermon is of the same stripe, although preached in a church, and on the holy Sabbath, he selected for its publication this paper. There are religious papers published in Boston,

5. Ibid.
6. Henry Sweets, *The Hannibal, Missouri, Presbyterian Church: A Sesquicentennial History*, 4.
7. *Hannibal Weekly Messenger* (hereinafter *HWM*), July 17, 1856.

and one of them of Mr. B[ennett]'s own denomination; but he very properly selected a political paper in which to publish his political sermon."

Joseph L. Bennett had been pastor of Hannibal's First Presbyterian Church from October 10, 1848, until the spring of 1853—from the time Sam Clemens was about to turn thirteen until he left Hannibal himself at age seventeen. In Hannibal, Bennett had adhered carefully to the theology of slavery. But in the East, freed from the constraints of Hannibal's slave culture, he had converted, like Theodore Weld and David Nelson before him, to abolitionism. In his Cambridge sermon he chose a text and message that would have sounded very strange in a Hannibal pulpit. Had he possessed the courage to present the sermon in Hannibal, it would have, at a minimum, resulted in his being run out of the state like Nelson. Very likely, he would have been arrested under the abolition law and tarred and feathered as well.

In Massachusetts, Bennett based his abolitionist sermon on Ezekiel, 22:29: "The people of the land have used oppression, and exercised robbery, and have vexed the poor and needy: yea, they have oppressed the stranger wrongfully." Bennett preached that slaveholders who had gone to Kansas to insure the state would enter the union as a slave state would incur the wrath of God. His sermon attacked the theology of slavery. The anonymous M. fired back: "Here is a wholesale slander against the ministers of the gospel of all denominations throughout the fifteen slave States. Have they ever profaned the Sabbath, or desecrated the pulpit by efforts to extend or perpetuate the system of slavery? Satan would blush at the utterance of so infamous a slander."

The Clemens women had not been pestered with the antislavery ideas of Reverend Bennett when he had been in Hannibal. "Mr. B[ennett] was a pastor of a church in this city for some years, and received an adequate salary for his services as such. He preached to the people Sabbath after Sabbath. He met them in social intercourse at the fireside, but he never inculated [sic] abolitionism, publicly nor privately, in Rome, he did as Rome did."[8]

The report of the sermon caused quite a stir in Hannibal. A week later, the editor of the *Hannibal Weekly Messenger* wrote:

> The friends of the Rev. Mr. Bennett, in this city are pained to hear that he has become a rank and violent abolitionist since his return to the east. . . . He can discover great evil and wrong where they do not exist, much easier and quicker than where they do exist; for while in Missouri,

8. Ibid.

in the midst of the evils of slavery, mixing daily with slave holders, he did not discover the wrongs nor cruelty of which he now complains. But soon after his return to the land of piety of steady habits, wooden nutmegs and oak bacon hams, a land where slavery does not exist, the scales fall from his eyes and he beholds the monstrous crimes of these men in Missouri who had supported, honored and flattered him, far beyond his deserts for several years.[9]

The conversion of Bennett to abolitionism was a brutal shock to the First Presbyterian Church. The church had long struggled to maintain its association with other new school Presbyterians. This was particularly difficult since many churches in Illinois and in the northeast United States were openly abolitionist. By 1853, the new school was teetering on the brink of a sectional break. With each national assembly, new school abolitionists continued their unrelenting attack on slaveholding. The *Missouri Courier* reported on a national assembly in 1853:

> The Presbyterian church, we see, as represented in Buffalo, is about to be rent in twain, as have seen the great and powerful church of the Methodists. The Northern Presbyterian is hereafter to look upon the Southern Presbyter as criminal in the sight of God and man for being a slave holder; and the Southern Presbyter will have, indeed, to be a meek and humble Christian if, under these circumstances, he can have any fellowship with his Northern brother.[10]

Hannibal First Presbyterian remained associated with the new school until 1858, when the tent of compromise collapsed. Southerners of the new school broke away to become the United Synod of the Presbyterian Church. Hannibal First Presbyterian did not join their southern brethren, but instead joined the old school Presbytery of Palmyra on January 27, 1859. In the old school they did not have to have their consciences pricked by abolitionists' barbs. They were secure in the knowledge that God approved slavery.

Other Churches in Hannibal

Sam Clemens was exposed to bitter and divisive fighting within the churches of Hannibal. During his youth, there were, in addition to the two

9. Ibid., July 24, 1856.
10. *Missouri Courier* (hereinafter *MC*), June 16, 1853.

Presbyterian churches, two Methodist churches, a Baptist church, a Christian (Disciples of Christ) church, a Catholic church, an Episcopal church, and a carefully controlled African church.[11] The polarizing effects of slavery reached far beyond Hannibal, and national churches were separating into proslavery and abolitionist camps. Local churches were succumbing to xenophobia. Perhaps Clemens's later religious cynicism was rooted in the struggles he observed as a boy.

The Methodists

In the mid-1840s, the Methodists split dramatically and publicly over the issue of slavery. Nationally the church divided into the Methodist Episcopal Church and the Methodist Episcopal Church, South. In the fall of 1845, the state conference of the Methodist Episcopal Church met in Columbia, Missouri, and elected to affiliate with the Methodist Episcopal Church, South. However, not all Missouri congregations followed the state organization into the new affiliation. The slavery issue divided churches at the local level as well, and disagreements played out on the pages of the local press. Almost immediately, the Methodist church in Palmyra banned Rev. W. S. McMurry for his suspected position on slavery, and McMurry promptly held a meeting at the courthouse. The only evidence against McMurry was his affiliation with the northern church. No one reported his having been involved in abolitionist activity or helping runaway slaves. He defended himself in the press, saying that he had "uniformly demeaned himself as a Christian and a gentleman."[12]

The Methodist church haggled over the division of church property for much of the decade. The compromise that had divided the church geographically was abandoned by 1848, and each church proceeded to establish congregations in both the North and South.[13]

The two Methodist churches of Hannibal dealt with the schism in different fashions. Though they both were staunchly proslavery, one congregation went into the southern church. The other elected to retain their affiliation with the old Methodist church and soon found itself the subject of suspicion and gossip. In response to allegations of abolitionist activity a decade after the split, the congregation that kept the old affiliation formed a committee to draft a statement paper for the local press. It declared that when the division came, the members of the Methodist church

11. *HWM*, November 4, 1858.
12. *PMW*, October 23, 1845.
13. *PMW*, June 1, 1848.

on Sixth and Market Streets "preferred to remain in the old Church—with our Mother—because she had given us no reason for withdrawing from her."[14] The declaration stated that the members of the local church had never been compelled to act upon the subject of slavery and their ministers had been law-abiding gentlemen, none of whom had ever spoken against slavery.

The group plainly stated that they had no connection with, nor sympathy for, the abolitionists, abolitionism, or any of the "ultraisms" of the day. The Hannibal Methodists who remained affiliated with the old church denounced abolitionists as "calculated to do incalculable injury to the cause of religion and good morals. They warned that these religious zealots threatened to destroy our 'Glorious Union.'" The theology being preached was identical with that preached before Methodist Episcopal Church, South congregations:

> That as citizens of this State—enjoying the privileges and blessings guaranteed to us by her Laws—we consider and acknowledge it to be our bounden duty as good citizens—which we claim to be—respect and uphold the Laws of the State, and therefore we condemn any and all who would directly or indirectly persuade or assist a slave to escape from his master or that would teach any other doctrine than that taught in the word of God: *"Servants, obey your masters."*

The Methodist church at Sixth and Market Streets maintained the northern affiliation until 1861, when the abolitionists finally seized control of the national organization. On January 4 of that year the congregation voted to join with other congregations in the border states.

The other Methodist church in Hannibal joined the Methodist Episcopal Church, South in 1845. A biography of the minister who served that Hannibal congregation from 1847 to 1850 survives. William Caples was a respected Methodist clergyman. He had begun as a circuit rider in the lonely pioneer frontier of western Missouri. Caples was a strong believer in slavery. One of his early postings had been to Keytesville, Missouri, where he replaced an abolition-tainted preacher who had been caught encouraging slaves to run away from their masters and was forced, himself, to flee.[15] As a result of the man's activities, Caples's biographer observed, "Methodist preachers were suspected men."

14. *MC*, August 31, 1854.

15. E. M. Marvin, *The Life of Rev. William Goff Caples, of the Missouri Conference of the Methodist Episcopal Church, South*, 66.

After the break with the old church, Caples was comfortable in the new organization. He was a public advocate for the principles of Methodism. In Hannibal, Caples held a public debate with a minister of the Christian church on the issue of baptism. Methodists sprinkled water on the heads of converts. Christians immersed individuals in water. Caples was opposed to dancing and to attending circuses. He was particularly opposed to women attending circuses. He felt that a woman seeing a circus would "come away with some loss of womanly sensibility." He also was troubled by agricultural fairs because while they might "in some slight measure promote the improvement of valuable farm products and stock, they would a thousand times more stimulate horseracing and gambling."[16] Caples also thought the theater, card playing, chess, and backgammon were sinful. Caples embodied the thought of the Methodist Episcopal Church, South with regard to slavery. His biographer recorded his positions on the issue:

> The first was that the Bible did not condemn slavery, but clearly in the Old Testament authorized it and in the New allowed it. It was established by statute in the civil code of Moses. It was recognized, and the duties it involved defined and enjoined, by the Apostle Paul. It is, therefore, not a question overlooked by the sacred writers, but distinctly under their cognizance and treated of by them. Clearly, if the ownership of slaves were sin, they had occasion to pronounce upon it. The Holy Spirit, speaking by them on this very topic, deals with the relation of master and slave, but never once condemns it.[17]

His position on abolition was more succinct: Abolitionism was the deadliest sin of modern society.[18]

Caples's position on slavery would lead him to join with the Missouri State Guard at the start of the Civil War. He was an eloquent public speaker, and his talents were recognized by commanding officers. He was sent north of the Missouri River after the fighting started to recruit and organize a unit of soldiers to serve in the Confederate Army.

Throughout Sam Clemens's youth in Hannibal, the Methodists' struggle over slavery would be in the news more than that of any other church group. They fought locally and nationally. When a Methodist church in Dubuque, Iowa, included a copy of *Uncle Tom's Cabin* in the church library, it triggered an outcry in Hannibal. A Hannibal correspondent asked,

16. Ibid., 131.
17. Ibid., 254–55.
18. Ibid., 255.

"What do you think of Northern Methodism now, sir?", continuing, "What next? Why not Garrison's *'Emancipator'* or the speeches of the free negro orator Fred. Douglass?"[19]

The Baptists

In the spring of 1845, Hannibal Baptists erected a new church on the corner of Church and Fourth Streets. The membership consisted of 145 white members and 60 slaves. Unlike the Methodists and the Presbyterians, the Baptists in the town stood undivided. That same year on May 10, a committee of 300 delegates from Maryland, Virginia, North Carolina, Georgia, Alabama, Louisiana, Kentucky, and the District of Columbia met in Augusta, Georgia. Because short notice was given of the meeting, delegates from the western states were not present. At this Georgia meeting, the Southern Baptist Convention was formed, sparked, of course, by slavery.

The board of foreign missions of the Baptist Church of the United States in Boston had for years refused to send slave owners abroad as missionaries. The position reflected the church's long-held, mildly antislavery position. As in other denominations, however, abolitionist thought was becoming more pronounced. Sparked by the missionary issue, the Southern Baptists soon fully embraced the theology of slavery—as did the Baptist church in Hannibal. Slaveholders could safely take their slaves to church, where, seated separately in the back, slaves would hear sermons admonishing them to obey their masters and assuring them that God wanted them to be good and obedient slaves.

Jacob Sosey, writing in 1849, in the *Palmyra Missouri Whig* praised the Southern Baptists. "The negro slaves are vicious and immoral," he wrote. The Southern Baptists were combating this problem with "training and indoctrination" of the young. He lauded the group for taking the position "that the religious instruction of the colored population was a duty incumbent on all Southern Christians." Sosey recognized that Southern Baptism had a very practical benefit for slaveholders. "What could be more beneficial to the master than to have faithful, honest and trustworthy servants?"[20]

Episcopalians, Catholics, and Christians

None of the other churches in Hannibal took a stand against slavery. Episcopalians, Catholics, and Christians all accepted slaveholders with-

19. *MC*, April 20, 1854.
20. *PMW*, June 28, 1849.

out exception and left the issue to the individual conscience. The position of the Episcopal Church is summarized in a piece published in *The Southern Episcopalian*, entitled "The Slave's Chatechism," intended to be used in instructing slaves.

> Who keeps snakes and all bad things from hurting you?
> God does.
> Who gave you a master and a mistress?
> God gave them to me.
> Who says you must obey them?
> God says that I must.
> What book tells you all these things?
> The Bible.
> What is the Bible?
> The Bible is God's Word.[21]

The Catholics' approach differed from that of the Protestant churches. The church was certainly not antislavery. The bishop of St. Louis actually owned slaves at one point, as did a seminary in Perry County, in south Missouri.[22] The Catholics baptized slave children. They also took the unusual step in slave culture of consecrating slave marriages. Thus, Catholic slaves frequently had family names in addition to first names. In the spring of 1851, in a country church not far from Hannibal, a Catholic priest married two slaves, Peter Paul Tolton, owned by the Hager family, and Martha Jane Chisley, owned by the Eliot family. Of course, the marriage required the consent of both owners. The owners of Peter and Martha agreed that the couple would live on the Eliot farm. Although Peter would remain a slave of the Hagers, all children would be property of the Eliots. This arrangement followed Missouri law, which dictated that the children of a slave woman belonged to the woman's owner. Thus sanctioned, Catholic slave marriages may have had more stability than relationships between slaves of non-Catholic slaveholders.[23]

The Toltons had three children. Their middle child's birth and baptism are recorded in the baptismal register of Saint Peter's Church, Brush

---

21. J. R. Balme, *American States, Churches, and Slavery*, 39.

22. Stafford Poole, *Church and Slave in Perry County, Missouri, 1818–1865*, xvi.

23. Sr. Caroline Hemesath, O.S.F, *From Slave to Priest: A Biography of the Rev. Augustine Tolton*, 8.

Creek, Missouri. It reads: "A colored child born April, 1854. Son of Peter Tolton and Martha Chisley. Property of Stephen Eliot. Mrs. Stephen Eliot Sponsor; May 29, 1854. Father John O'Sullivan." The child was Augustine Tolton, who would go on to become the first black Catholic priest in the United States.

Chapter 9

The Theology of Slavery

Why were niggers and whites made? What crime did the uncreated first nigger commit that the curse of birth was decreed for him? And why is this awful difference made between white and black?

Mark Twain, *The Tragedy of Pudd'nhead Wilson*

What did Sam Clemens and his classmates learn in Hannibal Sunday schools about slavery? They would have heard quotations from scripture that salved the consciences of those who used slave labor and elevated slave owners to an exalted position. To possess a slave was to fulfill a divinely sanctioned duty: The master received the labor of a race cursed by God to servitude; the slave, the benefit of a patriarch who cared for his every need. The churches also played an important role in controlling slaves; slaves were taught that their servitude had a biblical basis and that to question slavery was to question God Himself. Realizing the influence of religion, the town of Hannibal regulated church services for blacks and slaves. By city ordinance, slaves could only be addressed by white preachers or approved black ministers.[1] Christianity was tightly woven into the civil institutions of the day. Hannibal newspapers openly reflected the dominant thought of mainstream Protestant churches.

1. Minute Book of Hannibal, 1839–1849.

The Curse of Ham

As 1854 began, the *Tri-Weekly Messenger* ran the following: "Our young friends Chas. T. And S. L. Davis of Kentucky, lately presented to us a copy of Priest's Bible defence of the institution of slavery, containing 500 pages, to which is appended very full and copious notes by the Rev. W. S. Brown of Glasgow, Ky. Altogether it is a valuable work, well worth the perusal of any man and we return them our thanks for it."[2]

Interest in Josiah Priest's *Bible Defence of Slavery,* first published in 1851, was sufficient that the *Tri-Weekly Messenger* began selling the book from its office. Priest had written extensively on antiquities and the Bible. He believed that Native Americans were descended from the lost tribes of Israel. Priest's book was just one of several popular in slave culture which argued that a curse of slavery had been placed upon the African people following the great flood.[3]

Noah had three sons: Ham, Shem, and Japheth. After the ark came to rest, Noah planted a vineyard. From the grapes of the first harvest, he pressed the juice and made wine. Then the mischief began:

And he [Noah] drank of the wine, and was drunken; and he was uncovered within his tent. And Ham, the father of Canaan saw the nakedness of his father, and told his two brethren without.

And Shem and Japheth took a garment, and laid it upon both their shoulders and went backward, and they saw not their father's nakedness.

And Noah awoke from his wine, and knew what his younger son had done unto him.

And he said, Cursed be Canaan; a servant of servants shall he be unto his brethren.

And he said, Blessed be the Lord God of Shem; and Canaan shall be

---

2. *Tri-Weekly Messenger* (hereinafter *TWM*), January 24, 1854.

3. Ibid., January 28, 31, and February 2, 1854. Priest's was apparently one of the most popular books on the Bible defense of slavery. Other examples include James A. Sloan, *The Great Question Answered;* Frederick Dalcho, *Practical Considerations Founded on the Scriptures;* Nathan Lord, *A Northern Presbyter's Second Letter;* Alexander McCaine, *Slavery Defended from Scripture;* and Patrick H. Mell, *Slavery.* For an excellent discussion and analysis of these works, see Peterson's "Myth of Ham" and *Ham and Japheth: The Mythic World of Whites in the Antebellum South.*

his servant. God shall enlarge Japheth, and he shall dwell in the tents of Shem; and Canaan shall be his servant.[4]

This theological justification for slavery had long been employed; however, it took on new power as a response to the attacks of religious abolitionists. Here, slaveholders claimed, was biblical proof that God Himself sanctioned the institution. Slave owners were not the sinners portrayed by the abolitionists; they were enlightened patriarchs. But the story did more than just provide a divine origin for slave culture. It explained and justified the socially inferior position of the Negro. The "curse of Ham" story held that the races were created by God for a given purpose. Under the racist theory, Noah's three sons were the forefathers of everyone living on the earth. In the days before Darwin and Mendel, theologians were free to conjure pseudoscientific explanations for the world around them—and some of the ideas they concocted were pretty far-fetched. According to Priest, before the great flood all people had been red. However, Priest's theory required some extrabiblical divine intervention to account for subsequent variations in skin color. With no knowledge of DNA or the process of skin pigmentation, he concluded that Noah's son Ham was born black; Shem was red like his parents; and not surprisingly, Japheth, the best son of all, was born white. In an interesting blend of the Old Testament and pseudoscience, Priest argued that God foresaw the destiny of Noah's sons and signaled it by causing them to be born in three different colors!

Priest dismissed the possibility that the races could have evolved or adapted to their environment. Writing in the same decade Darwin published *Origin of Species* and without an understanding of the scope of geologic time, he disregarded the possibility of adaptation to environment by observing that no one had ever seen such change. "[Since] the appearance of the Negro race on the continent of America, has there one lineament of countenance, or trait of bodily formation . . . which promises even an approximation of a final change to white? Is the wool of such individuals as have not amalgamated with the whites and Indians, a whit less woolly than it was when they were first brought to this country?"[5]

Priest believed that divine will had created the differences in people, and descendants of Noah's sons had populated the globe with the black, red, and white races.

4. Gen. 9:21–27.
5. Josiah Priest, *Bible Defence of Slavery; or the Origin, History, and Fortunes of the Negro Race*, 32.

What's in a Name?

Another belief then common among people of European descent was that at one point, everybody on the planet had spoken Hebrew. Priest purported to explain what words meant in the Hebrew language in conjunction with the players in the Ham myth. This unique etymology was used to endorse the prevailing view of slave culture: blacks were treacherous, hot-blooded, oversexed, simple people who required close supervision. Priest explained that the name Ham signified the color black and the qualities associated it with:

> *heat* or *violence* of temper, exceedingly prone to acts of ferocity and cruelty, involving murder, war, butcheries, and even *cannibalism*, including beastly lusts, and lasciviousness in its worst feature, going beyond the force of these passions, as possessed in common by other races of men. Second, the word signifies deceit, dishonesty, treachery, low-mindedness, and malice.
>
> What a group of horrors are here, couched in the word *Ham*, all agreeing, in a most surprising manner, with the color of Ham's skin, as well as with his real character as a *man*, during his own life, as well as with that of his race, even now.

Naturally, under this theory the color white and associated qualities were admirable: "Japheth was a *fair white man*, on whose face and form there was stamped in the eye of his father, the sure sign of great intellectual endowments betokening renown, enlargement and rule among men, wherefore, he could give him no other name, than the important word *Japheth*, or the *fair* and ruddy *white* son, his fortunes remaining to be fulfilled in the course of time."[6]

The third son, Shem, was left the middle ground: "Shem, was the name of another of the sons of Noah; which word also had its meaning, and was *renown*, praise or greatness, prophetically pointing out the character of *his* race, but doubtless *more* particularly, the renown of the genealogy of the holy seed, or line of the Patriarchs, Prophets, the Jews, and of Jesus Christ, who came of the line of Shem."[7]

However, even though the red people, descendants of Shem, were to produce the Christian savior, Priest could not bring himself to believe in a non-white Jesus. Though of the line of Shem, Jesus, too, was miraculously

6. Ibid., 40, 43.
7. Ibid., 44.

made white by God. "The proof that he was a white man, is derived from a letter, written by a Roman Senator from Judea, in the time of Augustine Caesar, to Rome. In that letter, which is now extant, the man Jesus Christ is said to have been a man of surpassing beauty, having a bright fair complexion, with hair of the color of a ripe filbert, which is inclining to the yellow or golden color. His eyes were of the hazel or blue cast; his forehead high, smooth, and broad."[8]

Priest believed that God created the three races then sent each to the part of the planet to which it was best suited. He sent the superior white descendants of Japheth to the northern regions, the middling red descendants of Shem to the middle regions, and the cursed descendants of Ham to the "burning south." In the names of Africa, Priest found support for the story. Although the biblical Ham was to be the father of Canaan, a small parcel of land in modern-day Israel, the theology of slavery required him to also be the father of Africa. Priest explained, "Ethiope, which is also a Hebrew word, signifies blackness, a name given to the country, on account of the color if its first inhabitants." He went on, "Even the word Negro, is derived from the Hebrew word Niger, and signifies black. *Niger,* is a great river of Africa, and was thus originally named, on account of black men having first settled the countries of that river; and hence arose from earliest time the word Negro, and applied to the race of Ham, and no other people."[9]

Although Priest rejected adaptation as an explanation of change, he used physical attributes of blacks as proof that God intended them for Africa and slavery. In pseudoscientific language, Priest explained how black descendants of Ham were better suited by God to the southern regions.

> The great thickness of the skull bone is an admirable defense of the brain against the *sun*stroke. Were it not for *this,* that portion of the Negro population, who live almost continually in the open air beneath the fervor of a tropical sun, would soon be totally cut off, as it is well known that the whites cannot endure this kind of exposure without great danger, as many lose their lives this way, although their heads are covered with a hat, a turban or some such defense. But the Negro is *never* affected in this way by the sun; no, not even their children, though they are continually wandering on the wilds and in the deserts, bare-headed and naked.[10]

8. Ibid., 165–66.
9. Ibid., 48, 42.
10. Ibid., 49.

This thick skull supposedly made the Negro particularly well adapted to American slavery. "The great thickness and hardness of the heads of this people—the African race—is in another respect a singular providence in their favor, as a defense against the blows of angry masters, in a state of servitude—it being almost impossible to break their skulls even with a club. Priest also also claimed that the Negro's large feet were suited to the deserts and swamps of Africa. In the final analysis, Priest found in his own sense of revulsion the most basic proof that God punished the slaves and that the institution of slavery was appropriate. He simply found the physical appearance of blacks aesthetically displeasing. In a circular argument he described what he thought a typical black person looked like and declared blacks could not have been natural descendants from Adam. To hammer home his point Priest surmised: "When, for the first time, a child of the white race sees a Negro man, it is always frightened by the horrible apparition. Even to a man, or any person of adult years, the first sight of a black human being gives them a shock, or a feeling of the most singular character, mixed up of pity, disgust and wonder, not experienced by Negroes, on seeing a white human being for the first time."[11]

Crude stereotypes regarding blacks were supported by the theory. Ham had been cursed for a sin thought to be of a sexual nature—seeing his father naked—which explained the wild, insatiable sexual appetites presumed to belong to the African. Ham's lack of restraint was also used to explain intellectual slowness or dullness in blacks. Slaveholders had no doubts as to the natural supremacy of the northern European white man.[12]

Blacks Deserved Slavery

Under the curse of Ham theory, cruelty to black slaves was fully justified. The black race was serving a sentence imposed not by a court of law but by God. Accordingly, a slave could be lashed, chained, or sold away from his family, and his misery openly acknowledged in slave culture, but instead of evoking sympathy, the pitiable condition of the servants was written off as divine retribution. The theory was popular throughout slave culture, especially in political circles. In 1846, Georgia Senator

11. Ibid., 52, 170.
12. *The Southern States, Embracing a Series of Papers Condensed from the Earlier Volumes of De Bow's Review, upon Slavery and the Slave Institutions of the South,* 316–30.

Alexander Stephens declared in the United States Senate that the morality of the institution of slavery stood on "a basis as firm as the Bible." He also stated, "until Christianity be overthrown . . . the relation between master and slave can never be regarded as an offence against the Divine Laws."[13]

In Hannibal, local politicians frequently quoted the Bible to defend slavery. Thomas L. Anderson, the attorney who had volunteered to prosecute Thompson, Work, and Burr, built a successful career in part on the defense of slavery. He was elected to the U.S. House of Representatives, and in January 1854 he addressed citizens in a speech that reflected political support for the notion of a curse. It was typical of speeches he gave during the period and was reprinted in the *Messenger:*

> The institution of slavery is of very ancient origin, having existed for a period of more than 4000 years. The prediction of Noah, that the children of Ham were not only to be servants, but "a servant of servants," has been so fully verified as to render it a striking instance of scripture truth. Africa with its groveling millions is the theatre of beastly barbarism and degradation, no species of the human race descends as low in the scale of brutality as the Etheopian [sic]. The highest state of intellectual development, as well as the greatest degree of moral and social elevation to which they have ever attained, has been under the compulsion of slavery to a superior people. In no country does slavery exist in a more abject form than in Africa, and the removal of the negro to this country is to him an inestimable blessing, for in no country whatever, does he enjoy so many comforts and blessings as in our own. The negro has unquestionably the seal of Inferiority stamped upon him by the author of his being, and would seem by nature peculiarly fitted to become the "servant of servants," since he is not sufficiently endowed with the intellect, to enable him to contend successfully with the more gifted races of men in the struggles of life. If left in a community to themselves, tho' they may have been previously civilized, they soon retrograde and become literally companions for brutes, as history abundantly confirms. No person doubts but that the negro is a species of genus homo, but that he is an inferior being in the scale of animated nature, when compared with the Circassian or white man, is a fact, of which his own person abounds in proof, from the crown of his head to the soles of his feet' evidences, that have received the stamp of infaliability from the author of his being and which could be easy demonstrated, but I must pass on.
>
> Is slavery a sin? a violation of God's moral law? if so it ought to be abolished and that speedily, where men differ as to morality, the only re-

13. Henry Cleveland, ed., *Alexander H. Stephens, in Public and Private,* 87.

liable arbiter is the word of God. That which the Bible sanctions is right, and hence it is regarded, by all men in Christian lands, as an infallible guide in all their actions. Having thus premised I now aver that if the Bible is true, slavery is morally right.[14]

Anderson referred to abolitionists as "hypocritical monomaniacs." He noted that the Bible said Abraham had 318 trained servants in his household and between 1200 and 1500 slaves, including women and children, and finished by pointing to the commandment to covet neither a neighbor's manservant nor maidservant as proof of divine sanction of slavery. It was a stump speech typical of those delivered at dozens of political and religious meetings as well as at antiabolition and slave-catching, or vigilance society, meetings, during the 1840s and 1850s, when the secular and religious worlds were not divided.

As a child, Samuel Clemens was exposed to the Ham story. As an adult, thirty years after the Civil War, Clemens used the curse of Ham in his novel *The Tragedy of Pudd'nhead Wilson* as the climax to a central passage. The satire discusses antebellum attitudes on the subordination of blacks through the story of two boys, Chambers and Tom, one the child of Roxana, a slave woman who is one-sixteenth black, and the other the son of the master of the house. The "black" baby appears little different from the "white" baby, and Roxana switches the two in their cribs. The free boy grows up thinking he is a slave and being treated as inferior. The slave boy becomes the arrogant new master. When Tom discovers he is really the son of a slave, his world turns upside down. He begins acting in a subservient manner. He stops shaking hands with former friends, steps out of the way of rowdy, less-educated white youths, and keeps his eyes downcast. In summing up his predicament, Clemens wrote, "He said to himself that the curse of Ham was upon him."

14. *Weekly Messenger* (hereinafter *WM*), January 17, 1854.

Chapter 10

The Face of Domestic Slavery in Hannibal

I knew the man had a right to kill his slave if he wanted to, and yet it seemed a pitiful thing and somehow wrong, though why wrong I was not deep enough to explain if I had been asked to do it.

Mark Twain, *Following the Equator*

When people think of American slavery, they usually think of cotton, but no cotton was raised in Marion County. Nor were there plantations with large populations of slaves living in separate quarters behind big houses. Because few overseers were required, the myth has arisen that slavery was kinder and gentler in Missouri. As late as 1973, an official state manual stated: "In fact, the slave and his family and the master and his family were, more often than not, a team, sharing the burden of work together in the field."[1]

A team? Slavery in northeast Missouri had a far different character from that of the cotton or sugar plantations of the Deep South. Although some tobacco was grown in Marion County, there was no single profitable agricultural use for slaves.[2] Instead, slaves served several important purposes—few of which had anything remotely to do with teamwork. Slave labor was not utilized by a small number of elites, but was common throughout the culture. Because slaves could be leased even white people of very modest means—people as poor as the Clemens family—had slaves in their households.

1. James C. Kirkpatrick, *Official Manual, State of Missouri, 1973–1974*, 15.
2. Edwin Leigh, *Bird's-eye Views of Slavery in Missouri*.

76

The people of northeast Missouri were quite aware of the substantial value of their slaves both at home and nationwide. The August 28, 1856, *Palmyra Weekly Whig* observed, "It is said that the value of slave property of the South is not less than two thousand millions of dollars, a sum equal to one-fourth the value of all the other property in the United States, as shown by the last census." The *Hannibal Messenger* observed on February 3, 1859, "The slave property in Missouri increased three millions and a half of dollars from 1857 to 1858, according to official reports. It is constantly increasing in number and value, year by year, notwithstanding the interference of meddlers from abroad, and the misrepresentations of a few fanatics at home." Just as investors today monitor the daily vacillations of the stock market, the people of northeast Missouri took an active interest in the prices slaves brought at auction.

Newspapers routinely reported the results of sales, breaking the prices into age and gender categories. It is interesting to note that slaves were referred to as men, women, boys, and girls. Though the words *boy* and *girl* might be used in conversation by a white person when addressing an adult slave, in transactions involving the sale and lease of slaves, the terms denoted young people. When a slave lease or bill of sale refers to a boy, the word usually refers to a young male slave. The following reports are typical:

Sale of Negroes at Palmyra
    A friend who was present, has furnished us the following list of negroes sold at Palmyra on the 1st inst. The following belonged to the estate of Thos. Gatewood:
    Woman, aged 22, and two children, $1,025
    Woman, aged 29 and 3 yr. Old child, 885
    Woman, aged 40, and infant child, 605
    Man, aged 21 years, 810
    Man, aged 43 years, 700
    Boy, aged 7 years, 400
    Boy, aged 15 years, 700
    Girl, aged 10 years, 605
    Boy, aged 17 years, 700
    Girl, aged 9 years, 510
    Boy aged, 19 years, 850
        Amounting to $7,790

Six slaves belonging to the estate of Moses D. Bates were sold, as follows:
    Girl, aged 12 years, $550
    Boy, aged 22 years, 865

Girl, aged 10 years, 505
Boy, aged 8 years, 420
Boy, aged 10 years, 570
Boy, aged 6 years, 320
   Amounting to $3,250[3]

Slaves were also an extremely important source of revenue for local and state governments. Slaves, like land, were taxed, and they constituted a substantial portion of the taxable wealth. In 1847, taxes on slaves accounted for more than 10 percent of Marion County revenue. The 2,180 slaves of Marion County were valued by the assessor at $408,450. By comparison, money on hand and loaned on interest in Marion County amounted to only $63,907. Banking was not well established. That same year, real estate in the county was valued at $1,080,655. Slaves were assessed at the same rate as other property, .2 percent. The total 1847 Marion County budget was $7,434.60. The tax on slaves generated $816.90. By the autumn of 1856, the tax structure had changed, and slaves had become even more important. Taxes on them accounted for nearly 20 percent of the state taxes generated from Marion County: $1807.80 out of $9,899.50. According to the assessment, slaves constituted nearly 20 percent of the value of all property in Marion county: $903,900 out of $4,569,315.[4]

But the impact of slavery was not merely economic. Government, law, religion, economics, and social status were all inextricably tied to slavery, and just as each institution in Hannibal was supported in some fashion by slavery, so each institution had a stake in its perpetuation. Over time, the nature and extent of slavery in northeast Missouri has been obscured and minimized. In part this has been the result of the misinterpretation of census data. In Marion County slaves were counted and listed in the census records by their owners. In the 1850 census, there were 12,182 people in Marion County; 2,852, or 24 percent, were slaves.[5] There were 732 slaveholders listed in the census for the year, or 8 percent of the 9,259 white people living the county. It would appear from these raw numbers that there were relatively few slaveholders. However, there is more to the story. The total white population made up only 1,652 families; thus, 44 percent of the families owned slaves—a much greater and more significant figure. But even this is not an accurate picture of the distribution of slaves in the county or their use by white households.

3. *Hannibal Messenger* (hereinafter *HM*), February 11, 1858.
4. *Palmyra Weekly Whig* (hereinafter *PWW*), September 9, 1847, October 23, 1856.
5. *MC*, December 12, 1850.

The census only counted as slaveholders those who owned slaves. Slaves who were *leased* year-round—frequently excess slaves, more potential labor than the slave-owning family needed—were counted with their owners. Accordingly, people like the Clemens family, who were leasing slaves by 1850, were not counted as slaveholders. Some slaves were leased year after year by the same families. In 1850 Hannibal, only 122 families actually owned slaves; far more leased them. The actual number has been lost and will probably never be known, which helps perpetuate the myths that comfort local residents, who say that slavery was rare and humane in this part of the world. Perhaps they do not consider that slaves who were leased out may have been treated more cruelly and fed less well because the temporary masters had no financial incentive to protect their short-term investment.

Putting on Appearances

It was not just emigrants from the Old South who utilized slave labor in Hannibal. Having someone else to do the drudge work seemed to appeal across regional lines. Emery Heath, who had lived in the northeast United States and in Canada, came through Hannibal in November of 1858 and wrote to his sister in New York: "You asked me what kind of a place Hannibal was and how long I thought of remaining here. Well, Hannibal is a City of about Seven thousand Inhabitants and at least half of them are Eastern People and the first thing they do when they come here is to buy a Nigger and Niggers are well used here, too."[6]

The possession of slaves enhanced a person's social status in the community. John Rogers, an engineer constructing the Hannibal and St. Joseph Railroad, wrote to his sister in Massachusetts: "I wish I could be at some of Laura's parties she tells of— but my prospects for gaiety has brightened since I moved into town. Several young ladies have patronized me the *tallest kind* lately—as they say out 'ere. One of them owns any quantity of '*niggers*' & boasts of never having to put her own shawl on."[7]

There is ample evidence that hired slaves were considered necessary household "appliances" in most Hannibal homes when Sam Clemens was a child. In December 1854, a local newspaper noted, "There is quite a

6. Emery Heath to Miss Sarah Heath, November 25, 1858, author's collection.
7. John Rogers, Jr., to Ellen Rogers, October 26, 1856, the Rogers Papers, New-York Historical Society (hereinafter Rogers Papers).

demand for hireling slaves for the approaching year, our friends in the country who have good cooks, washers and ironers to hire will find good places and high wages for them in Hannibal." Another newspaper solicited classified ads of "[p]ersons having Negroes to hire," charging fifty cents for the first insertion and twenty-five cents thereafter.[8]

People who sought slaves to hire were frequently very particular about the gender and age of the slave they were seeking. Slaves could be leased by people with very modest means—and whites certainly took advantage of the easily rented labor they provided. Poverty was no bar to enjoying slave labor in Hannibal. There were eighty-four ads either seeking or offering slaves for lease between 1839 and 1865 in the Marion County newspapers that have been preserved. It seems unlikely that the newspapers carried even the bulk of slave-leasing transactions. Private arrangements between individuals were undoubtedly made by individuals through social, church, family, and business connections. Likewise, once a slave was leased to a holder, there was no reason the lease would not be renewed year after year without need for another posting in the newspaper. The ads provide a fascinating glimpse into slave life.

A Very Young Face: Real Hannibal Childhoods

The faces of slavery in Missouri were very young. Though Hollywood has portrayed the house slave as an old gentleman in a tuxedo or a plump woman with a bandana on her head, it appears that children as young as nine were sought as household servants in Hannibal and Palmyra. They were taken from their mothers and put to work emptying bedpans, bringing in firewood, tending fires, and doing other unpleasant tasks around the house. The following advertisements suggest the widespread use of children:

Negro Girl Wanted—I WISH to hire a NEGRO GIRL from 9 to 13 years of age, by the year. Any person having such a one, will please leave word at this office. A.B. COHEN

WANTED TO HIRE—For the ensuing year, a servant BOY, from ten to fifteen years of age, for which liberal wages will be given. Enquire of J. S. BUCHANAN, Journal Office.

8. *MC*, December 21, 1854; *TWM*, August 10, 1854.

FOR SALE—By calling at this office information can be obtained of a valuable NEGRO GIRL for sale, between 13 and 14 years of age. Apply immediately.

Negroes for Sale—A WOMAN, who is a fine cook, washer and ironer, having been raised to that business. Also, three boys, from eight to ten years old, sound and likely. For information, apply at this office.

Negro Boy For Sale—A likely negro boy, about 12 years old, will be sold at private sale, if application be made soon at the Messenger office.[9]

In Hannibal a slave's childhood was brief. Though slave children were usually kept with their mothers until about age nine, this was not always the case. Even babies were sometimes torn from their mothers. One traveler who passed through northeast Missouri in 1859 on his way to Colorado to mine for gold first encountered slavery when he crossed the Mississippi River at Canton. There he was shocked when a man offered to trade him a slave baby for his spare horse. The traveler refused.[10]

Extremely young slaves could be found on the auction block. An ad in 1840 listed "a likely NEGRO BOY, about three years old." The boy was sold to settle an estate. An 1857 ad listed slaves seven, five, and four years old. The *Hannibal Weekly Messenger* reported one sale in 1855 for which a four-year-old crippled girl was listed. She brought the lowest price in the lot, selling for a meager $155.[11]

As domestics, these children were the first up in the morning and the last to bed at night. A slave child would probably be the only black and the only servant in most Hannibal households. He or she bore a large responsibility and had a lonely existence with no one to turn to for comfort or support. These children often were depressed at having been removed from their families. The inhumanity of this system was recognized by the white people who used the children as slaves. Sam Clemens recorded his mother's remarks about their hired slave boy, Sandy:

We had a little slave boy whom we had hired from some one, there in Hannibal. He was from the eastern shore of Maryland and had been

9. *HM*, January 1, 1857; *Hannibal Journal* (hereinafter *HJ*), December 27, 1848; *TWM*, September 30, November 18, 1852, and June 17, 1854.

10. "Memoir of Franklin Harriman," Roberta and Hurley Hagood Collection, Hannibal, Missouri, 4.

11. *PMW*, March 7, 1840, May 14, 1857; *TWM*, May 10, 1855.

brought away from his family and his friends halfway across the American continent and sold. He was a cheery spirit, innocent and gentle, and the noisiest creature that ever was, perhaps. All day long he was singing, whistling, yelling, whooping, laughing—it was maddening, devastating, unendurable. At last, one day, I lost all my temper and went raging to my mother and said Sandy had been singing for an hour without a single break and I couldn't stand it and wouldn't she please shut him up. The tears came into her eyes and her lip trembled and she said something like this:

"Poor thing, when he sings it shows that he is not remembering and that comforts me; but when he is still I am afraid he is thinking and I cannot bear it. He will never see his mother again; if he can sing I must not hinder it, but be thankful for it. If you were older you would understand me; then that friendless child's noise would make you glad."[12]

Although Jane Clemens was aware of the hardships imposed on the slave child, Sandy, she did not hesitate to exploit his labor in her home. She was not the only slave master to indicate she had comforted a lonely slave child.

Another early settler of Marion County was a former Virginia schoolteacher named William Callaghan. One of his descendants, Harold H. Haines, discovered a bundle of his letters in a trunk in the 1930s in Marion County and published them along with family stories that had been handed down about Callaghan's slave, Isaac. Callaghan took possession of Isaac from Callaghan's father when Isaac was twelve years old. Isaac's mother remained in Virginia with his father. Haines recorded, "Sometimes Isaac felt blue and cried as he was young and lonely. William would put his arm around him, pat him on the head and talk kindly to him and soon Isaac would be happy again."[13] The strange mixture of compassion and cruelty was a hallmark of slavery. Aware of the consequences of their actions in taking children from their mothers and families, some slave masters sought to comfort their slaves and at the same time, perhaps, salve their own consciences. Such contradictions were inherent in the slave culture of northeast Missouri—an indifference to slavery's consequences coupled with a patronizing desire to comfort pet slaves.

Slave children were never truly secure in a home. Even if they were apparently situated for life in a setting, they could be suddenly and unexpectedly subjected to sale. Besides the obvious risk of death of a master, slaves were also at the mercy of their owner's creditors. In 1843, John Marshall Clemens sued William Beebe and won a verdict against him.

12. Neider, *Autobiography of Mark Twain*, 6–7.
13. Harold Haines, *The Callaghan Mail, 1821–1859*, 14.

The next year he had the sheriff seize a nine-year-old slave girl and sell her at public auction to satisfy the judgment.[14] A modern American can only imagine what thoughts went through the child's mind while she was examined, probably naked, before the sale—her mouth probed, eyes examined—made to walk to prove she had no physical defects. No one was there to comfort her. She was merely a piece of property sold at public auction along with tin plates, barrels, and sacks of salt. Sam Clemens turned nine that same year.

Living across the street from Sam Clemens was a cute little girl named Laura Hawkins. Hawkins, the girl Hannibal claims was the model for the character of Becky Thatcher, was also a slave owner. The Mark Twain Boyhood Home Foundation of Hannibal now owns her house. In the 1850 census she was listed as the owner of a six-year-old girl. It was not unusual for children in wealthier homes to be given a slave child who would grow and go off with the young master or mistress when they left home. The rest of the Hawkins family also had slaves. Laura's mother, Sophia, liked one slave so well that she buried her in the old Baptist Cemetery and put a stone marker on her grave—a rare thing for a slave. Nearly all are buried in graves that are either unmarked or have simple field rocks placed at the head. Like the nation's unknown soldiers in Arlington Cemetery, they are known but to God.

Though slaves in the country were frequently provided with very low-quality slave cabins, often crudely constructed log structures, domestic servants in Hannibal were kept in the houses or outbuildings of their masters. Architectural surveys of Hannibal's historic districts identified no slave quarters. It appears that slaves slept on pallets in kitchens, under the stairs, or in the existing outbuildings.

Uses to Which Slaves Were Put

Slaves were put to a variety of uses in northeast Missouri slave culture, the most common being housekeeping. The following ads are typical of those offering and seeking domestic servants:

Wanted to hire—By the year, a good House Servant for which liberal wages will be paid. Apply to J. D. Dowling

A Negro Woman for Hire—An excellent cook, washer and ironer. Apply to J. B. Brown.

14. Wecter, *Sam Clemens of Hannibal*, 112.

Cash will be paid for a good house servant. For one who is well acquainted with house work, and of good character, a liberal price will be given. Enquire at G. W. Bird, of Hannibal[15]

Slaves were leased for other purposes as well. Farm workers could be hired:

FOR HIRE!—A STOUT, able-bodied black man, a first rate farm hand. Also two black boys, one fifteen, the other sixteen years old. They are all stout healthy and hearty. For particulars enquire at BROWN'S DRUG STORE Hannibal, Mo.
For Hire,—A NEGRO MAN, Who is a good farm hand
Enquire of Henry S. Millan, Of Palmyra[16]

Slaves were also hired out to tend young children.

WANTED TO HIRE—A NEGRO GIRL, from 12 to 15 years of age, suitable for a nurse. Any one having such a girl to hire, will make it known at this office.[17]

Slaves were also leased for very specific purposes. The following ad offers a slave to be leased to operate the sawmill that is offered for rent as well.

NOTICE
WE will rent the SAW & GRIST MILL, on Salt river in Ralls county, belonging to the estate of Richard Matson, deceased, now occupied by Jas. L. Fisher, with the Houses, &c. about 30 acres of tilable land, and some Meadow. And we will hire a certain NEGRO MAN (the miller) with the mill, for the term of twelve months, on the first Saturday in September next, on the premises. Should the possession of the premises be ejected from the Administrators, the possession of the premises, &c. is to be given up, and payment to be made in proportion. Bond and approved security will be required.
JAMES CULBERTSON,
WM. H. VARDEMAN
Administrators[18]

15. *HJ*, December 27, 1848; *MC*, January 5, 1854; *Hannibal Commercial Advertiser*, June 22, 1838.
16. *Hannibal Daily Messenger* (hereinafter *HDM*), January 18, 1861; *PMW*, May 21, 1842.
17. *PWW*, April 8, 1858.
18. *MW*, September 5, 1840.

Slaves were also hired for large construction projects:

HANDS WANTED.
  The subscriber wishes to employ, immediately, FIFTY Negro Men, to
work on the Rail-Road. For stout, able-bodied men, higher prices will
be paid than can be obtained any where else in this section of country.
J. W. SHEPHERD[19]

The leasing of slaves was important to the local economy, and prices
for leasing slaves were frequently reported in the newspapers. Although
slaves could be rented by the week or month, most leases ran from Christmas to Christmas as in the following lease by Anna McCormack, who was
residing near Lexington, Kentucky, but owned two young slaves in Hannibal. It is very likely McCormack inherited her slaves. Her brother Henry
made arrangements to lease the slaves out for her.

I have this day hired of Miss Anna B. McCormack her certain negro
boy named Peter for the term of one year commencing on the 25th day
December AD 1860 and to terminate on the 25th day of December 1861.
And for his services during said period I promise and hereby bind myself to pay to the said Anna B. McCormack or order the sum of (40) forty
dollars at the end of said time. And also that I will furnish said boy Peter
with suitable food and clothing and pay all tax assessments and all bills
for medicine and medical attendance which may be had performed or
imposed upon said boy during the period aforesaid
  Witness my hand this the 29 day of Dec 1860
          Saml. A. Hatch[20]

Under Missouri law, the owner assumed the risk for the loss of a slave.
If a slave ran away while in the possession of a hirer, and the hirer had
used all reasonable diligence to prevent the escape of the slave and then
attempted to capture him afterward, the hirer was liable only for the
amount due under the lease and not for the full sale value of the slave. Of
course, if the owner could prove that the hirer had been negligent, then he
could recover the value of the slave from the hirer. What constituted reasonable diligence and care depended on the circumstances of each case.
Anna McCormack obviously had this risk in mind when she wrote her
brother in 1862:

19. *PMW,* June 29, 1848.
20. Author's collection.

I am already indebted so much to you yes indeed. I have troubled you no little about hiring and collecting. If I possibly can I will dispose of my servants before another year rolls around. Henry please get places for Emily and Pete where they will be strictly watched over. I think the reason Emily is so dissatisfied at Mr. M——s [illegible] is because she wants to hire her own time for a year or two past. She has a great notion of setting up for herself.[21]

If a slave died during the term of a lease, the hirer owed the owner only the prorated amount for the portion of the lease during which the slave was in service. If the slave died as a result of cruelty or abuse by the hirer, the owner could sue for the value of the slave. Slaves were sometime sublet, resulting in a chain of legal obligations from master to master to owner. Missouri case law covered this contingency as well. If a hirer of a slave hired him out to another who caused the death of the slave by his cruelty, either the owner or original hirer could take the guilty party to court for the value of the slave.[22] The existence of these cases is evidence that cruelty by people who leased slaves occurred.

In all other aspects, the person who leased a slave stood in the shoes of the owner. He could discipline the slave and direct his every move. Missouri's slave laws explicitly made the slave responsible to his "master," who could be either the slave's owner or the person who had rented or leased him for a period of time.

The obligation to provide clothing to the leased and owned slaves of slave culture gave rise to a class of goods designed for use by slaves. Designed to be sturdy and practical, "negro" goods were created. The style was so common that a category was even created at the Marion County Fair. Along with awards for such items as best cotton quilt and best hearth rug, these cheaper items were recognized. In 1856, the prize for "Best four leaf negro jeans" went to Mrs. T. Cleayer of Ralls County. In 1857, a prize of two dollars was awarded for the best pair of "coarse negro" shoes, and in 1858, a prize of four dollars was offered for the best example of "negro jeans" cloth.[23] The cheap but durable items provided by owners were augmented by the discarded clothing of Hannibal's whites and whatever clothing slaves could purchase with their own money.

21. *Ellett v. Bobb,* 6 Mo. 323, Mo. 1840; *Perkins v. Reeds,* 8 Mo. 33, Mo. 1843; *Perry v. Beardslee,* 10 Mo. 568, Mo. 1847; *Beardslee v. Perry,* 14 Mo. 88, Mo. 1851; Anna McCormack to Henry Bourne, December 13, 1862, author's collection.

22. *Dudgeon v. Teass,* 9 Mo. 867, Mo. 1846; *Adams v. Childers,* 10 Mo. 778, Mo. 1847.

23. *HM,* October 2, 1856, June 11, 1857, and January 1, 1858.

Emma Knight, who was born in slavery on the farm of Will and Emily Ely near Florida, Missouri, participated in the Works Progress Administration (WPA) slave narrative project. The project provided employment to writers, who interviewed former slaves about their experiences. Knight recalled:

> We didn't have hardly any clothes and most of the time they was just rags. We went barefoot until it got real cold. Our feet would crack open from the cold and bleed. We would sit down and bawl and cry because it hurt so. Mother made moccasins for our feet from old pants. Late in the fall master would go to Hannibal or Palmyra and bring us shoes and clothes. We got those only once a year. I had to wear the young master's overalls for underwear and linseys for a dress.[24]

Punishment of Slaves in the Home

Slave culture made no provision for slaves who were weary or merely had a bad day. To enforce his will, the master commonly administered whippings, most often using the cowhide, and beatings. In the patriarchal world of northeast Missouri, it usually fell upon the man in the family to administer punishment. Frequently, simple annoyance motivated a beating. In *Following the Equator*, Sam Clemens wrote about his father punishing a slave boy the family had leased to work around the house. Sam remembered how the lad's "trifling little blunders and awkwardnesses" provoked John Marshall Clemens from time to time to "cuff" him. In the original manuscript Clemens had used "lashed," but in the margin Sam's wife and frequent editor, Livy, penciled, "I hate to have your father pictured as lashing a slave boy." Clemens answered, "it's out, and my father is whitewashed."[25]

Sam Clemens recorded another occasion when his father came home to whip the family slave, Jennie. She was acting "uppity"—a term used by slaveholders to denote anything other than complete, smiling obedience. Jane Clemens threatened to lash Jennie with the family's whip. Defiantly, the slave woman snatched the whip from Jane Clemens's hand. Defiance was not tolerated by slaveholders; Jane Clemens was so angered that she sent for her husband. John Marshall Clemens hurried home, bound Jennie's wrists with a bridle rein, and flogged her with a cowhide.[26]

24. George P. Rawick, ed., *The American Slave: A Composite Autobiography*, suppl., ser. 1, 2:202.
25. Wecter, *Sam Clemens of Hannibal*, 74.
26. Ibid., 74.

Cruelty was common. Clemens recalled another incident when he was ten years old that resulted in the death of a slave. He saw a white over-seer "fling a lump of iron-ore at a slave-man in anger, for merely doing something awkwardly. . . . He was dead in an hour . . . it seemed a pitiful thing and somehow wrong. . . . Nobody in the village approved of that murder, but of course no one said much about it."[27]

Missouri law prohibited "wanton cruelty" to slaves. The law provided for the punishment of any person who cruelly or "unhumanly" tortured, beat, wounded, or abused any slave in his employment or under his con-trol. However, as with all criminal laws, the prosecuting attorney had discretion in whether to bring charges against a slave master. Prosecu-tors were elected and thus sensitive to the voters' mood. There was little concern for the lives of slaves. As Clemens observed about the killing he had witnessed, "[E]verybody seemed entirely indifferent about it—as re-garded the slave—though considerable sympathy was felt for the slave's owner, who had been bereft of valuable property by a worthless person who was not able to pay for it."[28]

Clemens described the attitude of the people in the slave culture of his youth:

It is commonly believed that an infallible effect of slavery was to make such as lived in its midst hard-hearted. I think it had no such effect—speaking in general terms. I think it stupefied everybody's humanity as regarded the slave, but stopped there. There were no hard-hearted peo-ple in our town—I mean there were no more than would be found in any other town of the same size in any other country; and in my experience hard-hearted people are very rare everywhere.[29]

If hard hearts were rare, short tempers and frustrated masters appear to have been common. When things went wrong, trifling things could set a master off. Slaves were ready scapegoats. In 1856, John Rogers, an engi-neer living in Hannibal, wrote to his family in Massachusetts describing an act of wanton cruelty committed by an officer of the Hannibal and St. Joseph Railroad. "I heard of a case today which shocked me as I know the parties. The treasurer of the road is quite a wealthy Irishman & lives close by where I board. The other day his wife for some offense, I don't know

27. Ibid., 99.
28. Article 8, section 8, *Missouri Revised Statutes of 1845*; *State v. Peters*, 28 Mo. 241, Mo. 1859; Neider, *Autobiography of Mark Twain*, 31.
29. Ibid.

what it was, threw a bowl of scalding hot preserves in the face of her black woman & then she & her husband beat her most immercifully."[30]

The narratives of former Missouri slaves provide more insight about the random violence suffered. Mary Armstrong recalled her childhood as a slave near St. Louis:

> That was in St. Louis whar I was born. You see when I was born, my mamma belong to old Wm. Cleveland an' old Polly Cleveland, an' they was the meanest two white folks what ever lived, 'cause they was always beatin' on their slaves. I know 'cause mamma told me, an' I hear about it other places, an' besides, old Polly—she was a Polly devil if there ever was one—whipped my little sister what was only 9 months old an' jus' a little baby, to death. She came an' took the diaper off my little sister an' whipped 'til the blood jes' ran jes' cause she cry like all babies do an' it killed my sister. I never forgot that.[31]

Ed Craddock recalled family stories of a particularly cruel act of retribution. "Stories told me by my father are vivid," Craddock said in an interview. "One especially, because of its cruelty. A slave right here in Marshall angered his master, was chained to a hemp-brake on a cold night and left to freeze to death, which he did."[32]

A drunken master had to be approached gingerly. William Black recalled: "At the age of thirteen my sister was bonded out to some man who was awful mean, she was a bad girl too. After we were freed she told me all about her old master. She said, 'One Christmas my master was drunk and I went to wish him a merry Christmas and get some candy. He hit at me and I ducked and run around the house so fast that I burnt the grass around the house and I know that there ain't any grass growing there yet.'"[33]

William Wells Brown, an escaped Missouri slave who published the story of his life in slavery in the nineteenth century, described a punishment unique to tobacco-producing areas. Tobacco was grown in Marion County. Brown attempted to escape, and when he was captured, he was returned to his master's farm in O'Fallon, Missouri.

> Major Freeland soon made his appearance, and took me out, and ordered me to follow him, which I did. After we returned home I was tied

30. John Rogers, Jr., to John Rogers, Sr., August 17, 1856, Rogers Papers.
31. Federal Writers Project, *Slave Narratives, Texas Narratives, Part 1*, 25.
32. Rawick, *American Slave*, 2:158.
33. Ibid., 147.

up in the smokehouse, and was very severely whipped. After the major had flogged me to his satisfaction he sent out his son Robert, a young man eighteen or twenty years of age, to see that I was well smoked. He made a fire of tobacco stems, which soon set me to coughing and sneezing. This, Robert told me, was the way his father used to do to his slaves in Virginia. After giving me what they conceived to be a decent smoking, I was untied and again set to work.[34]

Mary Bolden also recalled seeing slaves punished for attempting to escape. "When I was a small girl I can remember seeing the master and two other men whip three men slaves, for running off. The whipping was unmerciful."[35]

Newspaper stories of the times reflect the acceptance of whipping in the white community, as is shown in the following (which also expresses a patronizing view of the slave's religious understanding):

A negro woman, soon after having experienced religion, stole a goose to make merry with her consort from a neighboring plantation. *Of course, she was whipped, for the good of others as well as herself.* Soon after these circumstances, a communion was to take place in the neighborhood, and Dinah prepared to go. Her mistress remonstrated with her, and mentioned the goose affair as a sufficient reason for her not to offer herself on such a holy occasion; to which she replied: "Lor, Missus, I ain't agwine to turn my back on my bressed Massa, for no ole goose!"[36]

The master, who has stolen the woman's labor and had her whipped for stealing a goose, counsels her on the propriety of taking communion after stealing the bird. Note also the presumption that the slave stole the goose to celebrate with her husband. Theft of food in these stories is always attributed to moral failure on the part of the slave and never to hunger.

Whipping slaves was considered a master's duty. Whipping did not shock the consciences of the white people in slaveholding Missouri; rather, it was so ordinary an occurrence that it could form the basis of supposedly humorous stories. The master in the following story administers weekly whippings to his slave. Note the outcome of the negotiations between the slave and master in this humorous 1849 story from the *Palmyra Missouri Whig.*

34. William Wells Brown, *Narrative of William W. Brown, a Fugitive Slave,* 28.
35. Rawick, *American Slave,* 2:150–51.
36. *PMW,* March 13, 1856.

Capt. Stick and Toney.

By J. J. Hooper

Old Captain Stick was a remarkably precise old gentleman, and a conscientiously just man. He was too, very methodical in his habits, one of which was to keep an account in writing of the conduct of his servants, from day to day. It was a sort of account current, and he settled it every Saturday afternoon. No one dreaded these hebdominal balancings, more than Toney, boy of all work, for the Captain was generally obliged to write a receipt for a considerable amount across his shoulders.

One settling afternoon, the Captain accompanied by Toney, was seen "toddling" down to the old stable, with his account book in one hand, and a small rope in the other. After they had reached the "Bar of Justice" and Toney had been properly "strung up," the captain proceeded to state his account as follows:

TONEY, DR.

Sabbath, to not half blacking my boots, &c, five stripes.

Tuesday, to staying four hours at mill longer than necessary, ten stripes.

Wednesday, to not locking the hall door at night, five stripes.

Friday, to letting the horse go without water, five stripes.

Total. twenty-five stripes

TONEY, CR.

Monday, by first-rate day's work in the garden, ten stripes.

Balance due, fifteen stripes.

The balance, being thus struck, the Captain drew his cowhide and remarked—"Now, Toney, you black scamp, what say you, you lazy villain, why I should not give you fifteen lashes across your back, as hard as I can draw?"

"Stop old Mass," said Toney, "dar's de work in de garden, sir—dat ought to tak off some."

"You black dog," said the Captain, "haven't I given you the proper credit of ten stripes, for that? Come, come!"

"Please old massa," said Toney, rolling his eyes about in an agony of fright,—"dar es—you forgot—dar's de scouring of de floor—old missus say 'e neber been scour so good before."

"Soho, you saucy rascal," quoth Captain Stick, "you're bringing in more offsets, are you? Well now, there!" here the Captain made an entry upon his book—"you have a credit of five stripes, and the balance must be paid."

"Gor a mighty, massa, don't hit yet—dar's sumpen else—oh Lord! Please don't—yes, sir—got um now—ketching' de white boy and fetchin' um to ole missus, what trow rock at de young duck."

"That's a fact," said the Captain—"The outrageous young vagabond—that's a fact, and I'll give you a credit of TEN stripes for it—I wish you had brought him to MISTER—we'll settle the balance."

"Bress de Lord, ole massa," said Toney, "DAT'S ALL." Toney grinned extravagantly.

The Captain adjusted his tortoise shell spectacles, with great exactness held the book close to his eyes, and ascertained that the fact was as stated by Toney. He was not a little irritated.

"You swear off the account, you infernal rascal—you swear off the account, do you."

"All de credit is fair, massa," Answered Toney.

"Yes, but,"—said the disappointed Captain—but—but—still the Captain was sorely puzzled how to give Toney a FEW LICKS ANY HOW—"but"—an idea popped into his head—"WHERE'S MY COSTS—you incorrigible, abominable scoundrel? You want to swindle me, do you out of my costs, you black, deceitful rascal? And," he added delighted, as well at his own ingenuity as the perfect justness of the sentence; "I enter judgment against you for costs—ten stripes"—and forthwith administered the stripes and satisfied the judgment.

"Ki nigger!" said Toney; "ki nigger! What dis judmen for coss, ole massa talk 'bout. Done git off bout not blackin' de boot—git off 'bout stayin' a long time at de mill—and ebry ting else—but dis judgmen for coss gim me de debbil—bress God, nigger mus keep out ob de ole stable, or I'll tell you what, dat JUDGMEN' FOR COSS make'e back feel mighty warm, for true!"[37]

Another supposedly humorous story indicates how common random whippings by masters were. In this story, slaves are incidental to the story line. It is a tale of a young white traveler who courts a lady at a house where he is a guest. Seeking to impress the young woman, the suitor plays the banjo for her. Unfortunately, he plays too well, and the girl's mother decides he must be a disreputable "showman." The girl's father likes the young man and quarrels with the mother. Their argument is overheard by the house servant, "old Uncle Ben," who informs the young man, "Massa tuck you side, but old Missus carried de day. Massa's been rarin and tarin 'round de place, whippin de niggers for nuffin, he's so mad."[38]

If refined people with gentle ways found the thought of beating a slave repugnant, they could send the slave to the local sheriff or constable. For a small fee the officer whipped the slave the number of lashes the master or mistress designated. Likewise, masters could lodge their slaves in the jail for a small fee.

37. Ibid., June 14, 1849.
38. *HM*, April 30, 1857.

A Hannibal correspondent writing in 1849 in the *Journal* recorded his reaction to three whippings he had observed.

> I just happen to think of three cases of unmerciful flogging that have come within the limited range of my observation.—All three were whipped on slight suspicions and as it turned out were innocent. The back of one was almost literally cut to pieces, and the others were so mangled that it took skillful medical aid to preserve life. One of these latter belonged to a "good Christian lady" of the upper ten who stood by and saw every strip well laid on, the other to a leading member of the church. And what was done? Why a few dared to whisper that they thought those persons rather cruel; and that was all.[39]

Sex and Slavery

As bad as physical punishment was, some other aspects of slave culture were far crueler. The dirtiest secret of slavery was the sexual exploitation of slave women by white men. In an oft-quoted section of her diary, Mary Chesnut wrote the unspoken truth of slave culture. "God forgive us, but ours is a monstrous system, a wrong and an iniquity! Like the patriarchs of old, our men live all in one house with their wives and their concubines; and the mulattoes one sees in every family partly resemble the white children. Any lady is ready to tell you who is the father of all the mulatto children in everybody's household but her own. Those, she seems to think, drop from the clouds."[40]

This is not to say that women always turned a blind eye to their men's indiscretions with slaves. In 1845 a story from New Orleans got national newspaper coverage. A New York merchant had started business in New Orleans. He had a girlfriend in New York who was from a respectable family. When she visited the man in New Orleans, she was shocked to find him living with a "quadroon" (a light-skinned slave with one black and three white grandparents). The outraged woman tracked her boyfriend to an auction house, where she confronted him, drew a pistol, and shot him down.[41]

White men of Hannibal sexually exploited slave women. In the 1860 census, 16 percent of the slaves owned by Hannibal residents were "mulatto" or of mixed race. Sam Clemens dealt briefly with the community

39. *HJ*, December 13, 1849.
40. Mary Boykin Chesnut, *A Diary from Dixie*, 21.
41. *PMW*, July 9, 1845.

attitude toward female slaves in his autobiography. While apprenticed to Joseph Ament at the *Hannibal Courier,* he and the other white apprentices were required to eat in the kitchen with the Negro cook and her mulatto daughter. One apprentice, Wales McCormick, made advances to the daughter.

> Wales was constantly and persistently and loudly and elaborately making love to that mulatto girl and distressing the life out of her and worrying the old mother to death. She would say, "Now, Marse Wales, Marse Wales, can't you behave yourself?" With encouragement like that, Wales would naturally renew his attentions and emphasize them. It was killingly funny to Ralph and me. And, to speak truly, the old mother's distress about it was merely a pretense. She quite well understood that by the customs of slaveholding communities it was Wales's right to make love to that girl if he wanted to.[42]

Clemens noted that "the girl's distress was very real. She had a refined nature and she took all Wales's extravagant love-making in earnest." However, she could not fend off the unwanted affection. If she insulted Wales by word or gesture she was subject to up to thirty-nine lashes under the Hannibal Slave Ordinance. If the city law didn't suffice, there was a state law that provided that "insolent and insulting language of slaves to white persons, shall be punished with stripes."[43]

There is no surviving evidence of the adolescent Clemens having sexual encounters with her or any other slaves in Hannibal while he lived as a printer's apprentice. However, Clemens recorded in his personal notebook a dream he had in 1897 of a black woman trying to seduce him.

> In my dream last night I was suddenly in the presence of a negro wench who was sitting in grassy open country, with her left arm resting on the arm of one of those long park-sofas that are made of broad slats with cracks between, and a curve-over back. She was very vivid to me— round black face, shiny black eyes, thick lips, very white regular teeth showing through her smile. She was about 22, and plump—not fleshy, not fat, merely rounded and plump; and good-natured and not at all bad-looking. She had but one garment on—a coarse tow-linen shirt that reached from her neck to her ankles without break. She sold me a pie; a mushy apple pie—hot. She was eating one herself with a tin teaspoon.

42. Neider, *Autobiography of Mark Twain,* 88.

43. Chapter 150, section 22, *Missouri Revised Statutes of 1845 as Amended in 1855.*

She made a disgusting proposition to me. Although it was disgusting it did not surprise me—for I was young (I was never old in a dream yet) and it seemed quite natural that it should come from her. It was disgusting, but I did not say so; I merely made a chaffing remark, brushing aside the matter—a little jeeringly—and this embarrassed her and she made an awkward pretence that I had misunderstood her. I made a sarcastic remark about this pretence, and asked for a spoon to eat my pie with. She had but the one, and she took it out of her mouth, in a quite matter-of-course way, and offered it to me. My stomach rose—there everything vanished.

It was not a dream—it all *happened*. I was actually there in person—in my spiritualized condition. My, how vivid it all was! Even to the texture of her shirt, its dull white color, and the pale brown tint of a stain on the shoulder of it. I had never seen that girl; I was not acquainted with her—but dead or alive she is a *reality*; she exists and she was *there*. Her pie was a spiritualized pie, no doubt, and also her shirt and the bench and the shed—but their *actualities* were at that moment in existence somewhere in the world.[44]

In Clemens's dream, the black woman initiated the encounter. While it is possible that some slave women were able to manipulate relationships with white men to their advantage, and while there may have been some instances of genuine affection between white men and slave women, the consent of the slave was totally irrelevant. If a master wished to sexually exploit a slave, there was nothing to prevent it. She was mere property.

Generations of such exploitation resulted in white and fair-skinned slaves who were particularly prized by slave traders. Whites could be slaves under Missouri law. A person was considered a mulatto if one of his grandparents was Negro. A person with one Negro great-grandparent was legally white. Then as now, race was a legal and social concept, not a medical or scientific concept. A person was a slave if his mother was a slave—regardless of his or her appearance or ancestry.[45]

William Wells Brown reported seeing such a white slave woman being put aboard a riverboat in Hannibal in 1844. She was accompanying a coffle of fifty to sixty slaves. They were being sold south. Such women brought a premium in the slave markets of the south. Brown's description of her conveys the complexity of slavery and sexuality:

44. Albert Bigelow Paine, ed., *Mark Twain's Notebook* (New York: Harper & Bros. 1935), 351–52.

45. Chapter 114, section 1, *Missouri Revised Statutes of 1845 as Amended in 1855; Lee v. Sprague*, 14 Mo. 476, Mo. 1851.

a beautiful girl, apparently about twenty years of age, perfectly white, with straight light hair and blue eyes. But it was not the whiteness of her skin that created such a sensation among those who gazed upon her— it was her almost unparalleled beauty. She had been on the boat but a short time before the attention of all the passengers, including the ladies had been called to her, and the common topic of conversation was about the beautiful slave-girl. She was not in chains. The man who claimed this article of human merchandise was a Mr. Walker,—a well known slave-trader, residing in St. Louis. There was a general anxiety among the passengers and crew to learn the history of the girl. Her master kept close by her side, and it would have been considered impudent for any of the passengers to have spoken to her, and the crew were not allowed to have any conversation with them. When we reached St. Louis, the slaves were removed to a boat bound for New Orleans and the history of the beautiful slave-girl remained a mystery.[46]

The white slave's future undoubtedly was to serve as a concubine or to work in a brothel. It is not unusual that this story was published by an abolitionist press. The existence of white slaves severely strained the underlying, racist justification of slavery. Slave culture of northeast Missouri usually ignored white male lust while accepting stereotypes of greedy or lustful female slaves. The simple fact was that masters and their adult sons usually had access to the slaves.

Another Missouri slave recalled that her master sold a very pretty girl of about sixteen years downriver to another owner but then grew lonesome for the girl and bought her back. The other slave master then missed the girl himself and tried to purchase her yet again. But the first owner "thwarted all endeavors of the other man to regain her." When it became obvious the girl was pregnant, the master became extremely angry because he did not know who the father of the child was "himself, or the man to whom he had sold her." Thus the slave girl suffered both the humiliation of being a sexual tool and the jealousy of an owner who felt betrayed.[47]

The girl seen by Brown was not the only appearance of a white slave in Hannibal. The *Hannibal Daily Messenger* reported:

PRACTICAL AMALGAMATION—*A Slave Elopes with an Irish Girl.*--an affair of the heart—an elopement, came off in this city, Sunday, between

46. Brown, *Narrative of William W. Brown*, 32–33.
47. Rawick, *American Slave*, 2:279–92

a white boy, though born a slave, name Jessie Webb, and a white girl of the Hibernian extraction, both in the employ of T.R. Selmes, Esq.

Jess was formerly owned by Judge J. Gore, through whose instrumentality he got his free papers, and was to be free at the age of 23. Judge Gore hired Jess to Mr. Selmes last year, who was so much pleased with him that he bought his time, intending to give him a piece of land and "set him up" in Iowa, when he served his time out.

But Jessie becoming weary of "tending store," driving the delivery wagon, and the family carriage of Mr. Selmes, and falling desperately in love with an Irish girl, also in the employ of his benefactor, concluded to elope with his "lady" love and try life on his own hook, although he was morally bound to serve Mr. Selmes two years yet.

Everything was got in readiness, and the "loviers" stole gently away from the employer, early Sunday, through rain and mud, and took the packet for the North, intending, we suppose to make some point in Iowa, their Gretna Green, there marry and dream their souls away in love, and live on the balmy atmosphere, by watching the opening buds and flowers and inhaling their sweet odors.[48]

The writer presumed that the slave Jess would feel "morally bound" to remain in slavery.

Although white slaves were an incalculably tiny fraction of those held in bondage, they served a very important role in the development of the abolition movement. In the racist environment of the time, abolitionists were able to generate sympathy by exposing this system. Henry Ward Beecher, a famous abolitionist preacher and brother of Harriet Beecher Stowe, the author of *Uncle Tom's Cabin,* frequently featured a white slave girl named Fannie Virginia Casseopia Lawrence at churches and abolition meetings. Photographs of her were sold to raise funds. She had been purchased at auction and emancipated. Many whites who could accept enslavement of people of color would be outraged by the enslavement of a white-skinned girl like themselves. This tactic used the very racism that was at the heart of American slavery to attract converts to abolitionism.

A sad truth of slave culture was that masters frequently sold or leased their own children. Slaves were an asset. Assuming a live birth and survival of the mother, the slave owner who impregnated a slave merely increased his net worth. A new slave baby was a welcome addition to what we would call today "the portfolio."

In addition to whippings and sexual exploitation, slaves also had to endure separation of family members. In Hannibal, Franklin Harriman

48. *HDM,* April 10, 1861.

encountered a scene he remembered all his life. He observed a coffle of slaves marched onto a riverboat just as William Wells Brown had observed fifteen years earlier. As the boat pulled away, a Negro drayman came running to the riverfront. His wife was among the slaves being sold south. The drayman screamed and cried inconsolably as the steamboat chugged past Lover's Leap and disappeared downriver. Harriman recorded that he had never seen such agony.[49]

49. "Memoir of Franklin Harriman," 6.

Chapter 11

The Siege Begins

People would call me a low-down abolitionist.

Mark Twain, *Adventures of Huckleberry Finn*

To the white citizens of Hannibal, the wailing of the drayman on the levee was part of the background noise of slavery. The separation of a couple was no more troublesome than the whippings or the clinking chains and muffled sobs of shuffling coffles of slaves which the institution required. Particularly sensitive people might look the other way, but these unpleasantries were part of the great scheme of things in Missouri. The blind eye and the deaf ear were the best defense to the inhumane treatment of slaves. But across the river in Illinois and to the north in Iowa, increasing numbers of white people were expressing outrage at slavery. Thompson, Work, and Burr's attempt to entice slaves to run away was a seminal, and polarizing, event, creating increased hostility between slave culture and free-state culture. Until slavery was abolished, preachers, politicians, and editors in Marion County would argue that Missouri's contented slaves would not seek to escape their happy lives unless influenced by outside agitators. When a slave escaped, the masters looked not to themselves for the root causes of discontent. Instead, they blamed abolitionists.

Across the river in Illinois, the freedom movement continued to grow. In 1840, when the Adams County Anti-Slavery Society was but five years old, James G. Birney of Michigan ran for president on an abolitionist Liberty Party ticket. The Liberty Party advocated using the election process rather than violence to accomplish its goals. It was a hopeless, symbolic bid for the White House, but the ticket received thirty-six votes in Quincy and another three votes in rural Adams County. Missourians were paying attention, and they had little doubt where Birney had gotten his three dozen votes. The Presbyterian Mission Institute in Quincy was the headquarters of abolitionist activities. As slaves continued to run away, hostility toward David Nelson, Richard Eells, and their school escalated.

The abolitionists, conscious of their emerging power, began taunting their neighbors across the river. In May 1842, two slaves belonging to the estate of William S. Pemberton escaped from Lewis County just to the north of Marion. The administrator of the estate, J. W. Forman, did what slaveholders had done for years and took out advertisements in the Quincy papers seeking help in catching the runaways, but instead of the customary assistance, he received an anonymous reply from an abolitionist:

> To Mr. John W. Forman—
> Dear Sir: Perceiving your address in the *Herald*, published in Quincy, and also that you have some cash on hand to pay for the "souls and bodies of men" I would improve this opportunity to inform you of a few simple *facts*. 1st, That the road from the land of oppression to freedom's soil is somewhat lengthy, but often travelled, and pretty sure. 2nd, That the poor, oppressed, and down-trodden African has with us many strong friends, and that number increasing continually 3d, That the frequent escapes from slavery in your State, is some of the fruits of your persecutions toward the Abolitionists, especially in the case of Burr, Work, and Thompson. 4th, That many christians [*sic*] here are praying for the destruction of slavery—for the escape of the slaves to a land of freedom—and that their faith is not without works. 5th, The Abolitionists feel that all the opposition, persecution and hatred of slaveholders, is only a prima facia [*sic*] evidence of the wickedness of the system, and every act of hostility is only a stimulant to urge them forward in their holy enterprise.
> 6th, and lastly, I would inform you that in the case of those negroes which you advertised in the *Herald*, you need not give yourself any further trouble about them, for they are *"able to take care of themselves."* They have arrived among friends—They have proved to our satisfaction that they have souls and bodies of their own. You may pursue, but will not overtake; you may *seek* but *never find-*

The taunt provoked already irate Missourians, and a mass meeting was called at Monticello, Missouri, "for the purpose of adopting ways and means to counteract the nefarious operations of a banditti, called Abolitionists, whose head quarters are supposed to be in the vicinity of Quincy,

Illinois, whose frequent excursions and repeated thefts from the citizens of this State, call for prompt and decisive action &c."[1]

The meeting, like dozens to follow over the next two decades, was an exercise in backwoods democracy. Only white men could attend, but the gatherings were a grass-roots response. Politicians were present and frequently were elected to run the meetings. It allowed them to gauge the political winds. Many of the political figures who dominated late antebellum Missouri found their support base in these angry gatherings. However, these events went beyond mere politicking to become what a later generation would call brainstorming sessions. Ideas to restrain slaves and to interdict the abolitionists were proposed and debated. Many of the repressive slave and free-black laws adopted by the Missouri Legislature over the next two decades originated in such local gatherings held in groves, in churches, or on courthouse lawns.

Though Thompson, Work, and Burr had failed to bring slaves to freedom that summer night in 1841, they had accomplished one unintended goal that did a great deal for runaway slaves and those who aided them. They set up the bogeyman of the white abolitionist agent prowling slave territory, enticing slaves to escape. While fellow slaves and free blacks were providing food, shelter, and guidance to runaways, slave patrols and vigilance committees were harassing itinerant preachers, salesmen, and immigrants—all white. As the three abolitionists suffered in the dank Missouri State Penitentiary, they had no way of knowing they had put the hounds of the slave catchers onto the wrong scent for years to come. They did more to aid runaways than if they had succeeded in their original goal. They enabled black resistance workers in Missouri to carry on in relative safety for years.

The language of the resolution adopted at the Monticello meeting clearly shows the extent to which the image of the abolitionist as secret agent had taken root in slave culture. The resolution called for stern measures for the protection of Missouri slave property against the "predatory incursions of an enemy, whose known principles of warfare is fiend-like." Abolitionists, the resolution argued, prowled through the country using disguises and pretenses. They worked by day and by night inculcating "fulsome doctrines." Although the slaveholders knew very well that few slaves could read, they feared abolitionists scattering incendiary pamphlets among slaves and "poisoning their minds against their masters and exciting their dissatisfaction as to condition." The secret agents of

1. *PMW,* May 28, 1842.

abolition sought "in fact to steal and aid away all such as can be operated upon to make the attempt."[2]

The anonymous, taunting letter from Illinois, coupled with the success of Pemberton's slaves in eluding their pursuers, was proof to the mass meeting of "the perfect and complete organization of this band of robbers." Despite the efforts of their many sympathetic friends in Illinois, and despite the willingness of Illinois slave catchers to seek Missouri runaways for the rewards posted by irate slaveholders, the meeting recognized the "almost utter hopelessness of ever recovering a runaway slave who has once landed on the eastern shore of the Mississippi River."

To whites in slave culture, Illinois was becoming hostile, foreign territory. Where there had been a common sense of nationality, a division was emerging. Abolitionists, while still considered extremists by most people in Illinois and Iowa, were rapidly increasing. With growth came acceptance. Of course, some in Illinois opposed the emerging abolition movement. Many Illinois residents had commercial interests in Missouri. They recognized that the Mississippi was the highway of commerce in what was then the West. The needs of commerce dictated good relations with slaveholders not just in Missouri, but downriver in Kentucky, Tennessee, Arkansas, Mississippi, and Louisiana. Illinois conservatives and moderates sought to accommodate the interests of the slave states.

An Illinois Backlash

On August 21, 1842, a slave named Charley swam across the Mississippi River and made his way to Quincy. Soaking wet, no doubt confused and lost, Charley approached a free black man who lived in Quincy named Barryman Barnet. Barnet took Charley to Eells's house. Eells made certain they had not been followed, then he let the slave, still wet, into his house. He gave Charley a dry set of clothes and hurried him to his buggy. Together they drove toward the Presbyterian Mission Institute and the help to be found there.

Unfortunately for Charley and Eells, Charley's owner, Chauncey Durkee, was in Illinois looking for his runaway property, and he had a good idea where Charley would head. It was an open secret that the physician and professor at the institute helped slaves to freedom. Durkee and a posse of slave catchers were watching the road from Quincy to the institute. When Eells's carriage was spied by the Missourians, Charley hopped

2. Ibid.

from the buggy and fled into a cornfield. He spent the night alone in the Illinois countryside. An intense manhunt followed. Charley managed to elude the Missourians and some sympathetic Illinois men for a day but then was caught.

Eells was able to escape the pursuing Missourians and loop back to his house, but he had been recognized. The angry Durkee and his posse forced their way into Eells's residence. After a quick search they found the evidence they needed to arrest Eells: Charley's wet clothes. Eells was dragged before a Quincy court and charged with harboring a slave. After posting a five-hundred-dollar bond, he was released until trial.

Eells's arrest brought about another mass meeting, and this one involved many people in Quincy. Alarmed at the unrest on the west side of the river, Illinois antiabolition forces held a meeting at the Quincy courthouse. The large crowd spilled out of the building onto the lawn. A committee was elected to draft resolutions to reassure their unhappy neighbors to the west.[3] These Illinois citizens acknowledged that abolitionists in and around Quincy had been active in persuading slaves to leave their masters in Missouri. They admitted that slaves were hidden and protected in Quincy and then placed on "a line established for the purpose of running off the negroes after their arrival in this State, conveying them by this line to some point on Lake Michigan, probably to Chicago, and there shipping them for Canada." This activity was condemned by the crowd for breaking up friendly intercourse between the citizens of Illinois and Missouri, depriving Missourians of their property without compensation, and being illegal and unjust.

The meeting passed a number of resolutions to placate Missourians and called upon abolitionists to stop their "reprehensible and illegal" activities. Those present pledged not to harbor, protect, or assist slaves in escaping and to aid Missourians in recapturing their runaways. Ominously, the meeting warned abolitionists that enticing slaves away could have "fatal consequences." The meeting reaffirmed the popular idea that Missouri slavery was a state institution, guarded and protected by the U.S. Constitution, and the power to abolish it rested solely with the people of Missouri. Citizens of one sovereign state had no business interfering with another. Despite the legal language and appeals to the Constitution, the real bond between Illinois antiabolitionists and Missouri slave culture was something visceral. The common bond was racism. These men believed that blacks were inferior to whites. The meeting at Quincy adopted the following:

3. Ibid., August 27, 1842.

RESOLVED, That whatever rights the Creator may have endowed man at his creation, we believe it is inconsistent with his providence and contrary to the moral laws of his universe for two people so widely different as the blacks and whites—different in complexion—in their physical structure, and the organization of their minds, resulting from natural, moral and physical causes, to mingle together in the enjoyment of the same civil, political, and social privileges—and that we will oppose to the utmost of our power, all schemes having this object in view, as contrary to nature—degenerating to virtue—repulsive to sound and enlightened policy, and contrary to every dictate of patriotism.[4]

Governor Thomas Reynolds of Missouri sought the extradition of Eells to Missouri. Rather than face a Missouri court, Eells used the Underground Railroad along which he had sent many escaping slaves to make his way to Chicago. Only after Illinois Governor Thomas Ford refused to send Eells to Missouri because of threats of violence did Eells return to Adams County to face charges.

At trial he was convicted and fined four hundred dollars. Disillusioned, Eells left Quincy and the rigors of the abolition movement in the West. He died in the West Indies in 1846. His case, however, lived on in appeals carried out by the Anti-Slavery Society. His conviction was affirmed by the Illinois Supreme Court. The case reached the nation's top court in 1853. Representing Eells were Salmon P. Chase and William Seward, both of whom would later serve in Lincoln's cabinet. The two influential lawyers did not sway the United States Supreme Court, which upheld Eells's conviction.[5]

Missouri slaveholders had many friends in Illinois. S. Christy, a physician in Farmington, Illinois, sent a letter dated September 6, 1842, to P. C. Lane, the assistant postmaster in Palmyra. It is unclear from the letter whether the postmaster knew Christy or was selected because of his public position. Christy warned Lane about the extent and growth of the abolition movement. "We frequently wonder here why you Missourians do not take some efficient steps to check the stealing of your slaves; and then we think that probably you may not be aware of the extent to which it is carried, and the route they may be carried. Scarcely a night passes without that more or less negroes are carried through toward Canada by rapid marches. I am informed that no less than seven were conveyed through last week."[6]

4. Ibid.
5. Lee, *Slavery North of St. Louis*, 130; *PMW*, September 3, 1842.
6. *PMW*, September 24, 1842.

Christy went on to state that he was ready at all times to render any assistance or give any information to aid slave catchers. He called the abolitionists "fanatics who are the bane of every community." On the same date Peter Frans, the sheriff of Knox County, Illinois, also wrote to Lane:

DEAR SIR—I have now in my custody five negroes, supposed to be runaway slaves, who give their names as Hannah, Susan, Jerod, Anderson and William.—Susan is about 32 years of age—has a scar on the left cheek. Hannah is about 20. Jerod is about 12—has a scar in the upper lip. Anderson about four, and William two. They were taken from the house of a noted Abolitionist, where they were brought by another of the same genus.

As slaves are frequently stolen from your vicinity, I have supposed that these may have escaped from some one within the circle of your acquaintance.

Will you please give this publicity.

Yours, very respectfully,
                    PETER FRANS,
                    Sheriff of Knox county.

Despite such efforts, slaves continued to make the perilous flight to freedom. In October 1842, four Hannibal slaves ran away. The *Palmyra Missouri Whig* claimed the runaways were traced to a "nest of Abolitionists in Illinois." The paper called for citizens "to form associations, such as exist in other states for the detection of horse thieves" to catch runaway slaves and abolitionists.[7] A meeting was promptly held and an association formed by men from Marion and Ralls Counties. In each township a committee of six men was formed to pursue runaway slaves. A fixed system of rewards was established.

Missouri slaveholders saw themselves as being surrounded by hostile territory. That fall, in his annual message to the people of Missouri, Governor Reynolds stated: "Recent events have satisfactorily shown that the slaveholding citizens of this State are constantly exposed to the depredations of organized bands of abolitionists, residing in sister States, who seize every opportunity to seduce slaves from the service of their masters, and then aid them in making their escape into non-slaveholding States, and often providing the means of conveying them into the British colonies."[8]

7. Ibid., October 8, 1842.
8. Ibid., December 3, 1842.

With the prominent case of Thompson, Work, and Burr in mind, the governor proposed specific legislation making slave stealing a crime. Abolitionists were arguing loudly that Thompson, Work, and Burr had not fairly been convicted of stealing. The governor answered: "Although I am satisfied that such offences are properly punishable as larceny, yet as some members of the legal profession have expressed a contrary opinion, I would respectfully urge the propriety and necessity of placing this question, by suitable enactments, beyond all doubt, and providing such penalties as will put an end to the increasing evil. The Penitentiary for life, seems a punishment scarcely too severe for the perpetrators of such atrocious offences."[9]

Missouri Strikes Back

In early 1843, the Illinois Legislature made it illegal for citizens to aid a slave to escape from his or her master. The *Quincy Herald* was a staunchly proslavery newspaper. Under the headline "Take Care 'Nigger' Stealers" the paper praised the new law, which made enticing Negroes from their masters and hiding them, or running them off, a penitentiary offense. Offenders would be fined five hundred dollars.

> This is just as it should be; and if the well disposed part of the community—those who have a strict regard for the laws and for the constitutional rights of their neighbors—will take the trouble to be a little on the watch for these midnight robbers, we think the infamous practice of decoying negroes from Missouri will soon be done away with, and the now tarnished character of our city restored to its original purity.—We certainly do not wish to see any person sent to the penitentiary; but the man who would entice to this state, and then assist in running off to Canada, the negroes—the legal property of our neighbors in Missouri, more richly deserves such a fate than the horse thief, the incendiary, and we like to have said, the assassin. Let them beware.[10]

Perhaps sensing that abolitionists had lost the support of mainstream Illinois citizens, a group of Missourians took revenge on the Presbyterian Mission Institute. On the night of March 8, 1843, the institute's chapel was burned to the ground. There was no doubt that the fire had been deliberately set and the arsonists had left a trail. A light snow had fallen on

9. Ibid.
10. *PMW*, March 18, 1843 (reprinted from the *Quincy Herald*).

March 7. Footprints led from the scene of the fire to the shores of the Mississippi River. No one was injured in the fire. The institute lost a library and a cabinet of curios. Classes were suspended for a week. No one was ever prosecuted for the arson.[11]

Missourians felt that the tide had turned in their struggle with the abolitionists. To celebrate the "patriotism" of the Illinois Legislature in passing the law for the "suppression of the villainous practice of the abolitionists and others in stealing and decoying away slaves from this state," the citizens of Marion County in March 1843 invited citizens from neighboring counties and from the State of Illinois to yet another mass meeting in Palmyra.[12]

But Missourians were still conscious of the threat posed by abolitionists. Attendees at the meeting enacted a series of strong measures designed to more tightly control the lives of slaves. They went much further than had those at the fall meeting in Ralls County. They organized a "committee of vigilance and safety" of fifty-eight persons whose duty was to examine and scrutinize every person of suspicious character found in the county. Members were sworn to examine all itinerant preachers, salesmen, and immigrants. The committee empowered members to punish any abolitionist they found "as they deem necessary" and compel him to leave the county.

This meeting also established the first regular patrols throughout Marion County to check all blacks for passes and assigned them the new duty of examining all canoes, skiffs, and boats to see that they were securely fastened with chains and locks to prevent persons from crossing the Mississippi on them. These patrols became known in slave jargon as "patterollers" or "pattyrollers." There is a noted slave song about the "patterollers."

Run nigger run.
The patterollers get you
Run nigger run,
It's almost day.

That man ran
That man flew
That man tore his
Shirt in two

11. Ibid., March 25, May 6, 1843.
12. Ibid., March 25, 1843.

(Refrain)
That man ran,
he ran his best
he stuck his head
in a hornet's nest.
    (Refrain)
He jumped the fence
And ran through the pasture
White man run,
but the nigger run faster

A committee of six men was also established. Taking the example of the Minute Men, it was to be ready to pursue a runaway slave or a suspected abolitionist at a moment's notice when the alarm was given. This posse was to capture the slave as soon as possible. Any abolitionists would be "dealt with." Another standard system of rewards was established.

In another important first, the 1843 Marion County meeting called for the removal of free Negroes from the county. Although the Missouri citizens did not yet suspect them of aiding and abetting runaways, they did not like the example free Negroes set for slaves. Although the Missouri Constitution of 1820 made it illegal for free blacks to settle in Missouri, those already in Missouri had been allowed to stay. In addition, Missouri slaveholders often freed slaves who were old or sick, and some slaves had managed to purchase their freedom. Marion County slaveholders did not want their slaves to see other Negroes enjoying even the limited freedom afforded free Negroes. The committee resolved to tell free Negroes to depart Missouri as soon as they could go, and "upon refusal after due notice and time for preparation, said committee are hereby required to take all lawful means to effect their removal."[13]

Each person at the meeting pledged to inform on all persons giving or selling liquor to Negroes. They were bound not to sell or barter with slaves in any way and not to allow slaves to carry arms. To tighten control of the slaves in Marion County, they pledged each master to require slaves to report at home each and every Sabbath morning at sunrise and evening at sunset. This would cut down on the amount of lead time a slave escaping on Sunday would have. Slaves were traditionally allowed free time on Sunday. It was not unusual for slaves with spouses belonging to a different owner to go visit them. An astute slave could escape on Saturday night, and the owner would not be aware he was missing until

13. Ibid.

Sunday night or Monday morning. The meeting pledged members to use written passes and authorized the arrest of slaves caught without passes. Finally, the citizens at the meeting voted to thank the citizens of Illinois who aided slave catchers.[14]

The same group met again on April 1 and drafted a letter commending the *Quincy Herald* for advocating the constitutional rights of slave owners and attacking abolitionists. The group then planned a barbecue to be held at Hannibal on July 4, 1843. In an act of neighborliness, they announced "our friends in Illinois are hereby invited to participate with us in the enjoyments and convivialities of the day."[15] Such high spirits seemed warranted. Just two weeks after the April meeting two Marion County slaves made the dash to freedom. Hopes in slave culture were heightened when the two were captured more than thirty miles into Illinois by a pair of Illinois citizens. The two had been traveling with a white man who was acting as their guide and had instructed them on how to get to Canada. The white man was arrested along with the slaves and prosecuted under the new Illinois law. The case was cited by the Missouri press as proof that the law was working and that the people of Illinois would protect Missouri property rights.

Despite all these steps toward bringing the abolition problem under control, slaves continued to run and risk capture by the new Marion County patrols and increased vigilance in Illinois. And they were successful. In July another mass meeting was called for Hannibal "to propose ways and means to protect our slave property against Abolitionists."[16] The meeting was reported by a New York newspaper. Hannibal again received national attention.

> *Trouble among Slave holders.*—The incessant flight of fugitive slaves, and the insecurity of investment in such moveable property have awakened the *zealous indignation* among the slave holders in Missouri. A mass meeting of the citizens of the counties of Lewis, Clark, Scotland, Shelby, Monroe, Ralls and Marion, has been called to meet at Hannibal on the 21st August, to take measures to protect their slave property against the operations of the abolitionists. The abolitionists residing in Illinois have become *emboldened by success,* and so frequent and unremitting are their exertions, that the slaveholders have no *security whatever* against their efforts to carry off their slaves to Canada.[17]

14. Ibid.
15. *PMW,* April 8, 1843.
16. Ibid., July 22, 1843.
17. Ibid., September 16, 1843.

A correspondent writing in the *Missouri Whig* noted that many eastern newspapers were carrying notice of the meeting. In the East, the writer observed, money and assistance were being raised to help abolitionists in Illinois. He predicted that "dire trouble" was coming unless:

> some effectual remedy be soon applied to prevent our slaves from getting into Illinois, and some more efficient measures than have yet been adopted to resist the aggressions and depredations of those land pirates who are continually holding out allurements to our slaves of a safe and speedy conveyance into Canada, if they can once reach the banks of Illinois . . . scarcely a week passes without our ears being stunned with new aggressions of the Illinois abolitionists against our individual and social rights in the abduction of our slaves.[18]

The joy of spring had given way to the reality of summer 1843. Slaves were still escaping. The August 21 meeting drew citizens from eight counties. Because the circuit court was in session and the prominent attorneys of the counties—many of whom were important political players—were in court, the meeting was continued until the following month. It was followed by other meetings throughout the rest of 1843, the last being held on December 2 in Palmyra.

The frustrations of slaveholders can be seen in the radical ideas adopted at a meeting in Lewis County in November. At a gathering held in the village of Tully, Missouri, the citizens of both Lewis and Clark Counties adopted resolutions calling for a variety of radical measures. They called for reprisal kidnappings of abolitionists from Illinois—one for each escaped slave. They offered rewards of two hundred dollars for Eells of Quincy and one hundred dollars for Erasmus Benton Stillman of Fairfield, Iowa. They instituted a standard punishment of ten lashes for any slaves found traveling without a pass. The resolutions were printed in newspapers throughout Missouri and ended with a polite thank you to the antiabolition forces in Illinois for their advice and aid "so cheerfully given."[19]

In 1844, David Nelson, archenemy of northeast Missouri slave culture and founder of the church Sam Clemens attended with his mother and sister, crossed back into Missouri. Hoping to peacefully persuade slaveholders to abandon slavery, Nelson attempted to speak at a Presbyterian church in the town of Little Union in Marion County. However, men were

18. Ibid.
19. Ibid., December 8, 1843.

ready to stop him. When Nelson rose to address the congregation, his old enemy John Bosley stood and announced he would not allow the church to be polluted by the dissemination of abolitionism. Bosley was the same man who had attempted to shoot Nelson years before. Bosley told Nelson if he did not leave the building peaceably, he would use force to remove him.

Nelson was about to ascend to the pulpit. He hesitated, turned, and took one step down. He stood looking at Bosley, and after a moment, he composed himself and once again turned toward the pulpit. Bosley raised his voice and ordered Nelson to leave the church. Nelson ignored him and continued climbing the stairs to the pulpit. This time Bosley did not resort to firearms. He ran to Nelson, locked his arm about his head, and dragged him to the door of the church. That was all the force necessary to convince Nelson to retreat. Perhaps remembering the gunplay the last time he had been evicted from a Missouri congregation, he made his way back to Quincy and never attempted to speak in Missouri again.[20]

Jacob Sosey, editor of the *Missouri Whig,* satisfied that further violence had been avoided during the incident, reflected on the occasion and advocated a peaceable approach to dealing with abolitionists.

> When you discover an Abolitionist among you, do not resort to violence: rather use moral means. Let no man speak to an Abolitionist: let us hold no communion with them of any kind; let us pass them as we would some offensive and loathsome thing we dare not touch. Be assured this is the only effectual mode, as long as they stop short of the actual infraction of the law: and when they do not, let the offence be noted, and visited with the stern and rigid, but calm and dispassionate judgment of the law. Few, we apprehend, can long endure the treatment first recommended—the last will place them out of the way of harming us.[21]

This civil approach continued to be the general rule until December 1849, when attitudes changed radically. The decade saw many more public meetings on the issue of runaway slaves and abolitionists. As each year passed, more people attended the meetings, and the measures adopted to restrain slaves became harsher. In February 1847, Marion County slave patrols were still private affairs. At a meeting at Taylor's Mill north of Palmyra, the Anti-Abolition Society created a more rigid structure for the

20. *PMW,* August 26, 1844.
21. Ibid., August 28, 1844.

group. It provided for taxation of members and established a two-dollar-per-diem payment for men who pursued runaway slaves. The group increased the pursuit posse to nine members. To encourage slaves to turn on fellow slaves, it established a fund with which to pay fees to informers. Any Negro who turned in a runaway slave would be paid twenty-five dollars. However, still believing that runaway slaves were being "stolen" by abolitionists, the group offered seventy-five dollars (equivalent to about fourteen hundred dollars today) to any slave turning in a white abolitionist attempting to entice a slave from his master.

Geography bore heavily on the minds of members of Marion County slave culture. Speaking to the crowd at Taylor's Mill, H. S. Liscomb, leader of the Anti-Abolition Society declared, "located as we are, in the immediate vicinity of the largest western den of these rogues, I deem it wholly unnecessary to say a word as to the propriety or importance of the adoption of some such plan."[22] The culture was spiraling downward into an ever-more repressive regime. Lipscomb continued:

> The abolitionists have done us some injury, but they have done much more harm to the slave population. That confidence which once existed between the master and his servants, and which was the source of great advantage to all parties, is in a great measure destroyed. The master is compelled to be more strict and severe in the treatment of his negroes. While the abolitionists are trying to decoy negroes to Canada, to live and die in misery and want, they are increasing the burdens and hardships of the millions who must ever remain slaves.[23]

This was the world in which Sam Clemens was growing up.

Iowa Emerges as a Threat

Missourians continued to be encouraged by a few signs from neighboring Illinois. In May 1846 an abolition convention in Peoria was broken up by the local citizenry. The mob was chivalrous enough. They allowed the women in attendance to leave before scattering the delegates with a shower of eggs.[24] Still, there was no question that the number of abolitionists was growing.

22. Ibid., March 11, 1847.
23. Ibid.
24. Ibid., May 28, 1846.

Settlement continued in Iowa, and by 1848 there were substantial abolitionist communities there. In June of that year eight Missouri slaves made
their way north into Iowa. They were pursued by a posse to the town
of West Point, Iowa, where they were cornered and captured. The slaves
were tried before an Iowa judge, who ordered the slaves returned to their
Missouri masters. However, before the posse could escort the slaves back
south of the Des Moines River, a crowd of Iowans stormed the courthouse
and set them free.

An abolitionist newspaper was started in Fort Madison, Iowa, and the
town of Salem, Iowa, developed a reputation as a hotbed of abolitionism
that rivaled even the Presbyterian Mission Institute in Quincy. Missourians were alarmed by these developments. The *Hannibal Journal* observed:
"Heretofore our only danger has been from Illinois, in which direction
we had some safeguard in the fact that the Mississippi River intervened.
Now a more dangerous outlet is opened in the North in the facilities of
getting to Salem in Iowa, which is said to be the headquarters of these
depredators and in which direction there is no similar barrier, the River
Desmoin [*sic*] almost at all times being easily crossed by an individual
without assistance from others."[25] A siege mentality was growing in Sam
Clemens's world. Curiously, though, there was still some tolerance for
questioning the institution of slavery: Although it would be short lived,
the Marion County emancipation movement would have one last gasp at
the tail end of the 1840s. Among those who would adhere to its principles
was John Marshall Clemens.

25. *HJ*, June 29, 1848.

Chapter 12

The Emancipation and Colonization Movement

I had heard my father say, some years before he died, that slavery was a great wrong, and that he would free the solitary negro he then owned if he could think it right to give away the property of the family when he was so straitened in means.

Mark Twain, "The Private History of a Campaign That Failed"

John Marshall Clemens, an unabashed slaveholder, disciplinarian, and enforcer of slave laws, probably thought that slavery was a great wrong. His reasoning, however, would have been substantially different from his abolitionist opponents'. Clemens's concern focused not upon the injustice done to the Negro, but on the adverse effects the institution of slavery and the presence of free blacks had upon whites. This type of "emancipationism" was wholly different from abolitionism and, in fact, grew in northeast Missouri in reaction to the abolition movement.

The goals of the abolitionists and the emancipationists were radically different. Abolitionists generally sought an immediate, uncompensated end to slavery. Emancipationists encouraged individuals to free their slaves and send them to Africa. Emancipationists advocated a gradual end to slavery in which slaveowners would be compensated for the loss of their property. Abolitionists saw slavery as sinful. Emancipationists sometimes shared this view, but they often opposed slavery for economic reasons or because they believed the institution had a negative impact on whites. While abolitionists wished to grant slaves full citizenship, emancipationists advocated separation of the races through colonization of Africa.

Despite these clear distinctions, many Missourians confused the two movements. Their differences have often escaped Twain scholars as well. Clemens's biographer Dixon Wecter wrote that the statement by Clemens about his father considering freeing his slave was an "act of filial white-washing" and that "No further proof of that conviction survives."[1] But the emancipation movement was certainly in vogue with Whigs in Marion County. There is ample reason to believe John Marshall Clemens actually was an emancipationist and colonizationist. John Marshall Clemens was active in local Whig politics. Jacob Sosey ran the *Palmyra Missouri Whig,* the county's party organ. Henry Clay of Kentucky, a leading Whig and U.S. presidential candidate, was president of the American Colonization Society.

The *Hannibal Journal,* under the leadership of J. S. Buchanan, was a Whig paper and frequently ran articles from the *Missouri Whig.* Although the emancipation and colonization movement was losing favor throughout most of the South by 1831, the movement took root late in Missouri. The Missouri State Colonization Society was organized in 1839 with Beverly Allen as president. John Marshall Clemens might well have been a member of the state organization, though he might have been hard-pressed to come up with a membership fee. More likely, he simply adhered to the ideas of the organization. He could not have belonged to the Marion County chapter. It was not organized until the summer of 1847, following lectures by the Reverend R. S. Finley, agent of the American Colonization Society.[2] Clemens died March 24 of that year.

Sosey, editor of the *Palmyra Missouri Whig,* had long advocated the movement. In 1842, he printed the story of a Virginia man who liberated his slaves on death and left them each $150 with a request that they go to Liberia. In 1843, he printed another story:

> COLONIZATION.—The *National Intelligencer* of Saturday last says:— We are happy to observe various indications in all sections of the Union favorable to the philanthropic objects of the American Colonization Society. Among others we perceive that the New York State Society has resolved to raise *ten thousand dollars* for the cause during the present year, and the Connecticut State Society has entered into a like resolution to raise *five thousand dollars.* These resolutions evince a zealous and laudable spirit.[3]

1. Wecter, *Sam Clemens of Hannibal,* 74.
2. Harrison Trexler, *Slavery in Missouri, 1804–1865,* 411; *PMW,* June 24, 1847.
3. *PMW,* June 17, 1843.

In June 1845, the *Missouri Whig* was aiding fund-raising by the Missouri and Illinois Colonization Societies. Sosey ran an article on the society's goals in sending literature to seven to eight hundred clergymen, challenging each to raise one dollar from his congregation for the society's work. In July he ran a letter from Galway Smith, an emancipated slave who had immigrated to Liberia. Smith described how happy he and his colleagues were in Africa.[4]

This colonization movement was closely tied to the churches of slave culture in northeast Missouri. On June 19, 1847, Reverend Finley, son of the movement's founder, delivered the first in a series of lectures on African Colonization at the Methodist Episcopal church in Palmyra. After the first speech, Sosey praised Finley effusively and set forth the tenets of the emancipation and colonization movement: "In an intellectual point of view, there is no theme more attracting than the history of Africa, either ancient or modern; and certainly none is better calculated to awaken the sympathies of noble and generous natures. The American Colonization Society proposes to effect for Africa a stupendous charity; and this in a manner perfectly consistent with the constitution and laws, and all the private rights of citizens."[5]

Finley shrewdly positioned his organization as an ally of slave culture. The group's position on the legality of slavery was clear: The Missouri State Colonization Society believed that slavery in the United States was protected by the Constitution and various laws and that no citizen could be deprived of his slave without his consent. The group advocated only voluntary emancipation! The group also believed that the presence of free Negroes in the country was hurtful to Negroes, slaves, and whites alike and that all free Negroes should be colonized in Africa. Using a term that would acquire ominous connotations a century later, Finley characterized Africa as the Negro's "fatherland." Finley clearly stated the difference between his organization and the abolitionists'. " 'Colonization' is therefore antagonistical to 'abolition,' in its whole nature, spirit and intention. Abolition aims to liberate the slave, elevating him to an equality of condition with the master here in our midst. Colonization opposes this policy as unwise, unsafe, and in fact impossible; and ruinous, if possible, to all parties."

The organization could exist in Missouri slave culture because it was premised on the same ugly racism that supported slavery. Justifying the expulsion of free Negroes to Africa, Finley said, "With a few exceptions,

4. Ibid., June 18, July 23, 1845.
5. Ibid., June 10, 1847. See appendix.

the great body of this class are idle, lazy and unprincipled. They infect the slaves with their habits where their intercourse exists, and the tendency of their associations is to do harm to themselves, the slave, and the master." It is interesting to note that Finley did not observe that the free black communities were aiding runaway slaves—testimony to the powerful specter of the skulking, white abolitionist agent.

The racist worldview of the society reflected the hierarchical scheme of slave culture in Marion County. According to Finley, "returning" Negroes were taking American civilization to Liberia while ridding the United States of a problem. Agriculture, mechanism, commerce, all the branches of industry were flourishing in Liberia. Though they might be idle, lazy, and unprincipled as compared to whites, they would be superior to native Africans as a result of their exposure to whites in the United States.

Jacob Sosey was impressed: "Mr. Finley is a man of talents, and an interesting speaker; besides, he is profoundly versed in all that concerns the movements and intentions of the society. We again earnestly request our citizens of the town and country, to come and hear him; and we assure them they will be more than delighted."

After the first lecture, the society's Marion County chapter was formed. The new organization elected twenty officers, a hefty number for a county organization. Attorney Samuel T. Glover, who had served as defense attorney in the Thomson, Work, and Burr trial in 1841, was elected president. Eight men, including seven Marion County ministers, were elected vice presidents. Eleven men were elected as managers. They drafted a constitution that required a payment of five dollars for life membership and then annual dues of one dollar to include a subscription to the *Liberia Advocate*, the society newspaper.[6]

In mid-nineteenth-century Missouri, speeches, like trials, were popular public entertainment. It was not uncommon for a well-received speech to be printed verbatim in a newspaper. The speaker would be asked for a copy of his oration. Samuel Glover's July 27, 1847, address as new president of the Marion County Colonization Society was reprinted in the *Missouri Whig*. Glover was in his element. He was an intellectual, given to musing and analyzing the world around him. He was respected for his intellect, if considered a bit odd by his fellows. Glover traced the history of the emancipation movement to the spirit of liberty prevalent in the American Revolution. Thomas Jefferson, Benjamin Franklin, and George Washington had foreseen slavery becoming a divisive issue. The peculiar institution had been a threat to the Union since the nation's founding.

6. Ibid., July 1, 1847.

Jefferson, Franklin, and Washington, Glover said, had advocated removing slavery from the country.

There was always a sense in the slaveholding community of the "evil
and disadvantage" of slavery. However, the position of the Colonization
Society was that the decision of whether to emancipate a slave clearly lay
with the slaveholder and, collectively, with owners in all the slave states.
They would accept no outside interference. Glover argued to the Marion County Colonization Society, "In other words, it leaves the subject of
slavery where it has always been, in the sacred keeping of the constitution
and the laws and the sovereign pleasure of the owner. With the *slave* it has
nothing to do; with the *free negro* everything."[7] Free Negroes were the real
threat to society, Glover argued. Slaves who were set free found themselves worse off after manumission, he said, and they corrupted those
Negroes who remained in slavery.

Referring to the freeing of slaves in the Northeast at the beginning of
the eighteenth century, he warned of their growing population. If free Negroes were not exiled from the United States, there would soon be millions
of them. Glover saw only two options for society: abolition or colonization. Abolitionism meant mixing of the races—a horrid, frightening idea
to the slaveholding people of Marion County. Colonization meant the removal of free Negroes from the country. Advocates of colonization saw
Negroes as a rapidly growing, infectious population to be quarantined
and sought to build up an asylum on the coast of Africa and induce free
Negroes to emigrate there.

Glover again cited the Founding Fathers as proof against the abolitionists' way. Jefferson, Franklin, and Washington had known that it was unthinkable that free Negroes would ever be able to live peaceably with
whites, Glover said,

> That by any system, legislative or otherwise, the free negro ever could
> be made to rise up by the side of the white man in this country, dividing
> with him on terms of equality, the privilege of suffrage, the administra-
> tion of the laws, and the social rites, was to the founders of this society
> a matter of utter impossibility. They had seen with their own eyes, that
> the emancipated negro was never permitted to enjoy the slightest social
> equality, without dragging down to his level the persons with whom he
> associated.[8]

After that, Glover's speeches were periodically printed in the *Missouri
Whig* in 1847 and 1848. In December, he noted that the Colonization

7. Ibid., August 12, 1847.
8. Ibid.

Society's policies and Missouri's laws had the same goals. Again he emphasized the danger of free Negroes to the community: "Our free negroes are in the general a miserable and vicious population, whose influence is injurious and dangerous to the relations both of the bond and free. With the slaves their associations are especially unhappy; while the general interests of peace and order in society suffer more severely from them than any other class. It is all-important the evil which they do should be counteracted for the good of the country."[9]

Glover then recounted the measures taken by the territorial and state governments of Missouri to counter these dangers: the 1804 territorial law, subsequently codifed into state law, prohibiting slaves from testifying in court in criminal cases, except against Negroes or mulattoes, or in civil cases, except those in which Negroes or mulattoes were the only parties to the lawsuit, demonstrated and proved "the pre-existing degradation of this entire race, bond and free; and declares in no instance is there sufficient moral worth to trust one of them in testifying against a white person."[10]

Missouri had also long realized the danger of free blacks mixing with slaves, Glover said. State laws prohibited free blacks from associating with slaves at any unlawful meeting and from harboring or entertaining any slave without the consent of his or her master, and denied free Negroes and mulattoes the right to keep guns, powder, shot or any type of weapon without a license from a justice of the peace. In the constitution of 1820 the state had allowed for laws to prevent free Negroes and mulattoes from coming to and settling in Missouri on any pretext whatever—a power exercised by the legislature.

> Nothing can declare more positively than this clause of our Constitution, that the class of persons are odious to the State, and in some way hurtful to its interests, since on no "pretext whatever" are they to be allowed to pass its borders. In conformity to this solemn injunction of the Constitution, a series of acts have been passed by our Legislature, laying down a most rigid course for excluding them from the State. By some of these laws the offender has been required to be whipped; by some fine and imprisonment; and by others, hired out for a definite period of time.[11]

Despite these efforts, Glover maintained, free blacks did associate with slaves. It was natural for them to do so, as they were prohibited by custom

9. *HJ*, January 4, 1849.
10. Ibid.
11. Ibid.

from fraternizing with whites. The only logical solution, Glover argued, was for the state to export free Negroes to Africa. The Colonization Society was the necessary, "perfect, safe, humane and just" remedy for the free Negro problem in the state of Missouri. Colonization, while aiding the black man, "will therefore do more good for the white race."[12]

Impeding Economic Growth

Another criticism of slavery was that it impeded economic growth. One branch of emancipationist philosophy in Missouri held that slavery was unprofitable and inefficient. "A Slave Owner" wrote to the *Hannibal Journal* in 1848, referring to slavery by the familiar nickname "peculiar institution": "While, for a middle, mild and salubrious climate; rich soil; valuable minerals; abundant productions of every article necessary for the wants of man; water power, and the best navigation to every part of the world—our State is equal to the best, of our rich western States, and surpassed by none—yet it is an acknowledged fact, that we are behind many States, junior in years to our own, in all valuable improvements:— roads, mills, and manufactures; and, not only in these, but in population, means and enterprise." The writer pointed out that immigrants were bypassing Missouri and electing instead to go to Iowa, Wisconsin, California, or Oregon. Why? Because of slavery. The writer left aside questions of morality and argued simply that slavery was ultimately unprofitable for Missouri. "This fact has become so well known that a large majority, it is believed, of the largest holders of such labor admit it, and are ready to lead the way to effect a change." He went on to propose gradual emancipation. The state constitution should be amended, he argued, so that after three or five years, slaves should be freed at "21 or 25 years of age." He continued with the admonition, "we should only ask that Abolition thieves and party demagogues stand off—and the matter be managed by slave owners."[13]

Although it was illegal to print abolitionist material in Missouri, emancipation was a perfectly acceptable topic. The movement was gaining strength, particularly in the northeast corner of Missouri. However, it was not to last. Slaves continued to escape, and the abolitionist movement grew, triggering a backlash. People were beginning to feel threatened by any discussion of ending slavery—the heretofore comfortable parlor

12. Ibid.
13. Ibid., September 14, 1848.

discussions held by respectable slaveholding intellectuals, ministers, and lawyers began to seem wrong. In the resulting controversy, slave culture began defending slavery as a humanitarian institution.

The colonization movement in Missouri focused more on removal of free blacks and less on emancipation, but some members continued to advocate ending the institution. Abolitionists and colonizationists attacked each other fiercely. The letter below from Philo Carpenter, a noted Chicago Underground Railroad operative, was reprinted in the *Missouri Whig* to demonstrate the fanaticism of abolitionists in opposing colonization.

ABOLITIONISTS AND COLONIZATION.

We publish below a letter addressed by an abolitionist of Chicago, Ill, to the Rev. Mr. Finley, of the *Liberia Advocate,* published at St. Louis. It will appear by it what are the sentiments of this fanatical sect towards the African Colonization Society. The bitter hostility of this one, who cannot bear even to read a Colonization paper sent to him gratis in the hope of removing his *unhappy errors*, is a fair specimen of the whole race. They know nothing of slavery or its effects—the condition of our slaves—the character of masters—their humanity and kind treatment towards their slaves, nor the folly of what he calls "emancipation;" and if they refuse to learn, we can only say God help them:

Chicago, July 28, 1847
Rev. Robt. S. Finley,
Dear Sir—I have received three or four numbers of your paper, the "Liberia Advocate," published in St. Louis. I do not wish to take your paper gratuitously, and I will give you a reason why I do not wish to become a subscriber: I am an abolitionist, in every sense of the word, and am, therefore, wholly opposed to any, and all measures, that tend to heal slightly this great moral and political disorder. Your efforts for colonization may be well intended; I do not impugn your motives. Your efforts and those of your society have undoubtedly been a blessing to individuals, but I verily believe that they have tended greatly to strengthen the bands of slavery.

You cannot rationally hope to remove slavery from this land with your plans. Do you, thus, hope? Is the day-star of liberty arising under the auspices of the Colonization scheme? Is there the most distant prospect of colonizing on the coast or interior of Africa, the millions that are now toiling in bondage in this *Christian land*? And are you not strengthening the bands of the oppressor, by apologising [*sic*] for one of the most fearful sins of earth, by preaching to and teaching the dealer in human flesh, that it would not be good policy to let the oppressed go free, unless they could be sent out of the country? You would not say to the polygamist, hold on to your score of wives until we colonize them? No, you would say, cease from your unlawful practices—stop sinning.

Who, let me ask, originated the scheme of Colonization? Was it not slaveholders? And is it not true of their peculiar institutions, sustained and fostered, mainly, by them, for the express object of sending out of the country what they call a great nuisance—the free people of color. And, forming an excuse for those who act upon the principle the Philistines did, when they sent the ark of the Lord out of the country, and not on the principle that God directs—*Isa* 58, 6 and 7; *Jer.* 34; 8, 17.

I have not time or ability to continue these reflections to my own satisfaction, much less to that of others. I will close with a word respecting the friends of Emancipation. I believe you are laboring under a wrong impression when you think they are sinners above all other men. Believing as we do that we should have no fellowship with slavery, but rather rebuke it, we believe in using all appropriate means, moral, social and political, for its abolition. And now, dear sir, let me say, that if this is of God, it will prosper, and I entreat you to be sparing of your censure of the friends of emancipation, lest you be found to fight against God. A better cause than the emancipation of the colored man from temporal bondage has been "everywhere spoken against."—And is it not good evidence that Colonization is not the remedy for slavery, and that emancipation is, when the intelligent and discerning slave-holder, professing to believe that it is an ordinance of heaven, favors the former, and is hostile to the latter? Is it not a fact that when any thing effectual is attempted against the kingdom of Satan, that his servants will be enraged, whilst they care nothing about the means that produce little or no effect?

Yours, most respectfully
PHILO CARPENTER[14]

Free blacks also opposed the emancipation and colonization movement. At a meeting held in Columbus, Ohio, on January 29, 1849, a large group declared their intention to resist deportation to Africa and to seek the rights of citizenship. The meeting resolved: "That we will never leave this country while one of our brethren groans in slavish fetters in the United States, but will remain on this soil and contend for our rights, and those of our enslaved race—upon the rostrum—in the pulpit—in the social circle, and upon the field, if necessary, until liberty to the captive shall be proclaimed thru'out the length and breadth of this great Republic, or we called from time to eternity."[15]

14. *PMW*, October 21, 1847.
15. Ibid., February 15, 1849.

Both the meeting and the declaration epitomized the very danger slave-holders feared from free blacks.

Opposition to Colonization within Missouri

The continual abolitionist encroachments on Missouri forced citizens to curtail all discussion of ending slavery—even through emancipation and colonization. Many Missourians did not distinguish between emancipation and abolition. They considered any discussion of ending slavery to be abolitionist and illegal. Mass meetings across the state called for an end to all discussion or agitation on the slavery question as if that would make the problem go away. In response to emancipationist activity in Lincoln County, a mass meeting was held in June of 1849 and the following resolution adopted:

> That the institution of slavery having been adopted and recognized by the people of this State, both in their constitution and laws no person holding opinions adverse to it, has the right either moral or legal, to come into this community and disturb the peace of society, by agitation the question of the abolition of slavery, either by publications through the press, by sermons from the pulpit, or in any other form.
>
> And therefore, that in the discharge of our duties in maintaining our lawful rights, should any attempt be made to do so, we will promptly put a stop to it in the most summary manner—believing, as we do, that the peace and safety of society would be better promoted without such agitators, than with their residence among us, and we recommend to any one opposed to the exercise of our constitutional rights and privileges, to remove to some State or place where his conscience may be at ease, and he no longer disturb the rights of others.[16]

Jacob Sosey, editor of the *Missouri Whig* and a slave owner, wrote a rebuttal to the resolution in which he clearly defined the type of emancipationists who populated Marion County at this late date.

> We are opposed to all force, all mob power, and repudiate it. Now there are in this county many good citizens who would be glad to see a system of gradual emancipation adopted by the people of Missouri, by which in the course of fifty or one hundred years, the State might be freed of its negro population. They think this would be a benefit to the State. These

16. Ibid., June 7, 1849.

citizens are peaceable, quiet, unoffending, intelligent men—not fanat-icks [sic], crazed by one idea, not abolitionists attempting to establish in "the most summary manner," equality, political and social between the two races, or any equality at all, at any time, or in any way.[17]

When Sosey advocated debate on the issue, he, of course, had in mind people like John Marshall Clemens. He was writing of men who could buy, sell, and whip their slaves and still sit in the library, parlor, or church hall and discuss the possibility of, maybe, someday, in the distant future, freeing the slaves. He meant debate among men who understood that emancipation must either be voluntary on the part of the slaveholder or that he must be compensated. He was writing of men who were agreed that the Negro must be sent to Africa because the races could never coexist outside the strict controls provided by slave culture. That was the type of freedom of speech the Whigs of Marion County advocated in the Marion County Colonization Society.

The rising tide of opposition to abolitionists threatened to swamp the fragile sandcastle of the colonizationists. And indeed, when Jacob Sosey wrote in June 1849, the Marion County Colonization Society was already doomed. The day was rapidly approaching when no criticism of "the pe-culiar institution" would be tolerated in any Hannibal or Marion County paper. The press would soon march in lockstep in support of slavery. The emancipation and colonization movement in Marion County would per-ish largely through the act of one man. He and a few determined slaves would destroy it in a rapid series of unconnected events that would spill white blood, destroy property, and raise the specter of slave insurrection in northeast Missouri.

17. Ibid.

Chapter 13

1849 and 1850

Terror in Marion County

I remember all about it.

> Samuel L. Clemens to Frank Bliss, August 26, 1901

Progress, the patron saint of nineteenth-century America, shone bright in Hannibal in the waning days of summer 1849. During the first week of September the telegraph came. Until then news had traveled no faster than a boat could paddle on the Mississippi or a person could ride on horseback. But with the arrival of the telegraph, Hannibal was no longer an isolated frontier town receiving only what news happened to filter down from Quincy or up from St. Louis. The former frontier village was suddenly in instant communication with the rest of the nation. This event was a technological coming of age. Commercial, political, and personal information now flowed freely into the little town. The telegraph office became so important that the intersection of Main and Hill Streets, where it stood, became known as "Telegraph Corner."[1]

Shortly after the telegraph arrived a tragedy occurred that shook Hannibal's slave culture more than any crisis since that surrounding Thompson, Work, and Burr. The entire county was stunned when a slave committed a brutal rape and murder. Like the incursion of the abolitionists, a single act forever changed life in Marion County. In addition to the danger from abolitionists in Illinois and Iowa, white people in northeast Missouri now felt acutely aware of the danger from slaves themselves. After years of comforting themselves with the notion of the contented slave, Hannibal and Marion County had to face the very real murderous rage of one

1. *HJ*, June 1, 1849; J. Hurley Hagood and Roberta Roland Hagood, *Hannibal, Too*, 184.

slave. The response of slave culture was to clamp down ever tighter on slaves—and to further restrict the debate about slavery among whites.

Ben

On October 30, 1849, two white farm children took a gentle mare and rode into the woods near their home in rural Marion County to gather black walnuts. Although walnut shells are hard to break, the nuts are delicious and often used in candy and cookies. Rich in oil and calories, black walnuts were an important part of the early settlers' diets. Susan Bright was twelve years old, and her brother, Thomas, had turned ten that day. Their father was Michael Bright, a farmer. He had no reason to worry about the children. There had not been danger in the woods for years. The bears had all been killed, and there was not a hostile Indian within a hundred miles. The children probably felt happy on that lovely autumn day, plodding through the woods stuffing walnuts into a burlap bag—but the outing was to end in tragedy.

Also out that day was a slave named Ben. He belonged to Thomas Glascock, another Marion County farmer. Glascock was hauling stone from a nearby quarry for a building then under construction. Glascock had hired another white man, William Callaghan, along with his slave Isaac, to help with the work. While Glascock and Callaghan laid stone, Isaac and Ben drove two wagons back and forth to the quarry loading and unloading stone. On one of his trips Ben saw Susan Bright and her brother. What happened next would send waves of horror throughout the county.

Ben attacked Thomas first. The boy was in the woods about seventy yards from his sister. Ben took a club and smashed the boy's head. The doctor who later testified at the trial said Thomas had been struck three times. The forehead, crown, and left temple all showed evidence of crushing blows. Next Ben turned on Susan. He forced the twelve-year-old girl to the ground. As she lay on her back, he pulled her skirt above her waist, tore off her undergarments, and raped her. He tried to club her, too, and when the stick broke, he took out a Barlow knife and slashed her throat. He made a large "v" at the base of her neck and hacked several small cuts near her jawbone. What he did next would haunt the dreams of Marion County slaveholders for years to come. He mutilated the girl. He cut off both of Susan Bright's ears and part of her nose. He pulled out clumps of her hair and drove his fist into her face. When he was done the girl was a hideous sight.

Ben threw his knife down near the body and cleaned up as best he could—although he could not hide the telltale bloodstains on his shirt. He could not change into other clothing. He had only one set of summer clothes. Leaving the knife was his undoing. The handle had been broken before the knife was given to Ben. Witnesses later easily linked it to him. Ben went on to the quarry with the wagon and returned to the Glascock project with a load of rock.

Glascock and Callaghan asked Ben what had taken so long. He had been gone an hour and a half. Previous trips to the quarry had been much quicker. To explain away both his tardiness and the bloodstains on his clothes Ben said he had suffered a nosebleed and was sick. Glascock and Callaghan had no trouble believing him. Ben was visibly nervous and shaking, which the men mistook for symptoms of illness. Glascock sent Ben home for the day and thought nothing more about it.

That evening, the Bright children's parents became alarmed when the youngsters did not return for supper. Their father, Michael, went looking for them. He thought at first they had gone too far to return before nightfall and were staying with some neighbors. When darkness came he saddled his horse and set out to check nearby farms. When he did not find them, Michael Bright became anxious. Concerned neighbors formed a search party to comb the woods where the children had been gathering walnuts. That night the forest was filled with men and boys on foot or horseback calling for Susan and Thomas. Their voices silenced the usual nighttime sounds of the autumn Missouri woods: the haunting call of barred owls, the wail of coyotes, and the song of the whippoorwills.

Near dawn, one of the searchers finally found the children's bodies. Joseph Sallee, a mill owner in the area, found the children's mare first. She was standing patiently, tethered to a sapling. Susan Bright's sidesaddle lay neatly on the ground where the girl had put it when she tied the horse. Sallee, aided by his young son and a neighbor, intensified their searching. About fifteen yards away from the mare they came upon some of Susan's clothing. Sallee's heart must have pumped faster at the sight.

Then Sallee found Susan. The sunlight was just poking through branches of the walnut grove. The twelve-year-old was lying on her back. She was naked from her ankles to some ten or twelve inches above her hips; the tops of her stockings were turned down over her shoes. Although overcome by the horror of the girl's brutally disfigured face, Sallee took the time to rearrange her clothing. Social norms took modesty seriously. Although her features were horribly disfigured and bloody, Sallee called the boys over to identify her. Confronted with the gruesome sight, one boy managed to choke out, "that's her." The other was speechless. Sickened, he turned and walked away.

Sallee found Ben's knife and the broken club very near Susan's body. A little while later he found Thomas's body—far enough away that the girl could not have heard the thudding blows of the club on Thomas's head. The children had gathered about a peck of walnuts.

The quarry was nearby, and it didn't take long for the spotlight of suspicion to turn on Ben. One of the searchers recognized his knife by the break in the handle. A few inquiries revealed that Ben had been driving the rock wagon near the spot. He had been allowed to travel unescorted from the worksite to the quarry. The facts fit like a glove. News of the crime spread quickly, but no lynch mob formed. In some areas of slave culture, slaves suspected of even minor sexual offenses were quickly and brutally killed without the formality of a trial. In Ben's case, however, Marion County allowed the judicial process to work, just as it had with Thompson, Work, and Burr.

Three men went to arrest the slave. Remarkable restraint was exhibited considering the nature of the crime and the heated emotions it had evoked. The men took the back way to Glascock's farm so they wouldn't alarm Ben. They found the slave about a quarter of a mile from the house and approached him quietly. He and his master were taken to the murder scene. Ben was told neither why he was being arrested nor where he was being taken. The three arresting officers watched the slave closely, and Ben's reaction at the scene betrayed him. When confronted with the horribly mutilated body, Ben did not exhibit any "awe or feeling as might be expected on such an occasion."[2]

Ben denied killing the children and told the sheriff that he had lost his knife the previous Monday. But he did not deny that the knife was his. There was also considerable circumstantial evidence. There was Ben's absence from the job, and the blood Glascock and Callaghan had seen was damning. Ben was examined by a doctor, who found evidence in his trousers that he had had intercourse. The newspapers that covered the trial used ellipses for this part of the doctor's testimony and noted parenthetically, "This portion of the details will not admit of publication."[3] However, the paper did report that there was a bloodstain inside the pants and that the clothing had recently been washed. Ben also had "marks" upon his body that the doctor testified were consistent with some struggle by the Bright girl.

2. *MC*, December 6, 1849.
3. Ibid., December 6, 1849.

The slave of William Callaghan was arrested as well, but he was quickly cleared. Ben was confined in the Palmyra jail, where Thompson, Work, and Burr had been incarcerated.

The Lewis County Stampede

Just as the citizens of Marion County were absorbing the horror of the murders of the Bright children, another stunning blow was delivered. While the actions of the lone slave Ben were horrendous, they could be discounted as the acts of a madman. But the next week, a group of slaves in Lewis County, immediately north of Marion County, acted in concert. Nothing frightened the people of slave culture more than the possibility of an organized revolt. Twenty-seven men, women, and children belonging to four white families armed themselves, stole wagons, and attempted to make their way north to Iowa and freedom.

Two white families were alerted to unusual activities on their farms. James Miller awoke to find slave men taking his two guns from their rack. About the same time, John McCutchen, a neighbor on a nearby farm, heard voices in his kitchen. Both McCutchen and Miller escaped from their houses and alerted the countryside. An armed posse was formed and the slave patrol alerted. They soon located the runaway slaves at the McCutchen farm, where they were preparing to march to Iowa.

The alert spread through Lewis County, and by dawn thirty armed white men had surrounded the farm. When the slaves became aware of the whites, they called a council. Heartbroken to find themselves trapped and outgunned, they decided to make a stand rather than surrender to their masters. They turned their wagons into barricades and prepared to fight it out. They were hopelessly ill equipped for a fight: They had only three guns, some clubs, and a few knives. They had intended not to revolt, but to flee. The farmers were well armed with shotguns and rifles. As the sun rose, more and more whites came with their guns to the McCutchen farm.

About midmorning, when they believed they sufficiently outnumbered the slaves, the white men ordered the slaves to lay down their weapons and surrender. The slaves refused. An older black slave named John told the whites to go away, then, in a sad climax to the episode, he charged one of the white men, armed only with a hayknife and a club. The man fired his rifle. The bullet struck the determined slave, but John still ran. Another man loosed a shot, and John fell dead at his pursuers' feet, still clutching the hayknife and club. At that, the spirit went out of the other slaves. Knowing the situation was hopeless, they surrendered themselves back into slavery.[4]

The Marion County press blamed the "uprising," as it termed the aborted escape, on abolitionists. Wild rumors spread of a phantom boat lurking on the Mississippi ready to take the escaping slaves to Illinois. As always, slave culture looked outside itself for the explanation to slave discontent. "These are some of the fruits of abolitionists," the *Hannibal Journal* declared.[5] The people of Marion County began to eye slaves who spoke with one another or nodded or even waved with great suspicion. They imagined simple gestures to be secret signals. And a sense of unease grew.

The Trial of Ben

As they had for the earlier trial of Thompson, Work, and Burr, the authorities placed extra guards around the jailhouse. Despite angry talk of Ben being taken from the jail and burned, he was allowed to stand trial. Samuel T. Glover was appointed as defense attorney, and as in the previous trial, the courthouse was packed with the angry and the curious. The crowd flowed over into the courthouse yard. The outcome was a foregone conclusion.

Ben was convicted on December 4, 1849, and sentenced to be hanged on January 11, 1850. It was the first legal execution in Marion County, and people flocked from miles around to witness the spectacle. Gallows were erected north of Palmyra near Joseph Sallee's mill in an area large enough to accommodate the crowd, estimated at five to ten thousand, who came to see Ben die.[6]

The *Missouri Courier* stated: "There was a deep feeling of resentment throughout our whole country, against the perpetrator of so horrid, merciless and unprovoked a murder; and it was this feeling, more than that of vicious curiosity, that drew together so large a crowd."[7] After noon on the day of his execution, Ben was dressed in his grave clothes and placed in a wagon to ride to the scaffold. He was escorted by a strong guard of armed men. No attempts were made to seize him.

4. *PMW*, November 8, 1849.
5. *HJ*, November 8, 1849.
6. *PMW*, January 17, 1850.
7. *MC*, January 17, 1850.

Ben had remained aloof throughout his trial and incarceration. He had not confessed or expressed remorse for the Bright murders. He spoke only when he stood on the gallows, the noose tight around his neck and his coffin on a wagon nearby. Reported the *Missouri Courier,* where Sam Clemens was apprenticed, "He requested one of the two ministers who were attending him to proclaim his guilt, and exhort the negroes present to be warned by his fatal example, and then desired the other to pray for him."[8] During the prayer, Ben gazed around upon the crowd with an "expression of absolute indifference." At about 2 p.m., Ben was swung off the scaffold and allowed to hang for thirty-five to forty minutes before being pronounced dead and cut down. Within weeks of his death, the *Missouri Courier* had printed a booklet called the "Confession of Ben," which it sold for twenty-five cents each, five for one dollar, or twenty for four dollars. No known copies survive.

Sam Clemens is apparently responsible for injecting some questionable information into the historical record about Ben. In his "Villagers of 1840–3," an outline for a story based on his childhood, he made an entry about "The hanged nigger." He wrote, "He confessed to forcing 3 young women in Va, and was brought away in a feather bed to save his life—which was a valuable property." However, there is no evidence in the court records or newspaper accounts that Ben killed anyone in Virginia or that he was too valuable to be hanged there.[9]

Had this evidence existed at the time it would have been offered by the state at trial and would have shown up in the newspaper coverage of the incident. This story seems to be an invention of Clemens's, which, like other of his inventions, occasionally shows up in history books. The idea that troublesome and criminal slaves were sold by speculators out of state was common in the slave culture.[10] Perhaps the notion of a slave being so valuable he could get away with murder would have been important to some plot that Clemens was forming in his mind.

The rape and murder of Susan Bright and the murder of her brother Thomas had an immediate and chilling impact in Marion County. The worst fear of people living in slave culture was realized in that walnut grove. Slaveholders had long told themselves that slavery was the natural relationship between African and European Americans. Slaves were routinely alone with white women and children in northeast Missouri. The

8. Ibid., January 17, 1850.

9. Dahlia Armon, ed., *Huck Finn and Tom Sawyer among the Indians and Other Unfinished Stories,* 101.

10. Michael Tadman, *Speculators and Slaves,* 85.

motive behind the vicious attack was inexplicable in the traditional think-ing of slave culture. Doubtless many Hannibal and rural Marion County residents slept fitfully, wary of the slave sleeping on a pallet in the kitchen. Slave culture reiterated in Sunday sermons and newspaper stories that slaves were content to serve so long as they were left alone by abolition-ists and outside forces. Missourians reassured each other that slaves only ran away when they were beguiled by outsiders and that slaves would return to masters of their own free will rather than face the uncertainties of life in Canada or the free states. Ben was inexplicable.

Reaction among the Masters

The reaction in Marion County was immediate. Simple explanations were sought for Ben's and the Lewis County slaves' actions. A letter to the *Missouri Whig* shows the sentiment sweeping the county. Although there was absolutely no indication that Ben had been drinking when his crime occurred or when the Lewis County slaves had plotted their escape, one writer used the occasions to urge stiff punishment for those who sold liquor to slaves. "The influence of strong drink in inflaming the passions, and exciting the lower appetites of men, is freely confessed by all. While its effects are different on men of different temperaments, this particular effect is manifest especially among slaves, whose animal propensities are ever powerful, and need but a drop of the liquid fire to make them break forth into an ungovernable flame." The writer was clearly motivated by the Bright murders. "We have lately been forced to look at it in a far more unpleasant light; and in that same unpleasant light we may be speedily called to look at it again. Is it not better to view it dispassionately when written with ink, than to view it with boiling indignation when portrayed in the blood of slaughtered innocence?"[11]

The temperance movement had always been popular in Marion County, and by focusing on controlling liquor, residents, particularly those with slaves in their houses and on their farms, could at least feel they were doing something to increase their safety. The campaign led to a petition drive late in the year to urge the state legislature to pass a law prohibiting bars and saloons in any Marion County city, town, or township unless the majority of the residents there voted to permit the establishment. The peti-tion attacked such places as "where our slaves are made drunkards, and

11. *PMW*, January 24, 1850.

thereby rendered thievish, disobedient and dangerous, and their value greatly impaired."[12]

The most noticeable change in slave culture was the immediate end to all civil discussions about gradually ending slavery in Missouri. Sam Clemens was an apprentice at Joseph Ament's *Missouri Courier* when debate abruptly ceased. The sudden shift can best be seen in events at a rival newspaper.

The unsettling events of late 1849 and early 1850 happened as Joseph S. Buchanan, a moderate emancipationist and colonizationist who edited the *Hannibal Journal*, published a series of essays on slavery by another local emancipationist and colonizationist who questioned the institution. The writer, who used the nom de plume "Toss," referred to slavery as the "curse." Buchanan had the misfortune to run the first of seven essays on the day after the grisly murders were committed. The "Toss Letters," which ran between November 1 and December 13, 1849, would be the last serious debate over slavery in Marion County until 1865.

Although the essays definitely reflected a minority view, before the Bright murders, most slaveholders would have found nothing incendiary, offensive, or extraordinary in them. In the first article, Toss said that slavery was sinful.[13]

He began, "Has God given to man the permission to enslave his fellow man?" He answered the question by pointing out the obvious fallacy of equating Africans with descendants of Canaan, as in the curse of Ham theory. He found no evidence to support the proposition. Toss then attacked the idea that slavery was permissible because God had permitted the Israelites to take slaves. He pointed out numerous actions Israelites were permitted that were taboo by modern standards in slave culture. In addition to keeping slaves, Israelites could take multiple wives, wage aggressive wars, and put to death the murderer of a relative without judge or jury. The Lord also at various times permitted men to possess concubines.[14] Toss argued that these were unacceptable in mid-nineteenth-century American society and concluded that conduct acceptable among ancient Israelites could not be automatically considered moral. He then turned his attention to the list of items over which God gave men dominion in Genesis 1:26. He noted that "other men" were conspicuously

12. Ibid., December 12, 1850.
13. *HJ*, November 1, 1849.
14. Ibid., November 8, 1849.

absent from the list. He argued that the omission indicated that God did not intend slavery to be part of the natural order of things.

Toss then asked, "Does domestic servitude deprive the enslaved of any of their natural rights?" He argued that American society was founded on principles embodied in the Declaration of Independence, the Fourth of July, and Plymouth Rock. These icons reflected rights that existed in nature and had been recognized by the Founding Fathers. Toss argued that democracy in America was premised on the right to work for yourself and enjoy the fruits of your labor. Americans had the natural right to make their own decisions and to acquire knowledge. Stopping short of advocating universal suffrage, Toss argued that everyone had a right to "voice in organizing and regulating society." He reasoned that the right to marriage—a basic right denied to slaves—was sanctioned by God and endorsed by Jesus Christ. "If these things be true,—as they undoubtedly are—how can the institution of slavery be founded in anything but sheerest injustice?"[15]

Toss's third question was "Is the relation of master and servant a natural one?" He tackled this by arguing that the employer-employee relationship was the natural relationship between laboring men. It afforded natural checks and balances that protected the worker. Under involuntary servitude the slave has no say whatsoever.[16]

The final question in the essay was "Do any of the precepts or teachings of the Bible condemn domestic slavery?" Again, he used scripture to dismiss the Ham myth and concluded that the spirit of the Bible is "clearly at war with the institution of domestic servitude." The Apostles did not endorse slavery—Roman slavery died out because of Christianity.[17]

'Tis in the side of the conscientious slaveholder a thorn which continually pricks and though he may plaster it over with all the patent salves that can be fabricated out of distorted passages of Scripture, yet there constantly issues from the point a stream of poison which will ever keep a running sore, so long as he refuses to apply the sole antidote of manumission.

If an American citizen were to be forcibly taken to a foreign land and sold as a bondman, he would say that to keep him and his descendants in a state of perpetual servitude, would be cruel, tyrannical and unrighteous.—But he with impunity can deprive of their just rights

15. Ibid., November 15, 1849.
16. Ibid., November 29, 1849.
17. *HJ*, November 22, 1849.

those who were torn from their birthright hearths and native shores by the merciless hand of the assassin and robber.[18]

Then, in the last of the seven installments that Buchanan ran, Toss attacked slavery as the possession of stolen property. It is an acknowledged principle of law, he wrote, that if a man gets a piece of property illegally, the property shall be restored to its rightful owner. Toss pointed out that the United States had banned the slave trade since 1807 and that importing slaves was illegal. Toss argued that the present slaves' ancestors had been illegally taken as well. "All are stolen," he argued, "let us return them their rights, educate them, send to school until age 10 and then to sabbath schools. Let them marry."

Toss then attacked the impact of slavery on blacks.

> The whole system of this diabolical institution tends to degrade the negro and takes from all encouragement to industry and well-doing. The law protects the person and property of the free citizen, and to it he can have recourse for justice in case of injuries inflicted by another. The negro may be allowed fat meat and corn bread enough to sustain life, and rags sufficient to cover a part of his nakedness; he may be kicked and cuffed about all his days and be brought almost to the verge of the grave by the lash, and what can he do but passively submit? True, a neighbor may "bring suit" and have the negro sold to the highest bidder, perhaps to another tyrant, while the master pockets the money—sweet consolation this to abused humanity! But is even this ever done?

To the failure of the law to protect the slave from abusive masters was also added the charge that the law provided disproportionate punishments for offenses committed by slaves and whites. "Furthermore, in case of misdemeanors against the laws of society by negroes, there is no intermediate punishment from the post to the gibbet. In some States the slave is hung for theft or house-burning, crimes for which the white man is only calaboosed for a term of years. Is this just, is this right?"[19]

Having made his case that slavery was wrong, Toss was never allowed to finish the series. In the climate following the murder of the Bright children and the flight of the Lewis County slaves, criticism of slavery could not be allowed. Under the bold headline **ABOLITIONISM!** the *Hannibal Journal* ran the following a few days before Christmas:

18. Ibid.
19. Ibid., December 13, 1849.

For several weeks past, we have been publishing a series of articles on the subject of slavery, written by "Toss," a correspondent, and was not aware that it was so strongly tinctured with *abolitionism*, until some of our worthy patrons made complaint. We were absent when the last two numbers were published, which we hope will be a sufficient apology for their appearance. We must admit that our correspondent has shamefully imposed on us—and can say to those who have formed a wrong impression in relation to our sentiments on the slavery question, that we look to a higher aim and a nobler design, than to take sides or tamper with Abolitionism, Free Soilism, Abby Kellyism, Disunionism, or any of the disgusting, contaminationisms of the day. Our readers can be assured, that hereafter we will be more particular about communications, and no such fanatical trash can again be admitted into the columns of the "Journal." Several of our honest and intelligent citizens have been unjustly censured with being the authors of these articles—but to clear this prejudice, we will state that Toss is a citizen of Ralls County.[20]

The next week Buchanan stated in the *Journal* that he would publish an explanatory letter from "Toss," but it never appeared. The paper sputtered on for a few more issues and died about the same time Ben swung from the scaffold. Buchanan sought to sell the paper. In January, he advertised the *Journal* office for sale "at a bargain" and offered his house and lots in town "dog cheap."[21] His son, Robert S. Buchanan, and a partner, Samuel R. Raymond, took over the paper in February 1850. They lowered the annual subscription rate from two dollars to one and renamed the paper the *Hannibal Weekly Dollar Journal.* Like all newspapers of the time, they had agents in various cities. Their agent in St. Louis was the newly relocated Samuel T. Glover.

The *Hannibal Weekly Dollar Journal* soon folded. The date the newspaper ceased publishing is unknown, but Raymond and Buchanan had legally dissolved their partnership by March of 1851. The last surviving copy is from June 1850. Sam Clemens's brother Orion said that the *Journal* "stunk" and died of "absurd flights" of "vicious imagination."[22] In response to a drive by out-of-town Whigs to start another Whig newspaper in Hannibal, Orion, who had begun his *Hannibal Western Union* in September 1850, acquired the *Journal*'s name and subscription list in September 1851, renamed the paper the *Western Union and Journal,* and honored unfulfilled subscriptions of the *Journal.* Orion never ran an antislavery editorial.

20. Ibid., December 20, 1849.
21. Ibid., January 17, 1850.
22. *Hannibal Western Union,* August 14, 1851.

After Ben's execution and the debacle of the Toss editorials, no anti-slavery piece would appear in any Marion County newspaper until the Civil War. Ben did more than kill two children out gathering walnuts. He extinguished debate. The line of socially permissible conduct and acceptable discussion shifted dramatically, and restrictions on slaves tightened. And as the shock waves from the Bright murders were still reverberating through Marion County, another slave rose in anger.

Hilliard Small

Less than a month after Ben was executed, another Marion County slave shook slave culture with a daring act of sabotage and escape. Hilliard Small was a light-colored, freckled slave belonging to Lewis Bryan in Palmyra. Unlike other runaways who simply fled, Small sought to inflict damage on slave culture as he left. On February 12, 1850, in the early hours of the morning, Small took a horse from the Bradley and Lee Stable in Palmyra with which to make his escape. After securing the horse, he set fire to the stable.

The blaze was fierce. The wooden stable was filled with hay and straw. The flames spread so quickly that it was impossible to save anything from the building. Nineteen horses died. Five buggies were destroyed. Saddles, harnesses, bridles, carriage-maker tools, oats, and corn went up in the blaze. A northeast wind carried sparks and burning bits of hay to other buildings, and the entire town was in danger. Several roofs were soon ablaze, and residents were kept busy putting out small fires throughout a harrowing night. It wasn't until the next morning that Hilliard Small was discovered missing.

A reward of $150 was offered for his return, but Small managed to elude the slave catchers who pursued him. A week later, Small was spotted in the northern part of the county in the North River bottoms, on horseback and carrying a gun. He appeared to be accompanied by a dog. Many people assumed Small was headed toward Iowa.

A month later the *Missouri Whig* reported that two slave catchers near Jacksonville, Illinois, fifty miles to the east of Hannibal, had attempted to capture a runaway they believed to be Small. The runaway had put up a ferocious fight, and although badly wounded, he had managed to get away on foot.[23] Faint from loss of blood, Small collapsed near a railroad. He had the good fortune to be found by a sympathetic white Illinois

23. *PMW*, March 21, 1850.

farmer. The man took Small to his house and dressed his wounds. The next morning he told Small to take the first horse he could catch from his farm and make his escape. Small did as he was told. When Small abandoned the horse, he made sure the kind man was notified so he could retrieve his property.

Hilliard Small was never captured, and the people of Marion County seethed. His act of arson was blamed on abolitionist influence. For years abolitionists had advised slaves running from their masters to take horses, boats, food, clothes, and anything else they considered essential to escape. Abolitionists advocated providing slaves with compasses and matches.[24] Now it appeared to those in Marion County that despite their best efforts, abolitionists' advice was reaching slaves, and that one had been swayed to commit a vicious act of sabotage.

The Depiction of Dangerous Slaves

After the Bright murders, the Lewis County stampede, and the Hilliard Small escape, Hannibal newspapers regularly ran articles about dangerous slaves. The image of the stupid, childlike slave who needed kind but firm guidance lived on, but another image was added—that of the slave as dangerous beast. In May 1850 Hannibal newspapers reported the shooting of a slave. When the white man who had leased the slave had attempted to whip him, the slave had resisted and drawn a knife. The master picked up a nearby shotgun and lodged a "full charge of fowling shot in the body of the negro." The man who shot the slave was arrested and examined by the circuit judge. There is no record of his having been prosecuted.[25]

The concern over the threat from slaves is also reflected in the nature of stories from out of the area that Hannibal editors chose to print. Orion Clemens selected for inclusion in the *Hannibal Journal* some that clearly warned slaveholders to beware of resisting slaves.

We learn that a most brutal murder occurred yesterday morning on the farm of Mr. Nathan Newby, about five miles from our city in this county. Mr. Newby had occasion to punish one of his negroes for some act of disobedience, but the negro resisted, when Mr. Newby called another

24. Ibid., February 19, 1842, April 2, 1842.
25. *MC*, May 2, 1850.

negro to his assistance, who coming up behind seized the refractory negro around the waist; the first one drew a knife from his coat pocket, and with a single back-handed blow, gave the one holding him a fatal stab in the groin, severing an artery and causing almost instant death. He then struck at Mr. Newby but inflicted only a slight wound on his arm. The murderer then fled, but was soon arrested. We don't know what course has been taken since his capture.[26]

Another article read,

FATAL AFFRAY.— On Sunday night last, two negro men, Adam an [sic] Edmund, belonging to Mr. Hayden and Mrs. McClane, of this city, got into a quarrel, which ended in the former stabbing the latter several times with a knife. One of the wounds in his side is very large, and the doctor's opinion is that it will prove fatal. Adam was arrested by the Marshall, but he has since succeeded in making his escape.[27]

The shift in the portrayal of blacks is dramatic yet complicated. It must have been very difficult indeed for young Sam, who was only fifteen at the time, to resolve the conflicting ideas around him regarding slavery. Had John Marshall Clemens lived to experience the events, how might his ideas of emancipation and colonization have been changed?

The Marion County Colonization Society was killed by events—just as surely as the Bright children were killed by a slave. There is never mention of another meeting of the county organization in any Marion County newspaper. It disappeared from the ideological map. Attorney Samuel Glover left Marion County for St. Louis shortly after Ben's trial. No one in Marion County would ever again publicly advocate freeing slaves and sending them to Africa. There was no moderate position in northeast Missouri slave culture after 1849: Only public support of slavery was acceptable. To question slavery in any fashion was to brand oneself as an outsider and an abolitionist. It was a dramatic change.

In other parts of Missouri the colonization movement shifted focus from emancipating slaves to ridding the state of free blacks. In October 1850, a petition was presented to the state legislature in Jefferson City asking the state to "take some decided and efficient step in aid of the noble enterprise of African Colonization" and requesting money for the

26. *HJ*, April 13, 1853 (reprinted from the *Weston Reporter*).
27. *HJ*, June 2, 1853 (reprinted from the *Cape Girardeau Eagle*).

removal of free Negroes to Liberia. The movement did not confine its activities to slave states. The racist vision of a whites-only America appealed to many in free states as well. In 1850, a petition was presented in Ohio praying for the "removal of all persons of negro, or part negro blood," from the state. The news was circulated widely in Missouri as proof that the free Negro was no more desired in the so-called free states than in the slave states.[28]

The Missouri Legislature eventually responded—in 1856, they allocated three thousand dollars a year for ten years to aid in the removal of free colored people from Missouri. However, it was a token effort. Even with the limited goal of removing free Negroes, the colonization movement in Missouri was far more talk than action. By 1851, only 21 Missouri blacks had been sent to Africa. Looking at the math shows how feeble this effort was. The 1850 census counted 2,618 free blacks and 87,422 slaves in Missouri. Nationwide, the Colonization Society had sent 6,116 emigrants to Africa by that year. There were 424,183 free blacks and 3,200,600 slaves in the United States in 1850. By 1856, the number of Negroes who had emigrated from Missouri with Colonization Society money had risen to an inconsequential 83.[29]

The society's public supporters were gone. The stakes had shifted. Now the lives of slaveholders were at risk. The property of slaveholders was at risk. There was no room for compromise. Hannibal's citizens believed that you were either for society as God intended it, with white people discharging their duty as caretakers of a cursed people, or you were a traitor and heretic. Fatherless Samuel Clemens was observing it all from the office of Joseph Ament's *Missouri Courier.* The murders had made a deep impression on him. He would be haunted by slavery all his life. Torn between loving the culture that raised him and despising the brutality that sustained that culture, he would use slavery as a major theme in many of his important works.

In 1901, fifty-one years after Ben the slave was hanged, Clemens wrote his publisher wanting data about the case to incorporate in a planned book on lynchings in America. "He raped a young girl and clubbed her and her young brother to death. It was in Marion County, Missouri, between Hannibal and Palmyra. I remember all about it."[30]

28. *PMW,* November 21, 1850, August 1, 1850.

29. *HWM,* February 28, 1856; *PMW,* April 17, 1851; Trexler, *Slavery in Missouri,* 411.

30. Wecter, *Sam Clemens of Hannibal,* 215.

Slaves in Hannibal had short childhoods. Young girls were frequently put to work tending white children. Tintype, mid-1850s, author's collection.

James Clemens, Jr., was a director of the Phoenix Insurance Company of Saint Louis. A cousin of the Hannibal Clemenses, he frequently loaned the family money. After John Marshall Clemens died, James's aid enabled Jane to live in the small house preserved today as the Mark Twain Boyhood Home. The company advertised regularly in the Hannibal press offering insurance on "slaves employed on land or on boats."

This woodcut of abolitionists James Burr, George Thompson, and Alanson Work (seated) sharing their Palmyra, Missouri, cell with two slaves appeared in *Prison Life and Reflections.* The white men are chained at the ankle to the wooden wall. The slaves are handcuffed to each other. Though ineffective at spiriting slaves away from Missouri, the three abolitionists proved to be excellent propagandists and martyrs. John Marshall Clemens served on the jury that sent them to prison for twelve years.

Insurance on Negroes.

The Boston Union Mutual Insurance Company takes risks on slaves. Applications may be made to the undersigned, agent.   JOSEPH P. AMENT.
Hannibal, Nov. 20, 1851.

Joseph P. Ament, who employed Samuel Clemens as an apprentice at the *Missouri Courier,* also sold life insurance on slaves.

Cash for Negroes!

I TAKE this method of informing the people that I am prepared at all times to pay the highest cash prices for *NEGROES,* and can at all times be found at the stable of Shoot & Davis.

FRANCIS DAVIS.

Hannibal, August 14, 1851.
aug14 7t.

Slave dealers thrived in Hannibal in the 1850s. They paid cash for slaves then usually resold them in the markets of the Deep South. As the decade progressed, a few dealers began to keep slaves on hand for sale. This advertisement ran in Orion Clemens's *Journal and Western Union* in the late summer and fall of 1851.

☞ There is quite a demand for hireling slaves for the approaching year, our friends in the country who have good cooks, washers and ironers to hire will find good places and high wages for them in Hannibal.

The leasing of slaves for use as domestics allowed slaveholders to derive income from their human property. Although the modern image of the domestic slave is of a middle-aged woman with a bandana or an older man in a tuxedo, children were frequently used.

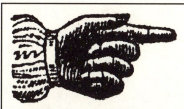 # HANDS

WANTED

The subscriber wishes to employ, immediately, FIFTY Negro Men, to work on the Rail-Road. For stout, able-bodied men, higher prices will be paid than can be obtained any where else in this section of country.

J. W. SHEPHERD.

Palmyra, June 29, 1848.

Missouri's first railroads were constructed with slave labor.

When the offices of Orion Clemens's *Hannibal Journal* were destroyed by a fire, he and Sam began publishing the newspaper from the little house in Hannibal that is now the Mark Twain Boyhood Home. This 1898 postcard identifies the house as the Mark Twain Printing Office. Courtesy of Dave Thomson.

TOM SAWYER
AND
HUCKLEBERRY FINN

THE MARK TWAIN CAVE IS LOCATED TWO AND ONE HALF MILES SOUTH FROM THIS SPOT. FROM A LITTLE LOG HOUSE ACROSS THE RIVER THREE MILES NORTH FROM THIS PLACE MARK TWAIN STARTED HUCKLEBERRY FINN ON HIS TRIP DOWN THE RIVER. TOM SAWYER'S ISLAND IS SOUTHEAST FROM HERE ONE MILE DOWN THE RIVER. HERE HUCKLEBERRY FINN AND NIGGAR JIM STOPPED FOR A FEW DAYS ON THEIR WAY DOWN THE MISSISSIPPI.

1934

This sign, a Missouri state historical marker erected in 1934, stood near Nipper Park in Hannibal for years. After protests, the word *Niggar* was ground off. The sign was quietly removed and stored in the late 1980s. It has since disappeared. Courtesy of the Hannibal Free Public Library.

John Rogers worked as an engineer on the Hannibal and St. Joseph Railroad beginning in 1853. A native of Massachusetts, he wrote frequently to his family describing slavery as he observed it in Hannibal. In 1859, he left Hannibal to begin a career as an artist. This was his first commercial sculpture—"Slave Auction." Courtesy of the New-York Historical Society.

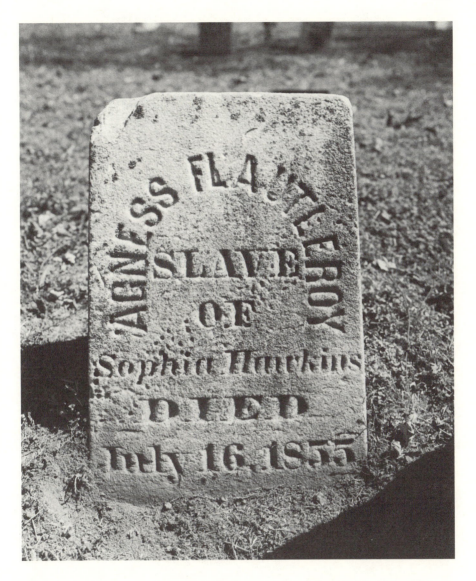

Marker for the grave of Agness Flautleroy, slave of Sophia Hawkins, old
Baptist Cemetery, Hannibal, Missouri. This is the only known marked grave
of a slave in Marion County from the time of slavery. Sophia Hawkins was
the mother of Laura, childhood friend of Sam Clemens. Laura Hawkins is
identified in Hannibal as a model for the character Becky Thatcher. In the
1850 census, Laura was named as the owner of a six-year-old slave girl.
Next to Flautleroy's marker is a crude concrete marker with the name
Petunia scratched in it. It may mark the grave of Flautleroy's daughter,
Laura Hawkins's slave. Courtesy of Dave Thomson.

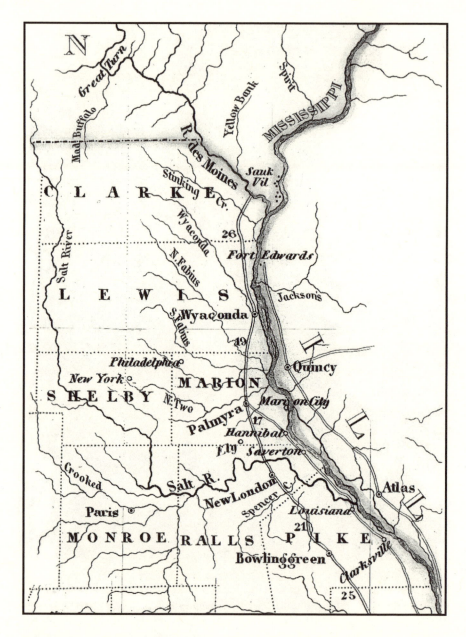

This 1845 map, from *Meyer's Hand-Atlas*, published in Hildburghausen, shows the close proximity of Quincy, Illinois, to Marion County. The Sauk villages shown near the top of the map, between the Des Moines and Mississippi Rivers, are in the area disputed in the Honey Tree War of 1839. Courtesy of Dave Thomson.

White slaves were a fact of life in Hannibal. Under Missouri law,
a person was a slave if his or her mother was a slave.
Photographs of white slaves such as Fannie Virginia Casseopia
Lawrence were utilized by the abolitionist movement to whip up
antislavery sentiment. Author's collection.

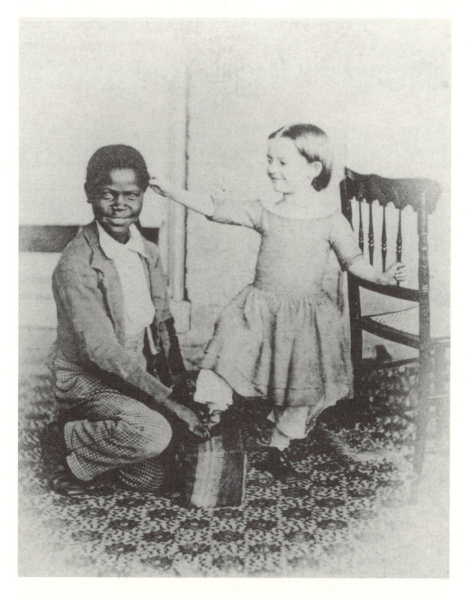

Young slaves were preferred by many as domestic servants. Here a slave boy puts a shoe on his young master, who reaches out to touch the slave's hair, a gesture believed to impart good luck. Carte de visite photograph, circa 1860, author's collection.

Chapter 14

Sam Clemens and the Press in Slave Culture

Surreptitiously and uninvited I helped to edit the paper when no one was watching; therefore I was a journalist.

Samuel Clemens to W. H. Powell, December 1907

Two years before the murders of the Bright children, another indelible incident had occurred in the life of Sam Clemens. March 24, 1847, was a dark but liberating day for young Sam. John Marshall Clemens, justice of the peace and failed businessman, died in poverty in an apartment above Grant's Drug Store in Hannibal, Missouri. He was forty-nine years old. His son Sam was only eleven.

John Marshall's death came when he was a candidate for circuit clerk of Marion County. Had he been elected to that position, he would have been responsible for maintaining important deed records and the circuit court's records in the county. The position would have paid considerably more than did that of justice of the peace. But real success was always just beyond the reach of John Marshall Clemens, and death deprived him of this final opportunity to obtain financial security.

His obituary, a tribute reserved for respected members of the community, praised his public service.

Judge Clemens has been for many years a citizen of North Eastern Missouri and of Hannibal. He had been honored by several public stations which he filled with credit to himself and advantage to the community. He was noted for his good sense and a clear discriminating mind. These added to a high sense of justice and moral rectitude, made him a man of uncommon influence and usefulness. His public spirit was exercised zealously and with effect upon every proper occasion.[1]

Young Sam probably read the obituary. In all likelihood the family saved a copy, and perhaps the words of praise had some formative influence upon the intelligent child. John Marshall Clemens was buried in the Baptist Cemetery on the west side of Holliday's Hill. In those days before segregation, slaves and masters were buried in the cemetery.[2]

The death of his father was quite a blow to Sam. The impact can only have been amplified by Sam's view through a keyhole of Hugh Meredith performing a partial postmortem upon Clemens's body.[3] The death of John Marshall Clemens certainly brought change to the Clemens household. Already plagued by money problems, the family was pushed to the brink of disaster. But as tragic as the death of John Marshall Clemens was to his impoverished family, the outcome would be historic for American literature. But for this tragic event, Sam might never have been exposed to the world of newspaper work and might not have begun a career that would propel him to become Mark Twain.

Jane Clemens moved the little family from the apartment above the drugstore first to a house that they could not afford, and then back to the small house on Hill Street that has now been preserved by Hannibal as the Mark Twain Boyhood Home. The land and house were owned by a relative, James Clemens of St. Louis, who helped the struggling family.[4] It was the house John Marshall Clemens had built for the family but then been forced by debt to abandon. Sam's older brother, Orion, helped as well with contributions from his earnings as a printer in St. Louis. Pamela Clemens, his sister, gave piano lessons in the parlor of the little house.

1. *Hannibal Gazette* (hereinafter *HG*), March 25, 1847.
2. The bodies of John Marshall and Benjamin Clemens were later removed to Mt. Olivet Cemetery. After emancipation, the Baptist church in Hannibal kicked its black members out of the church. Most white people quit burying in the old Baptist Cemetery, though blacks continued burying there until the 1950s, and the old cemetery fell into disrepair. Mt. Olivet became the fashionable cemetery for white Hannibal Protestants.
3. Wecter, *Sam Clemens of Hannibal*, 116. However, in private correspondence, noted Mark Twain scholar Lou Budd expressed doubt that a postmortem actually occurred. He pointed out that not much would be visible through a keyhole and that a genuine postmortem would have produced buckets of blood and could not have been performed on a table or bed in the house.
4. Wecter, *Sam Clemens of Hannibal*, 121.

A week after the death of John Marshall Clemens, Henry La Cossitt, the *Gazette* editor, published a small article about the virtue of working at a newspaper. Though the Clemens family was probably too consumed with mourning and their worsened financial condition to notice, the tiny article presaged the great opportunity that awaited Sam. La Cossitt wrote, "There is something in the very atmosphere of a printing shop, calculated to awake the mind and inspire a thirst for Knowledge."[5]

Out of necessity, Sam began to earn his keep by doing odd jobs for local merchants. In later life he recalled working in a grocery store, blacksmith shop, bookshop, and drugstore, but those were only fleeting part-time jobs. Perhaps as early as September 1847 he began working for the *Hannibal Gazette*, delivering the newspaper to local subscribers.[6]

But part-time jobs were not enough. Jane Clemens was overwhelmed, and it was necessary to apprentice Sam out to learn a trade. It is possible that Sam actually began his apprenticeship under La Cossitt, but if so, Clemens offered no memory of it. In September 1847, La Cossitt advertised that he was seeking an apprentice. La Cossitt sought a fourteen- or fifteen-year-old from the country. Sam was only eleven and lived in town. If Sam did apprentice with the *Gazette* it was only for a few months. His real apprenticeship began in the spring of 1848.

On May 3, 1848, a twenty-four-year old journalist by the name of Joseph Ament purchased the *Hannibal Gazette* and moved his own *Missouri Courier* to Hannibal. He set up shop in the old *Gazette* offices on the top floor of a two-story brick building on Main Street above Brittingham's Drugstore. He took on twelve-year-old Sam Clemens as his apprentice. Throughout his two-year apprenticeship with Ament, Sam would work with T. P. McMurry, journeyman printer, as well as fellow apprentices William T. League, Richard Rutter, and Wales McCormick. The social status of an apprentice was hardly higher than that of a slave. If Sam had run away from Ament, the publisher could have resorted to the law to compel his return. Young Sam went to live at the printing office. He received no wages. His compensation consisted of food, a place to sleep, and two suits of clothes a year—and the opportunity to learn the printing trade.

This early work meant a hardscrabble existence for Sam Clemens. Food was meager, and Sam and Wales McCormick took to stealing onions and potatoes from the cellar and cooking them surreptitiously at night in the stove at the print office. The clothes he received were just as bad. Joseph Ament gave the pint-sized Clemens his oversized hand-me-downs to

5. *HG*, April 1, 1847.
6. Wecter, *Sam Clemens of Hannibal*, 122–23.

wear. Young Sam's bed was a pallet on the floor of the printing office, and he had to take his meals in the Aments' kitchen with the slave cook and her mulatto daughter—a certain loss of dignity for John Marshall Clemens's son.[7] The daughter was the unfortunate girl that Sam's fellow apprentice pursued sexually.

In many ways Sam Clemens's duties at the paper were similar to those of domestic slaves in Hannibal. He built the fire in the morning in the little shop. He brought water in from the community pump down the street. He swept the office. He picked up yesterday's type from the floor and sorted it into pieces to be reused and those to be melted down and recast. He watered down the paper stock on Saturday and turned it on Sundays. When the weekly paper was printed, he folded and delivered copies around town—and he learned to set type.[8]

The last was a crucial development in Clemens's life. Print was set by hand in midcentury. Sam Clemens had to learn to distinguish the 154 different pieces of type at use in the paper and to sort them by sight and feel into the type case. The type was kept in slanted trays on boxes at hand height. The upper case was divided into ninety-eight compartments, which held capital letters, numerals, and various accent and punctuation marks. The lower case held the small letters in fifty-six compartments. It took skill to tell the difference among d, q, and p or between u and n, particularly in the dull light of the print shop. Sam had to learn not only to pick the letters from the cases quickly, but also to drop them back in nimbly, quickly, and accurately.

Sam would be given a written article to set, often one of the racist articles or a story written in dialect. With the article before him on a table, he held a small metal tray called a composing stick in his left hand and selected the proper letters one at a time with his right. The job required intelligence, good eyesight, and a good memory. The longer the phrase Sam could hold in his head, the more pieces of type he could set between glances at the article. He had to recall the standard spelling of words and be able to remember the butchered spelling and syntax of dialect.

There was more to the job than just selecting the proper letters. Sam had to be certain that stories contained the proper spaces between words and sentences. Lines and columns had to be straight. The result had to be esthetically pleasing as well as correctly spelled. Printers were not tolerant of either too much or too little white space on the page. One cost the printer money; the other sacrificed legibility.

7. Ibid., 202–4.
8. Mark Twain, "The Old-Fashioned Printer."

When Sam had filled a stick, he had to place the lines of type into the wooden galley tray. When he had set enough type to complete a page, he tied off the block of type with a piece of string and transferred it to the "imposing stone," a flat marble table designed to hold the type perfectly flat. He then made a proof from the page, and Joseph Ament read it, hence the term *proofreading*. Any errors were corrected, and finally an iron frame was placed around the page, and the columns locked up with wooden blocks called "furniture" and wedges called "quoins."

While performing these tasks, Sam Clemens stood on a box to work on equipment designed for adults. In the masculine environment of the press he smoked a cigar and went about his task with great diligence. He might have been, to modern eyes, a slightly comical sight at twelve years old, a stub of cigar protruding from the corner of his mouth, bent over the type cases, setting type by the hour. Clemens aspired to set ten thousand letters a day by the time he had finished his apprenticeship, although some journeymen could set up to fifteen thousand.[9]

Pages were produced one at a time in the 1840s and 1850s in much the same fashion as Gutenberg had printed the first Bible in the 1450s. Printing had not changed much in 400 years. A strong man pulled a lever that impressed the type onto a sheet of paper called newsprint. After it dried, it was folded and distributed. After the paper was printed, the type was taken up line by line. It was cleaned and distributed into the cases to be reused. Any broken pieces were swept up and put into the "hell hole" to be melted. It was a demanding job, but one that inspired many young men to follow a life of letters. Benjamin Franklin and William Lloyd Garrison had been apprenticed to printers and had mastered the trade to become journeymen. Furthermore, like Sam Clemens, their love of language had carried over to a lifetime of writing.

Sam took pride in his craft and later wrote home from New York City, where he was working as a free-lance compositor:

> They are very particular about spacing, justification, proofs, etc., and even if I do not make much money, I will learn a great deal. . . . Why you must put exactly the same space between every two words, and *every line must be spaced alike*. They think it is dreadful to space one line with three em spaces, and the next one with five ems. However, I expected this, and worked accordingly from the beginning; and out of all the proofs I saw, without boasting, I can say mine was by far the cleanest. In St. Louis, Mr. Baird said my proofs were the cleanest that were

9. Edgar M. Branch et al., eds., *Mark Twain's Letters, 1853–1866*, 20.

ever set in his office. The foreman of the Anzeiger told me the same—
foreman of the Watchman the same; and with all this evidence, I believe
I *do* set a clean proof.[10]

Sam Clemens stayed with Ament until January 1851, when he went to
work for his brother Orion, who had returned to Hannibal from his stint as
a printer in St. Louis. Orion first published the *Western Union* newspaper
in Hannibal on September 5, 1850.[11] A few months later Sam came to work
for him, continuing to set type and print under the editorial guidance of
his older brother. Also working as apprentices under Orion were Sam's
younger brother, Henry, and a young man named Jim Wolfe. The change
in employment officially marked the beginning of Sam's writing career.
The first known article authored by Sam appeared in the *Western Union* on
January 16, 1851, and featured Jim Wolfe as the object of Sam's humorous
ridicule. After a fire in the adjoining grocery store, owned by A. C. Parker,
Sam wrote the short essay "A Gallant Fireman," which featured Wolfe
speaking in dialect and using malapropisms, "If that thar fire hadn't bin
put out, thar'd a' bin the greatest confirmation of the age!"[12]

The following year Orion Clemens bought the defunct *Hannibal Weekly
Dollar Journal*, changed the name to the *Hannibal Journal and Union*, and
subsequently shortened it to *Hannibal Journal*. A fire destroyed the *Hannibal Journal* office in January 1852. The newspaper temporarily reopened in
a new office over Stover and Horr's Clothing Store on Main Street. In May
1852, the *Journal* was located above T. R. Selmes's on Main Street nearly
opposite the post office. Just two months later on July 1, 1852, Orion began
publishing the newspaper in the living room of his mother's little house
on Hill Street. It would have been a busy little building with the press in
the small parlor. In addition to housing the newspaper, Jane Clemens took
in boarders. Apprentice Jim Wolfe moved in with the family and shared
a bedroom with Sam. A cow wandered into the house one night while
the press was there. She ate two composition rollers and knocked over a
case of type.[13] Whether Jane Clemens leased a slave to help with the extra
work is unclear, but the 1850 census indicates that she did not own one at
the time.

10. Branch, *Mark Twain's Letters, 1853–1866*, 9.

11. The first surviving copy of the *Western Union* is volume 1, number 6,
dated October 10, 1850.

12. Edgar M. Branch and Robert H. Hirst, eds., *Early Tales and Sketches*, 62.

13. *HJ*, January 29, 1852, May 27, 1852, July 1, 1852; Wecter, *Sam Clemens of
Hannibal*, 243–44.

Hannibal Newspapers and Their Role in Slave Culture

Newspapers had a unique role in slave culture. As the only medium, they had a monopoly on news. There was no television, radio, or Internet. The world was a slower, much quieter, less cluttered place. When Sam Clemens began his apprenticeship, Hannibal had no telegraph. News arrived at a leisurely pace. Editors swapped copies of their newspapers via the steamboats that plied the Mississippi, Missouri, and Ohio Rivers. By law, the postal service would deliver a copy of one newspaper to another for free. If an editor wished another editor to reprint a particular story, he would often put in a remark with the story. Otherwise, editors frequently and freely borrowed from one another. In addition, editors often communicated by private letter with individuals—thus the term *correspondents*—in other towns. Individuals in the community would also bring in interesting tidbits from letters they received from friends and family in far-off places—which, in practice, could mean anyone more than a day's ride away. But the editor had sole power over what was printed in his newspaper. Newspapers had distinct points of view. A paper was usually associated with a political party, often indicated in the paper's name. Both Palmyra and Quincy had a *Whig*. Other papers were *Democrat*s or *Republican*s.

Abolitionist newspapers were considered a serious threat in Missouri. The success of newspapers like the *Liberator,* published by William Lloyd Garrison, was viewed with great trepidation in Missouri. Elijah Lovejoy had paid with his life for his determination to publish first in St. Louis and then in Alton, Illinois. Sam Clemens came to the world of newspapers as a seismic shift was occurring in Marion County and among its newspapers. As outside threats to their slave property increased, the people of northeast Missouri grew intolerant of debate over slavery. Clemens was at Ament's *Missouri Courier* during that shift in 1849 and 1850.

After that time, the newspapers of Sam Clemens's world were curiously consistent on the issue of slavery. They had always been crucial to the maintenance of the institution. The newspaper was itself a market for slaves, with advertisements and legal notices announcing slave auctions and individual slaves for sale. The papers also kept people informed on the value of their human stock by reporting prices and trends across the country. Beyond their importance to the economics of slavery, newspapers fulfilled another function—similar to that of churches in slave culture. They churned out a constant stream of racist propaganda that perpetuated and supported slavery. The psychic burden of keeping people in bondage must have been very high indeed, because there seems to have

been no end to the need to portray blacks in a bewildering set of contra-
dictory stereotypes, all of which justified keeping slaves in bondage.

The newspapers were chock-full of stories about slaves—most of them
fiction—many were racist jokes. Negroes were portrayed as bumbling id-
iots who required wise guidance, but also, on occasion, as loyal and trustworthy. They were constant companions, but also dangerous, untamed
beasts who could turn on their masters in a heartbeat. They were almost
always sexually dangerous—people who could not control their appetites
and needed white slave owners to restrain them.

Modern readers find these stories offensive. Although some may elicit a
laugh, the humor is sad because it is had at the very real cost of another's
liberty. (In November 1905, Sam explained in "A Humorist's Confession,"
an interview for the *New York Times:* "The hard and sordid things of life
are too hard and too sordid and too cruel for us to know and touch them
year after year without some mitigating influence, some kindly veil to
draw over them, from time to time, to blur the craggy outlines, and make
the thorns less sharp and the cruelties less malignant.") But if the modern, literate world is to understand the man who would create Jim in *Adventures of Huckleberry Finn,* it must first know fully and realistically the
world that created Sam Clemens. Like images in the crude propaganda of
totalitarian regimes of the twentieth century, the picture of the Negro is
roughly drawn. But the material of racial hatred did not issue from a central authority. It is difficult to say whether the material molded attitudes
in northeast Missouri slave culture or reflected them. The probability is
that it did both.

It is difficult to determine what moral or social lessons Sam Clemens
learned from the hate-laden newspaper articles he read as he grew up.
But without question, he learned one very important technique as he set
the type for racist stories in the *Hannibal Courier* and later for his brother
Orion's newspapers, the *Western Union* and the *Hannibal Journal.* Sam
learned the technique of writing in dialect—a skill that would be a strong
positive factor in his later contributions to American literature. To understand Sam Clemens, it is necessary to examine what he probably read and
what he most certainly set in type.

In a culture where it was illegal to teach slaves to read, society took
great delight in the butchered syntax and limited vocabularies of slaves.
Malapropisms were used extensively in these comic articles. The ignorance projected or imposed upon the slave was a great joke and at the
same time justified keeping the slave under the protection of the wiser and
better-educated master. Editors butchered spellings and used ellipses to

catch the pronunciations of slaves. Clemens would later use these techniques for Jim's speech in *Adventures of Huckleberry Finn* as well as for that of his other black characters. The practice was well established before Clemens began working at the newspaper. The same techniques were used in the popular minstrel shows that Clemens loved throughout his life, but minstrel shows were rare in Hannibal. Racist stories showed up regularly in the newspapers. The following are selections from newspapers published in Marion County while Clemens was a boy. In these stories, which Sam Clemens may have read, slaves are portrayed as foolish children needing the supervision of white masters:

"Cato, what do you suppose is the reason that the sun goes to the south in winter?"

"Well, I don't know, massa, unless he no stand the 'clemency ob de norf, and so am obliged to go to de souf, where he 'sperience a warmer longemtude."

A black fellow who was disposed to walk uprightly, took his child to be christened, and when the minister asked what name should be given to it, he seriously said, "Scripture name by all means—call um Belzebub."

"I say, you darkey," said a tall Kentuckian to a negro who was taking an awful big horn at the bar of one of our Mississippi Steamboats—"I say, you darkey, do you belong to the temperance society?" "No, massa, I b'long to Misses Hall," was the reply.

"Sambo, are you afraid of work?"

"Bress you, massa, I no 'fraid ob work. I'll lie down and go asleep by him side."

"Wonder what's de reason dis saw mill won't go?" asked a country negro who hadn't seen much of the world, addressing his most 'high larn' village friend. "Det circumstanc argufies easy enough, nigga,'" replied Congo, "de reason is caus dare am not sufficient number of water."[14]

The following is one of several ventriloquist stories told at the expense of blacks. Interestingly, it is set in the free state of Pennsylvania.

14. *PMW*, February 4, 1843, January 22, May 7, 1845, August 6, October 15, 1846.

Watermelon Extraordinary.—"How much do you ask for that melon?" said a cute, dapper looking chap, to a sturdy darky, who was mounted on a cart before one of the principal hotels in Philadelphia, a day or two since.

"For dis big un? Why, massa, I reckon he's wuf tree levies, I does."

"Is it ripe?"

"O yes, massa, he's ripe, shu. I dun plugs um dough, if you say so."

With that, the darky out with his jack-knife, and was making the first incision in the melon when it gave a long deep, piercing, "O!"

"What do you stop for?" said the gentleman.

"I tot him holler, I did."

"Come, cut away, and see if it is ripe."

He gave another poke with his knife, and this time the melon shrieked out, "oh, murder! You kill me!"

Before the last word was out, the melon went tumbling on the ground on one side of the cart, and the darkey on the other, bellowing, "O de Lord! O de Lord of Hebens!"

Picking himself up, he half scrambled, half ran a few paces from the cart, and turning to behold the fragments of the melon, continued, "Whew! Dis nigger nebber stan dat, it holler murder!" while Wyman, the celebrated ventriloquist, walked quietly away, amid the shouts and roars of the bystanders.[15]

This story encourages readers to laugh at what the characters see as important:

WHAT YOU TAKE.—The following though not new, should not be lost; particularly at this time, when everything tending to the "development" of people of color, is yet much in vogue.

Two interesting negro lads were standing in the streets of Charleston, gazing into the market, which everybody knows is proverbial for its supply of all manner of luxuries.

"Jim," said one, " 'spose you hab you choice now of all de good tings in that market—what you take, nigger?"

"What I take! Why I'd take all de possum fat and all de hominy—ob course I would—now what you take? Hey!"

"Hum! How you 'spect me to choos when you's took every tingas nice? Com along nigger."[16]

In other dialect stories the childish observations of ignorant slaves are

15. *HJ*, October 28, 1847.
16. Ibid., April 12, 1849.

used as devices to mock the pretensions of white people or deride the views of political parties.

[on Polk's position regarding annexing Mexican territory]

"Hallo! Jim! You great six-footer you. What are you beating that poor old nigger for?"

"Why, Lor bless your soul massa, I is tryin' to conquer a peace! Ye see dis old nigger keep up a fuss all de time 'bout me takin' his tater patch. I ax de ole fool if he didn't know 'twas my destiny, an' if he ever hear 'bout de Angler Saxums, as how dey was bound to take ebery ting dey could. But he jes go on sayin' it was his'n. Den I jis takes half his patch from him, and told him help umself if he could. Den he git mad an' told me I'd better not. Den I gives um jesse a few times, an' he kicks back, an' now I is tarmined to conquer a peace, as Massa Polk says, an' take de hull patch from him for his sass."

[on gambling]

Very Uncertain.—"Boy, who do you belong to?" asked a gentleman the other day as he stepped on board of a steamboat, of a darkey list-lessly leaning, on the guards. "I did belong to Massa Williams, sir, when I came aboard, but he's been in the cabin playin poker' wid the captain 'bove an hour; I don't know who I do belong to now."

[on politicians]

A negro, undergoing an examination at Northampton, when asked if his master was a christian, replied, "No, sir-ee, he's a member of Congress!"

[on gentlemen]

The following is the negro's definition of a gentleman: Massa make de black man workee—make de hoss workee—make de ox workee—make ebery ting workee, only de hog; he, de hog, no workee: he eat, he drink, he walk about, he go to sleep when he please, he live like a gentleman.[17]

Dialect Stories Set by Sam Clemens

The next two stories were printed at Ament's *Missouri Courier* while Sam worked as an apprentice typesetter. He undoubtedly read and quite

17. Ibid., June 10, 1847 (reprinted from the *Hamilton (Ill.) Intelligencer*), September 30, 1847 (reprinted from the *Hamilton (Ill.) Intelligencer*); *PMW*, June 8, 1848; *TWM*, March 19, 1853; *PMW*, August 23, 1849.

possibly set the type for these articles. It is important to note their portrayal of blacks because they can provide a baseline to measure the mental, interpersonal, and emotional growth in Sam Clemens's lifetime.

> A rich anecdote is told of a negro boy in the western part of the State [Virginia], who, during the alarming prevalence of the cholera, heard his father say that the disease would soon be along their way, left his work on the plantation and betook himself to the woods. Here he was found by his overseer soon after, fast asleep. Being taken to task by him for leaving his work, he excused himself on the ground that not being prepared in mind to die, 'he had gone to the woods to meditate.'
> "But," said the overseer, "how was it that you went to sleep?"
> "Well I don't know, massy, how dat was, 'zactly" responded the negro, "but I speck I must *over-prayed* myself."
>
> "Julius, is you better dis morning?"
> "No. I was better yesterday, but got over it."
> "Am der no hopes den ob your discovery?"
> "Discovery ob what?"
> "Your discovery from de convalescence dat fotch you on yer back?"
> "Dat depends, Mr. Snow, altogether on de prognostifications which amplify de disease.—Should dey terminate fatally, de doctor tinks Julius am a gone nigger; should dey not terminate fatally, he hopes de colored indiwidual won't die till anoder time. As I said before, it all depends on the prognostics, and till these come to a head, it is hard telling whedder de nigger will discontinue hisself or not."[18]

Sam Clemens experimented with writing black dialect throughout his career in short stories such as "Sociable Jimmy" and "A True Story" and later in a novel, *Adventures of Huckleberry Finn.* The exchange between Jim and Huck when Huck asks the runaway slave if he was a rich could easily have been printed in the Marion County newspapers when slave culture prevailed.

> Jim knew all kinds of signs. He said he knowed most everything. I said it looked to me like all the signs was about bad luck, and so I asked him if there warn't any good-luck signs. He says: "Mighty few—an' dey ain't no use to a body. What you want to know when good luck's a-comin' for? Want to keep it off?" And he said: "Ef you's got hairy arms en a hairy breas', it's a sign dat you's a-gwyne to be rich. Well, dey's some use in a sign like dat, 'kase it's so fur ahead. You see, maybe you's

18. *MC,* February 21, 1849, May 7, 1853. See appendix for more stories.

got to be po' a long time fust, en so you might git discourage' en kill yo'sef 'f you didn't know by de sign dat you gwyne to be rich bymeby."

"Have you got hairy arms and a hairy breast, Jim?"

"What's de use to ax dat question? Don't you see I has?"

"Well, are you rich?"

"No, but I ben rich wunst, and gwyne to be rich ag'in. Wunst I had foteen dollars, but I tuck to specalat'n', en got busted out."

"What did you speculate in, Jim?"

"Well, fust I tackled stock."

"What kind of stock?"

"Why, live stock—cattle, you know. I put ten dollars in a cow. But I ain' gwyne to resk no mo' money in stock. De cow up 'n' died on my han's."

"So you lost the ten dollars."

"No, I didn't lose it all. I on'y los' 'bout nine of it. I sole de hide en taller for a dollar en ten cents."

"You had five dollars and ten cents left. Did you speculate any more?"

"Yes. You know that one-laigged nigger dat b'longs to old Misto Bradish? Well, he sot up a bank, en say anybody dat put in a dollar would git fo' dollars mo' at de en' er de year. Well, all de niggers went in, but dey didn't have much. I wuz de on'y one dat had much. So I stuck out for mo' dan fo' dollars, en I said 'f I didn't git it I'd start a bank myself. Well, o' course dat nigger want' to keep me out er de business, bekase he says dey warn't business 'nough for two banks, so he say I could put in my five dollars en he pay me thirty-five at de en' er de year.

"So I done it. Den I reck'n'd I'd inves' de thirty-five dollars right off en keep things a-movin'. Dey wuz a nigger name' Bob, dat had ketched a wood-flat, en his marster didn't know it; en I bought it off'n him en told him to take de thirty-five dollars when de en' er de year come; but somebody stole de wood-flat dat night, en nex' day de one-laigged nigger say de bank's busted. So dey didn't none uv us git no money."

"What did you do with the ten cents, Jim?"

"Well, I 'uz gwyne to spen' it, but I had a dream, en de dream tole me to give it to a nigger name' Balum—Balum's Ass dey call him for short; he's one er dem chuckleheads, you know. But he's lucky, dey say, en I see I warn't lucky. De dream say let Balum inves' de ten cents en he'd make a raise for me. Well, Balum he tuck de money, en when he wuz in church he hear de preacher say dat whoever give to de po' len' to de Lord, en boun' to git his money back a hund'd times. So Balum he tuck en give de ten cents to de po', en laid low to see what wuz gwyne to come of it."

"Well, what did come of it, Jim?"

"Nuffn never come of it. I couldn' manage to k'leck dat money no way; en Balum he couldn'. I ain' gwyne to len' no mo' money' dout I see de security. Boun' to git yo' money back a hund'd times, de preacher says! Ef I could git de ten cents back, I'd call it squah, en be glad er de chanst."

"Well, it's all right anyway, Jim, long as you're going to be rich again some time or other."

"Yes; en I's rich now, come to look at it. I owns myself, en I's wuth eight hund'd dollars. I wisht I had dé money, I wouldn't want no mo'."[19]

Like the previously noted political propaganda, these stories, so common in Clemens's youth, helped to maintain slavery's social structure. For slave masters to preserve a feeling of superiority, it was obviously necessary to keep pumping up their belief system. Although disguised as humor, these articles served a serious social function. Repeated by the fireside in Hannibal homes, they served as teaching tools for the young. What better way to impart social knowledge than through humor? It was the perfect supplement for the more serious lessons taught in the Sunday schools of slave culture.

19. Mark Twain, *Adventures of Huckleberry Finn*, 44–45.

Chapter 15

Runaway Slaves and Slave Resistance

A sort of regular recurring duty imposed on the local press of this portion of Missouri, of late days, is the chronicling of frequent departures of slaves for parts unknown.

Palmyra Weekly Whig, October 23, 1856

The year 1847 held another horror for Samuel Clemens in addition to the death of his father. In August, when the summer heat beat down on Hannibal and the temperature hovered in the upper nineties, Sam went with his playmates John Briggs and the Bowen brothers, Bart, Will, and Sam, to find refuge in the cool water of the Mississippi. They rowed out to an island for a day of swimming and fishing. They were in a slough, or channel that ran between the island and the Illinois side, when they discovered the body of a runaway slave. It must have been a frightening experience. The boys released the body from a snag, and it rose head-first from the murky green water. The *Hannibal Journal* reported the event. "While some of our citizens were fishing a few days since on the Sny Island, they discovered in what is called Bird Slough the body of a negro man. On examination of the body, they found it to answer the description of a negro recently advertised in handbills as a runaway from Neriam Todd, of Howard County. He had on a brown jeans frock coat, home-made linen pants, and a new pair of lined and bound shoes. The body when discovered was much mutilated."[1]

Clemens claimed in his autobiography that Benson Blankenship, older brother of his friend, Tom, had secretly been taking food to the slave on the

1. *HJ*, August 19, 1847, quoted in Wecter, *Sam Clemens of Hannibal*, 148.

island, but there is no proof of that. The body of the slave, which floated up ghostlike from the river, epitomized one of the great contradictions of slavery. The slave had lost his life seeking freedom. But in Hannibal's worldview slavery was established by God for the well-being of both slave and master. Every need of the slave was met by the system. What slave in his right mind would flee?

White slave culture offered several answers to this troublesome question: Slaves were childlike creatures, easily led astray by cunning abolitionists, who tricked them into leaving the natural order of slavery. Despite abundant proof to the contrary, in their newspapers Joseph Ament and Orion Clemens both took the editorial position that slaves didn't often run away from Hannibal. Both editors sought to assuage the fears of slaveholders wishing to settle in the area. Orion wrote (and Sam may have set) the following story:

> Emigrants from slave states, who hold large property in slaves, generally seem to prefer settling on the Missouri river. They imagine that their property cannot be safe anywhere near the Mississippi. This is a mistake. Ten slaves run away from the Missouri River, where one leaves this section. The negroes in this part of the State, hardly ever run off, because they are well acquainted with the difficulty of getting away. On the Missouri, they think that all is safe, if they can succeed in reaching the Mississippi. Not long since, three or four men in one week, were over here from the Missouri River, in search of runaway slaves.
>
> The Island opposite this city is about six miles wide, and sixty miles long; and it is too thinly populated, and the people too well disposed towards us to admit of underground railroad accommodations.[2]

When Joseph Ament ran practically the same editorial a year later, in June of 1852, he added: "For the four years we have been residing immediately upon the river, we have not known a single slave to escape, out of the hundreds owned and hired by our citizens; and is rarely ever the case that one makes the attempt." This editorial "white lie" was typical of the time. In an essay he submitted to Philadelphia's *American Courier* during the same period, Sam Clemens wrote a glowing description of Hannibal. In the essay, dated March 25, 1852, Clemens described the Mississippi River, the growing transportation system of the Hannibal and St. Joseph Railroad, and the natural wonder of the cave south of town. But he completely omitted any reference to slaves or slavery.[3]

2. *Western Union* (hereinafter *WU*) May 29, 1851.
3. *MC*, June 24, 1852; *American Courier*, May 8, 1852. See appendix for complete article, one of Clemens's first published works.

Despite such pretense, the truth was that escaping slaves were a very serious problem in northeast Missouri. The region's peculiar geography made it far easier to escape from Missouri than from most slave states— not easy, but easier. An enterprising slave in Hannibal could go east or north toward freedom. More important, Missouri was in constant contact and commerce with the free areas surrounding it. This provided slaves with the chance to communicate with those who wanted to help them get to freedom. Between 1850 and 1860, the number of slaves escaping declined nationally, while increasing in Missouri.[4]

It is no wonder that Mark Twain's *Adventures of Huckleberry Finn* would be built around a runaway slave. Runaways were a constant feature of his childhood. Missouri slave culture even joked about them. One Marion County merchant ran an advertisement that boldly declared, "Running Away!" There followed a list of the clothing, boots, shoes, and food items he offered for sale, and he closed, "Please call before they are all run off." Runaways were an accepted topic for humor. "Darkness has fled, as the man said when his negro absconded" was a one-liner run in a local paper. The *Hannibal Journal* poked fun at a mistake in a runaway advertisement. "A Southern advertiser, describing a runaway negro, says, 'he is thirty-five feet of age!' Tall age that. That darkie was exactly six years high." Despite the jokes, running away was deadly serious business. Not only did local slaves run away to the North and East, but countless slaves from the interior of Missouri made their way toward the Mississippi or the Des Moines River.[5]

The Des Moines River had a substantial advantage over the Mississippi for the escaping slave. There were many low spots where one could simply wade across. The Mississippi could be treacherous. In the days before the U.S. Army Corps of Engineers narrowed the river with wing dikes that keep the channel scoured, the river was wide and dangerous. It could be a challenging swim. Eddies and undertows could drown the tired or inexperienced swimmer. The patrols made certain that boats, rafts, and canoes were kept locked tight. Any unchained craft were destroyed and their owners fined.

Running for freedom was no lark, yet men, women, and children risked their lives to do so. Frustrated slave catchers would kill a slave rather than let him reach freedom. The *Hannibal Journal* recorded such an incident in 1849. Two white men from Shelby County immediately to the west of Hannibal were hunting game when they saw two Negro men in a field. When the Negroes saw the white men, they fled. The whites knew

4. *Eighth Census of the United States, 1860.*
5. *PMW,* October 24, 1850, May 28, 1846; *HJ,* October 11, 1849.

immediately by their behavior that they were runaway slaves and pursued them. They stalked the slaves for several days, never able to catch them. Frustrated, when the pursuers got within rifle range, they shot one of the two runaways. They hoped that the other man would become demoralized and surrender, but he left his dying friend and ran off. The whites were distracted by the slave they had shot. This allowed his comrade to make his way to freedom. It took the wounded slave three hours to die.[6] Rather than let him go, his pursuers preferred him dead. The value of a dead slave was no more than that of one who had escaped. However, he could still be used: His execution might serve as a warning to others.

A runaway slave in Missouri was also at risk from exposure to the elements. In the Christmas Eve edition of 1857, the *Hannibal Messenger* reported that a female runaway slave had frozen to death in a winter storm. Likewise, merely getting to Illinois or Iowa did not ensure freedom. The rewards offered for captured slaves increased dramatically for those caught outside Missouri. Slave catching in Illinois and Iowa could be very lucrative. Upon return to his Missouri master, a slave who was captured was sure to be whipped, jailed, and perhaps sold. The recaptured slave's life would be hell for a time.

On the run, he or she would never know who could be trusted until the safety of the free black community in Chicago was reached. There the slave could breathe a little easier in the knowledge that a pursuing master would meet an angry mob of free blacks. Some law enforcement officers in Chicago were sympathetic to runaways and helped shelter them until they could get passage on a Great Lakes steamer to Canada. Despite the great odds against them, people of all ages made the run for freedom. They went singly and in groups. Some escapes were well planned and obviously aided by abolitionists, both black and white, in Illinois and Iowa. Others were audacious spur-of-the-moment breaks. Some flew in the face of common sense. Some ended in death, and some in capture, but many slaves made it to Chicago and Canada.

There is no doubt that slaves communicated among themselves and planned escapes. In one week in 1851, an outbreak occurred in northern Marion and southern Lewis Counties. On a Sunday night, a mother and three of her children disappeared in northern Marion County. While the slave patrols were searching for them, nineteen slaves, belonging to at least three different masters, just across the line in Lewis County disappeared on the following Wednesday night. It was a coordinated escape. There is no record of their capture. Another blitz occurred in November

6. *HJ*, September 20, 1849.

1853 when eleven slaves escaped simultaneously from Palmyra.[7] Obviously these were carefully planned efforts. While a single escapee without a plan might be able to hide and scrounge his or her way across the countryside, groups would have difficulty hiding and foraging for food.

Several groups of four made breaks from Marion County. Four men left together on July 3, 1852. Obviously they appreciated the true meaning of Independence Day and intended to celebrate on their own. They belonged to three different masters: Moses Bates, James McWilliams, and Robert Masterson. Their owners placed an advertisement in a Hannibal newspaper which ran for six weeks after they took off. The ad is typical of the manner in which runaways were described. The first man was Scott, a forty-four-year-old, five feet, six inch, stout man with large short arms. He left wearing tow linen pants, a light yellow jeans coat bound with black and black buttons, low-crowned white fur hat, and coarse, heavy shoes. The next man was Ellick. He was twenty-one years old and was described as a copper-colored or dark mulatto. Ellick was wearing a brown jeans sack coat, pale blue striped cassimere pants, blue cloth cap, and large, heavy, coarse shoes. Manuel was also a mulatto. The portion of the advertisement with his age has been damaged, but it appears to say that he was sixteen or twenty-six years old. He was wearing striped cassinet pants, black cloth coat, plush silk hat. Dan was twenty years old and described as a copper or dark mulatto wearing a brown jeans coat, "janes" pants, well-worn hickory shirt, and a black cloth cap. It is interesting that three of the slaves were described as mulattoes. In one of the horrible ironies of Missouri slave culture, it is possible that the owners Bates, McWilliams, and Masterson, all prominent men in Marion County, were pursuing their own progeny.

The advertisement was not necessarily intended to alert the people of Marion County to the escape, who had probably already heard about it. The advertisement states that they were believed to have crossed the Mississippi at Marion City and to be on their way to Canada. Owners hoped that the advertisement would make its way to Illinois and Iowa through newspaper exchanges and alert slave catchers along the way. In typical fashion, the owners offered a tiered reward. The slaves were worth twenty dollars each if taken in Marion County, fifty dollars each if taken elsewhere in Missouri, and one hundred dollars each if taken in another state.[8]

7. *PMW,* May 15, 1851; *TWM,* November 3, 1853; *MC,* November 10, 1853.
8. *MC,* August 19, 1852.

Families often escaped together. In one week in 1857, two family groups escaped from Hannibal. A man, twenty-eight, his wife, twenty-five, and her brother, fourteen, escaped. They took off about the same time as two men, a woman, and her child escaped from another owner. There were as many ways to escape from Missouri as there were willing individuals. Of course, the most successful ways were probably used by the people who were not caught and had the good sense not to record how they had escaped in case they ever needed to use the ruses again. Unfortunately, our best knowledge about how slaves attempted to escape comes from those who had the ill fortune to be captured. Many slaves simply walked north toward Iowa. Rowing across the Mississippi was also popular. Two Marion County men escaped together in a skiff they stole in Marion City in the spring of 1854. Sometimes escaping slaves had arranged to rendezvous with a boat from the Illinois side. A white man from Illinois was caught rowing a skiff with a black couple in 1858.[9]

The biggest obstacle to a slave was his or her physical appearance. All blacks were presumed to be slaves under Missouri law. Therefore, any black person who was in a suspicious place was regarded as a runaway. One very ingenious slave nearly made his way to the Mississippi River at Hannibal with a brilliant disguise. He came from Lafayette County in the middle of the state. As late as 1852, it was not that unusual to see an occasional Indian in Missouri. This slave, whose name has been lost to history, made a wig to resemble Native American hair. He wore a turban headdress, blanket, leggings, and moccasins. He adorned his costume with what a Hannibal newspaper characterized as "appropriate trinkets."

The disguised slave left home on Saturday and began walking toward Hannibal. His disguise worked very well for a time. He traveled all day Sunday. When he met up with travelers who insisted on speaking with him, he faked an accent and told them he was on his way to Hannibal to see the Indian agent to get money to return to his mountain home. He was captured well inland of Hannibal when a Mr. Spencer, "who is always eyeing runaways and thieves with the keenness of a Marshal Felps, detected his lips as being too thick for an Indian."[10] The bold slave was returned to his master.

A written pass could be a valuable asset to a slave and, of course, was the main motivation behind the law forbidding the teaching of reading and writing to all blacks in Missouri. Three runaway slaves from Marion County were captured in Illinois in July 1854. All had forged passes, and

9. *HM*, September 3, 1857; *PWW*, May 11, 1854, December 2, 1858.
10. *MC*, May 20, 1852.

one had a bill of sale supposedly executed by his master to himself. When the railroads came along, two enterprising slaves carried forged passes and rode from inland Missouri to St. Louis, where they rowed across to Illinois. The owner sued the new Pacific Railroad for allowing them to escape.[11]

After a lifetime of having their labor stolen, slaves frequently took what they needed from the masters before heading out. One very bold Hannibal slave decided he preferred to ride to freedom, rather than walk to Iowa. His master, Temple Davis, lived about two miles outside Hannibal. The slave walked into town on Sunday evening and hired a horse from a local stable. The slave said he wanted to ride out to the farm of a man named Donnelly. The owner of the stable knew the slave and his master. He was glad to get the slave's money. The next morning, Davis discovered that his slave had not returned. When he went into town to make inquiries, he discovered from the stable owner that the slave was supposedly going to Donnelly's. The owner, no doubt, thought the slave was overstaying his visit with the slaves there and was prepared by go fetch him. But by chance, he encountered Donnelly in Hannibal and was told that the slave had never come near his place. The truth dawned on Davis and a search ensued.

The slave had last been seen going north on the road to Palmyra. He rode by the house of a former owner named Fuqua. It is heartening to envision the slave respectfully tipping his hat to his former owner with an "afternoon Massa." Then he continued north toward the Des Moines River. It would have been very shallow and easy to ford in January. His feet in the stirrups would not have gotten wet. The *Hannibal Daily Messenger* stated the slave had at least one free brother who lived in Keokuk. Freedom and help were just a day's ride away.[12]

The separation of families led slaves to run away. Sometimes they simply went to see loved ones. Other times freed slaves took great risks to liberate members of their families still in bondage. One slave was captured in Hannibal while visiting relatives. A thirty-year-old man named Milton had been sold by a Hannibal family named Dickson to another family who lived far to the south in Jefferson County. He evidently missed his own family and ran back to Hannibal to visit them. He was visiting slaves belonging to George Mahan (father of the man who would purchase Sam Clemens's boyhood home in Hannibal and open it as a museum). Milton

11. *PMW,* July 13, 1854; *Hannibal Whig Messenger* (hereinafter *HWGM*), September 20, 1855.
12. *HDM,* January 8, 1861.

became sick while visiting his relatives and was discovered. In his weakened state, he was easy prey for Mahan. He was captured and returned to his owner.[13]

Isaac McDaniel, a former slave, freed his wife and several other slaves in a bold escape from Marion County. McDaniel was married to a slave belonging to John Bush, one of the first pioneers to settle in Marion County. McDaniel had been a slave in Marion County himself and had established quite a reputation as a preacher of the gospel. Being a black preacher meant he had the approval of the county and city governments to preach. He had earned enough money to purchase his own freedom. Though he was free, he continued preaching the gospel in Marion County to slaves and free blacks. McDaniel used his position as a minister and a free man to travel into Illinois and up to Chicago. His reputation was spotless among the slaveholders of Marion County. When he returned to Missouri in October 1856, he began negotiatiating to purchase his wife from John Bush. The slave owner agreed to sell the woman to McDaniel, never suspecting that McDaniel had bigger plans. He had made detailed arrangements with abolitionist friends. McDaniel stole a horse and buggy from Bush, and along with his own wife, he took four or five slaves from the neighborhood. The entire episode had been well planned on both sides of the river, and none of the slaves were ever heard from again.[14]

Many slaves helped themselves to clothing when they escaped. This made it more difficult for owners to describe them in newspaper advertisements. As it was impossible to disseminate photographic images by wire or to publish them in print, owners had to describe slaves with words. Some owners were better at this than others, but if an escaping slave had only one set of clothes, he or she was easier to describe. For instance, one woman was a "bright Mulatto woman" twenty-two years of age wearing a "dress of white oznaburg, red handkerchief round her head." Another was described as a sixteen- or seventeen-year-old-boy named Dick wearing a "blue military roundabout, and buckskin pants."[15] These descriptions greatly aided white slave hunters to identify the runaways.

Advertisements demonstrate how having a change of clothes could make identification difficult and give the escaping slave a slight advantage. One describes a runaway man and says, "it is not known what kind of clothes said boy wore; but it is supposed he took with him several

13. *PMW,* January 1, 1849.
14. *PWW,* October 23, 1856.
15. *PMW,* October 24, 1850, June 5, 1851.

valuable articles of wearing apparel." An 1840 advertisement describes "an old Negro Woman, low in stature, of black complexion, small face, named Mary Ann. The clothing which she took with her consists of a cloak, a blue and a yellow linsey dress, and some calico dresses."[16]

Better quality clothing could also help the runaway slave to look like a free person in Illinois or Iowa. Clothes issued to slaves, even new clothes, were generally of inferior quality and worn only by slaves. Slaves were also given well-worn hand-me-downs from the master—frequently with little regard for fit or style. Stolen clothing might also give the slave something to barter for food or assistance on the road.

Having light-colored skin could also be an advantage. In 1856 a slave woman and a free black man named Sandy living in Palmyra planned an escape. The woman was a mulatto and could pass for white. She had escaped from a man named Pond who lived in the country. The man hid her at his house and found a nice dress for her. Then he took her to the house of a German immigrant and said that the slave was a white woman who needed to get to Quincy to see a sick brother. Another German immigrant, who was helping to paint the house, agreed to drive the lady to Quincy in a buggy.

At first, the plan worked exceedingly well. The slave woman rode up to the Quincy ferry and even made it onto the boat. But when the ferry docked at Quincy, the woman's master came aboard for the return trip to Missouri. He had come to Illinois to search for her. He walked up to her and took both her and the German prisoner. But for the chance encounter, she likely would have made it to Chicago and then Canada. One can imagine the woman's despair as she looked at Quincy and realized how tantalizingly close she had come to reaching help. The German told the sheriff about Sandy, and he, too, was taken into custody. The German managed to convince the authorities that he had not known the woman was a slave, and he was released. Sandy, however, paid with his freedom for the attempt to free the slave woman.[17]

Reaching Illinois did not mean freedom. Slave catchers, aware of increased rewards for Missouri slaves captured in other states, were not deterred by state borders, nor were they necessarily discouraged by the passage of time. Rewards typically increased over time. An 1853 ad offered one hundred dollars in state and two hundred dollars out. It was possible of course that abolitionists would come to the rescue of a slave captured

16. Ibid., May 28, 1842, December 12, 1840.

17. *Southern Sentinel* (hereinafter *SS*), April 23, 1856; *HWM*, May 1, 1856; *PMW*, April 24, 1856.

in Illinois. When one Missouri slave girl was caught in Alton, Illinois, the abolitionists in that town raised twelve hundred dollars to purchase her from her master.[18] Abolitionists and free blacks would often try to free slaves who had been taken into custody by law enforcement officers or slaveholders themselves. The abolitionists in Chicago could be especially aggressive. In 1854 three St. Louis slave catchers tracked a runaway slave to the windy city and met their quarry in the street. An angry free Negro intervened, and one of the slave catchers shot and wounded him. A riot almost followed. Angry Negroes surrounded the slave catchers, and the slave was spirited away. The Missourians were outraged when law enforcement officers arrived on the scene and arrested the three of them. The Missouri slave catchers were charged with assault, riot, and attempt to kidnap. The slave went free.

Jacob Sosey, editor of the *Missouri Whig*, fumed: "This is the kind of justice extended to the people of Missouri, and the slave-holding States, by the *hypocritical thieves of that mob-ruled, treason-hatching city of Chicago*. They first steal a man's property from before his eyes, and then incarcerate him in a dungeon, because he endeavored to reclaim that property peaceably." The abolitionists in Chicago could be overly vigilant. In 1857 a white Pennsylvania man, who was caring for a young black boy at the request of the boy's mother, passed through Chicago on his way to Monmouth, Illinois. Suspicious, abolitionists took the boy from him until he could prove that the child was his ward, not his slave.[19]

One poor runaway slave woman was freed by abolitionists in Illinois only to be recaptured a year later, a victim of overconfidence. In 1856, the woman fled from a man named Martin in Monroe County, west of Marion. He tracked her to Quincy, where he captured her, but then a crowd overwhelmed him and set the woman free. She fled to Chicago. She stayed there for a while, but then she became comfortable in Illinois and returned to Quincy to live as a free woman. She made the mistake of traveling to see friends in Missouri. She was identified onboard a packet headed to the small town of Louisiana, Missouri. When the steamboat docked at Hannibal, she was hustled off and locked in the city jail.[20]

Another obstacle to runaways was the Illinois Black Laws. Passed in 1853, they made it illegal for blacks to enter and stay in Illinois. A Negro could be seized by a sheriff and his services auctioned off. The Negro would work as an indentured servant for a period of time and then be

18. *TWM,* January 22, 1853; *HWM,* January 22, 1853.
19. *PMW,* September 21, 1854; *SS,* September 16, 1857.
20. *HM,* October 8, 1857.

expelled from the state. Unscrupulous whites could easily take such servants into Missouri and sell them. However, Illinois abolitionists resisted these laws. On one occasion, abolitionists in Quincy bid for the freedom of such a slave and on his behalf challenged the constitutionality of the state law. The abolitionists posted a bond for the runaway and spirited him out of state, at which point the legal issue was moot.[21]

Not everyone was lucky enough to be saved by the abolitionists. In September 1853, two slaves belonging to John R. Flourree of Ralls County were captured near Lancaster, Illinois, by two Kentucky slave catchers. The slave catchers had to fend off abolitionists in Warsaw, Illinois, and make their way to Canton, Missouri. A determined white abolitionist followed them to Canton and tried to persuade the sheriff there to release the black men. However, the tables were turned, and the abolitionist found himself arrested. The story so pleased Hannibal editors that it was run in three newspapers, Orion Clemens's *Hannibal Journal*, the *Missouri Courier*, and the *Tri-Weekly Messenger*.[22]

Runaway slaves from Hannibal were often caught just across the river, as five were in 1857, or in nearby Illinois towns, like two captured near Mendon, Illinois, in 1858. The slaves were all taken to jail. Many escaped slaves from the interior of Missouri were arrested in or near Hannibal before they could try to cross the Mississippi. A slave from Boone County was captured in Marion County in May 1842. Some—like the dead slave found by Sam Clemens and his friends in 1847, who was from Howard County—lost their gamble at the river. Both runaways had traveled nearly one hundred miles. Slaves from Monroe County (immediately to the west of Marion) were also frequently caught in or near Hannibal. At least one free black man from Illinois was arrested in Hannibal while he was trying to "steal" his enslaved children.[23]

In 1853 four armed runaways from Marion County were arrested when one went into town to purchase food. He was caught and forced to betray the others. They surrendered after they were surrounded by the slave patrol. Orion or Sam Clemens commented in the *Hannibal Daily Journal*, "Each negro was well armed with pistols, knives, &c., and no doubt had

21. *HWM*, December 8, 1853.

22. *HJ*, September 21, 1853; *MC*, September 22, 1853; *WM*, September 24, 1853; *TWM*, September 27, 1853.

23. *HWM*, September 3, 1857; *PWW*, September 9, 1858; *HJ*, August 19, 1847; *PMW*, May 28, 1842, May 20, 1843, September 12, 1850; *HWM*, July 19, 1855, September 9, 1858.

they not got confused, would have resisted stoutly any attempt to arrest them."[24]

Captured slaves were confined in the city jail. Under Missouri law, owners had three months to claim their slaves. The sheriff posted advertisements for the owners to come forward. If owners did not claim their property and pay the reward and expenses of capture and board, the county would auction the slaves off at the courthouse in Palmyra.[25] However, incarceration was not the end of the line for some runaway slaves. In 1855 a slave escaped from the Paris jail in Monroe County. In February 1859, three blacks and two white men escaped from the county jail in Palmyra. Two of the blacks were slaves who had been held for "safekeeping" by their masters. The third black man was charged with tampering with slaves and inducing them to run away. Two years later another three slaves, all being held for safekeeping, escaped from the county jail when two white criminals made a break for it, one an accused murderer and the other a burglar. There is no record of any of these jail escapees ever being recaptured.

Hiding Out

Some slaves made no attempt to get to Canada or the free states. There were plenty of wild wooded hills along the Mississippi and the smaller rivers where slaves were able to hide out for months. In September of 1844, a slave owner ran an advertisement seeking the return of his twenty-three-year-old slave girl, who had run away on February 29. The owner believed she was hiding in the country between the North River and the South Fabius River.[26] Another owner was grateful that he had been able to catch his runaway slave in the rolling hills just south of Hannibal. In 1855, John P. McMillin wrote to thank the *Whig Messenger* for its help in the capture. The runaway was caught sleeping in Colonel Wellman's stable. The frightened slave informed on three other runaways living in the woods near Saverton, a little river town just a few miles south of Hannibal. He identified them as George Welky, nearly grown, and Tom and

24. *HJ*, May 27, 1853.
25. *PMW*, August 20, 1842; *HDM*, March 1, 1861; *HJ*, May 27, 1853; *PWW*, September 9, 1858; *HM*, September 3, 1857; *PWW*, September 9, 1858; *HWM*, December 23, 1858.
26. *PMW*, September 4, 1844.

Henry Waters, ten or fifteen years old. The captured slave said they had been hiding out and living off the land for two or three weeks.

The runaway described the clothing the other slaves were wearing and warned that they were armed. George had a double-barreled pistol. They were "on their way to Louisiana to meet some 'friends [Negro thieves] from the State of nuts'," evidently referring to Illinois abolitionists. The letter writer asked the good people of Hannibal for assistance. "The negroes say they have been supported and fed in your city for one week and I feel sure that the young gentlemen of Hannibal would like to convince abolitionists that it is not a safe place to hold their meetings and feed runaways." The editor of the paper, William League, reflected the twisted thinking of slave culture on the capture of McMillin's slave in a separate article, "the recapture of the slave has doubtless saved him from the horror of being carried off to hopeless captivity by abolitionists."[27]

Carrying Mail Back on the Underground Railroad

There is evidence that slaves in Marion County were in contact with their runaway friends and family members in Canada, Detroit, and Chicago. Delphia Quarles was a free black woman living in Hannibal.[28] She played a fascinating role in Hannibal's history. She was a mail courier for the Underground Railroad. Slaves were mentally isolated from the outside world. Under the 1847 Missouri statute, which had merely codified the custom and practice of most slaveholders, it was illegal to teach reading to any Negro, mulatto, or slave. This was designed to limit their opportunity to learn about the abolition movement and the Underground Railroad as well as to keep them from forging passes and communicating with others.

But by the late 1850s, the Underground Railroad had become so sophisticated that operators could not only slip slaves from northeast Missouri into Iowa and Illinois, but also get mail from the successful runaways back to the homefolk in Marion County. Mail served to inspire and give courage to those who wished to make the run themselves. Delphia Quarles must have been able to read, for surely most of the recipients of the mail she delivered could not. Unfortunately, the vigilantes in the Marion

27. *WM*, August 16, 1855.
28. *HM*, October 15, 1857.

Association, an antiabolitionist group, got wind of her activities. At a mass meeting in the county in 1857, they passed the following resolution:

> Resolved, That there is a combination of free negroes in the City of Hannibal, who corrupt all the slaves that hold intercourse with them, and that there is a certain free woman in that city, named DELPHIA QUARLES, who has received several letters from fugitive slaves living in Chicago and has slyly distributed them among the slaves of Miller Township, causing in-subordination among them.
>
> Resolved, That the Committee notify said woman to leave this State in ten days, and in the event of her failure to do so, that the Committee wait upon her in due time.[29]

The thinly veiled threat to "wait upon her in due time" meant death. Quarles appears to have taken the threat seriously. There is no further mention of her in Hannibal or Marion County records after publication of the resolution.[30] One interesting possibility is that Quarles had formerly been the property of John Quarles, Sam Clemens's uncle in Ralls County, or married to Daniel Quarles, whom John Quarles emancipated.

Suicides and Mutilation

Some slaves were unable to escape slavery by making the arduous run to Canada and chose suicide over continued bondage. In a number of cases, mothers killed their children before killing themselves. In 1841, the following story was reported in the *Palmyra Missouri Whig*:

> INFANTACIDE,—HORRIBLE DEPRAVITY.
>
> a negro woman belonging to Mr. William Woods, of this county, says the Liberty Far West, on Monday last, destroyed her three children, the oldest about eight years of age, by drowning them in a creek. The wretched woman informed a negro man of what she had done, and where the children might be found; also, of her own intention to drown herself in the Mississippi River. The children were found laid out and protected by some boughs to shade their faces. As nothing has yet been heard of the unhappy mother, it is supposed she carried her threat into effect.[31]

29. Ibid.
30. Ibid.; *PMW*, October 22, 1857.
31. *PMW*, June 26, 1841.

The mother's shading the faces of her dead children is particularly touching. In 1856, another area slave committed suicide, but first managed to sabotage his master's crop. The *Hannibal Messenger* reported that a man belonging to Charles C. Carter set fire to Carter's wheat and ran off. The slave drowned himself in the Salt River.[32]

Slaves in mid-Missouri had a harder time escaping than did slaves close to the Illinois or Iowa borders. Stories of their suicides appeared in the Marion County press. On April 28, 1857, a slave woman living in mid-Missouri hanged her four- or five-year-old son from the cross-beam in the kitchen of the master's house. Then she took the other end of the same rope and hanged herself. A man hanged himself with a log chain in nearby Macon County in April of 1859. That same month, a woman in Howard County chopped three fingers off her left hand to avoid being sent to the slave market in St. Louis. Slaves sometimes committed suicide after failed escape attempts. Orion Clemens reported one such slave who committed suicide in the jail awaiting return to his master in mid-Missouri. Orion commented, "He was confined there for attempting to run away and it is supposed preferred death to being whipped for the offence." The thought that he preferred death to slavery did not occur to Orion.[33]

32. *HM*, September 25, 1856.
33. *PMW*, May 21, 1857; *HWM*, April 21, 1859; *HDJ*, September 21, 1853.

Chapter 16

Battling Abolitionists in the Press

The Enemy Without

Unassailable certainty is the thing that gives a newspaper the firmest and most valuable reputation.

Mark Twain, *Roughing It*

The mounting list of runaway slaves and the increasingly harsh measures taken to deal with them foreshadowed the much greater conflict to come between the slave and free states. But long before the Civil War there was a war of ideas. Invective and misinformation were hurled by both slave culture and the forces of freedom. Battles were fought through the newspapers, where each side engaged in what would later be termed propaganda. Sam Clemens came of age in this environment and was a full-fledged partisan in the struggle. The newspapers for which he worked were active in the word wars, both attacking the enemy and bolstering morale at home. In Sam Clemens's Hannibal, all the newspapers—and it was an active newspaper community—were united in supporting the institution that defined their culture and society. In articles, letters, and editorials, they fought the abolitionists regularly and bitterly.

Missouri, the peninsula of slavery, perceived itself as suffering great indignities at the hands of abolitionists and runaway slaves during the 1850s. It is important to remember the substantial portion of Marion County wealth invested in human property. An escaped slave was an expensive loss to both the owner and the government (through lost tax revenue). But there was much more at issue: The flight of slaves challenged the very fabric of slave culture and, to people who believed slavery divinely ordained, God's plan for the universe. Thus, slaves, normally

182

loyal, obedient, simple creatures, were being beguiled by tricky abolitionists. Then, like an infection, the idea of running off could spread throughout the slave population. A New Orleans doctor actually came up with a disease, "drapetomania," to explain slaves running away. A proverb frequently heard in Marion County described the phenomena: "a white man is uncertain and a nigger *will* run off."[1]

The people of Marion County had known that the enemy lurked in Illinois since the case of Thompson, Work, and Burr in 1842. By 1848, they knew that the abolitionists were also working in Iowa.[2] Antislavery forces were operating presses, and slaveholders believed they were sending agents to work among the slaves and to steal them. Abolitionists were thieves and fanatics. Just as segregationists in the South would later dismiss the civil rights movement as the work of outside agitators, slave masters a hundred years earlier attributed their problems to the abolitionists. If a master in Marion County had any trouble with his or her slaves, the explanation was simple:

> It is our opinion that the emissaries of Negro-stealing societies are prowling about the country, exciting the slave population to insubordination, and enticing them away from their masters.—It would be well for everybody to keep a good look out for such characters; but at the same time, due care should be taken to avoid punishing the innocent for the sins of the guilty. Several stampedes among the Negroes have taken place recently in this vicinity . . . there is no doubt at all but they were aided in making their escape by Northern Abolitionists. They crossed the river at Quincy.[3]

Without fail, slave culture fell back on the explanation that slaves could not be dissatisfied with their lives since God had created them for that role. Likewise, slave culture had a difficult time believing slaves themselves capable of planning and organizing successful escapes. The real enemy clearly lay outside. Of course, there really were abolitionists in Iowa and Illinois who were quite anxious to help slaves escape. And as the 1850s progressed, the state boundaries between Iowa, Illinois, and Missouri came to more closely resemble international borders, borders that had to be guarded and patrolled. Ferries, which were the only public

1. *Southern States, a Series of Papers,* 322; E. F. Perkins, *History of Marion County, Missouri,* 263.

2. *HJ,* June 29, 1848. See appendix.

3. *MC,* November 10, 1853.

transportation across the Mississippi River in the 1850s, were a particular problem.

The legislature of Missouri enacted strict regulations regarding the liability of ferry operators. The law provided that any ferryman or keeper of a ferry on the Mississippi or Des Moines River who transported a slave into Illinois or Iowa without written permission from the master or owner of said slave would have to pay the owner double the slave's value. To make it even more difficult for runaway slaves to get from the interior of the state to the borders, the same law had stiff penalties for ferry operators within Missouri. Anyone who allowed a slave to cross any river—even within the state—by ferry without the permission of the owner or master of the slave could be forced to pay the owner the value of the slave.[4]

Even with the penalties in place, the vigilance committee ("patterollers" in slave parlance) of Marion County kept a wary eye out for slaves sneaking eastward on the ferry. The committee also interrogated people who had taken the ferry from Quincy. Itinerant preachers, traveling salesmen, and immigrants who could not give a proper accounting of themselves were sent packing. A bill posted on the ferry warned that if an expelled abolitionist returned a second time he would be subject to fifty lashes, and upon a third trip would be hanged until he was "dead! dead!! dead!!!"[5]

Rumors and Labels

The rumor is a staple of the small community, and northeast Missouri was a chain of small towns, with Hannibal the largest, strung along the Mississippi River. A malicious suggestion could ruin a person. Any hint that someone was an abolitionist, and he or she was tainted. Preachers and public speakers were particularly vulnerable to false stories and innuendo. Entire organizations could be damaged. This happened in Hannibal after a March 1850 Sons of Temperance meeting. Someone, perhaps a citizen who resented the self-righteousness of the teetotalers who publicly took their pledges and marched in parades wearing sashes and banners, started a rumor that a speaker had stood before the sober and religious crowd and declared that "a liquor dealer was worse than a slaveholder as a slaveholder was worse than a horse-thief."[6]

4. *Missouri Revised Statutes of 1845, as Amended in 1855,* March 5, 1855; *PWW,* March 4, 1855.
5. Perkins, *History of Marion County,* 263.
6. *MC,* March 21, 1850.

Now everyone in Hannibal in 1850 knew that a horse thief was pretty low. While they apparently were not hanged with the regularity seen in old cowboy movies, they were considered despicable. But the many slave-holders in Hannibal were considered respectable people. In fact, they were among the most powerful people in town, and they certainly did not take to being publicly insulted. The rumor caused such a stir that a meeting was held and a series of resolutions passed denying that the "abolition-tinged" statement had ever been made at a Sons of Temper-ance meeting. The resolutions were further attested by four of Hannibal's leading citizens. They were then published, not just in the local *Missouri Courier* and *Hannibal Journal*, but in the *St. Louis Intelligencer, Palmyra Whig, Paris Mercury,* and *Quincy People's Journal* just in case the rumor had crept beyond the city limits. Charges of abolitionist leanings were not something to be taken lightly.[7] The allegation apparently did not taint the antidrinking crowd for long, and the teetotalers were soon back in the public's good graces. But the episode demonstrates the seriousness with which even rumors were treated.

In Hannibal, there was hardly anything too vile to write about an abo-litionist. The editors of the Hannibal newspapers were united in their opposition. Joseph Ament, Sam Clemens's first newspaper taskmaster, was vociferous in his hatred of all things associated with abolitionism: "A petition was presented to Congress the other day asking an exten-sion of 'the *blessings* of slavery over every State in the Union.' A good idea!—an excellent pill to cram down the throats of those wide mouthed Abolition fanatics who are constantly harping on the '*evils* of slavery.' If slavery be an evil, it does not injure them; yet they are everlastingly peti-tioning Congress for its abolishment. It is time their *cant* was stopped by the ridicule of encounter petitions."[8]

In that very religious time, the greatest insult of all was to label some-one an unbeliever and a blasphemer. And so that charge was hurled at the abolitionists. While Sam Clemens was working for Joseph Ament, he may well have set the story about a New York abolitionist meeting on May 7, 1850, where William Lloyd Garrison "reviled the Bible, Jesus Christ, and the religious churches of every denomination, and denounced slavery." To drive home the depths to which the heathen abolitionists had sunk, Ament fumed, "He [Garrison] was followed by other speak-ers, among whom was Fred Douglass, the negro."[9] One can only imagine

7. Ibid.
8. Ibid., April 4, 1850.
9. Ibid., May 22, 1850.

how Hannibal readers cringed at the thought of a Negro addressing a white audience.

As Missouri found itself estranged from the free states surrounding it, Missourians became aware of the danger of traveling with their slaves beyond the state's borders. Cases involving stolen slaves made their way into the courts, and Missourians were occasionally successful in recovering money for the losses. In 1850, a jury in Henry County, Iowa, awarded a Missouri man $2,900 in damages and nearly $1,000 in court costs from Iowa residents who had helped his slaves escape.[10]

William League published the *Whig Messenger* in Hannibal. In 1852 he reported the story of a Virginia man who was moving to Texas with eight slaves. He took a boat to New York, where he was to transfer to a ship for the Texas run. While he was changing from one craft to the other, abolitionists helped his slaves escape. The man located them and sued for their return, but a state judge declared the slaves were free under New York law. The man sued the shipping line for the $5,000 value of the slaves. Many similar losses were reported in the Hannibal press. Orion Clemens's paper reported in August 1853 that "The abolitionists of Alleghany City recently robbed a Missourian of a negro woman and three children and ran them off to Canada."[11]

Many free-state courts were unsympathetic to Missouri slave owners. Chicago was a particular problem, and that was where many runaway slaves headed. In June 1851, a Missouri slave was found there by his master and arrested by a deputy marshal under the Fugitive Slave Law. The slave was well guarded, and despite the protests of several hundred people—many of them black—he was held in jail. The slave was not liberated by the mob, but a judge set him free with a ruling that infuriated the people of Hannibal. In what Missourians viewed as a dirty trick, the judge waited until the slave owner rested his case. Then he ruled that the slave owner had failed to prove that the slave had not returned to Missouri since his escape and been brought voluntarily by the slave owner into Illinois—an act which would have freed him under state law! The judge also found that there was no proof that the man was the slave sought by the warrant since the document described the runaway as "copper-colored." Several pieces of copper were introduced into evidence, and not a single one was the same color as the man! In slave culture "copper" was just one of the adjectives used to describe variations in skin color. Joseph

10. *PMW,* June 20, 1850.
11. *WM,* December 1, 1852; *HJ,* August 26, 1853.

Ament expressed the view of Hannibal's citizens: "Such a contemptible evasion of the law is worse than open resistance."[12]

Sometimes the black community of Chicago arose in open resistance to the seizure of runaway slaves. In a later case, when a U.S. marshal had writs to arrest more than a dozen runaway slaves, word of his intentions leaked out. Abolitionists and Negroes mobilized to stop him. They were "thick as blackberries. Large crowds soon collected on the street corners, and barber shops were closed, and the occupants, together with all the free Negro men in the place, were soon seen parading the streets in their holiday attire." The marshal asked for help from the military, but only one company of militia in the city was willing to mobilize. The *Chicago Tribune* was accused of issuing a handbill calling on people to watch out for "kidnappers." Crowds gathered at the railroad depot to prevent any slaves being taken away. The *Missouri Whig* reported that there was a secret association with more than seven hundred members "armed to the teeth" and ready for any act of violence to aid runaway slaves. Jacob Sosey wrote that "something should be done, and must be done soon, or the property of Missouri will depreciate within the next two years, at least twenty millions of dollars, for in that time there will be railroads from Chicago, touching the Mississippi opposite Missouri at half a dozen different points, and then the negro stealers of Chicago will carry on their business a hundred fold more largely than they have ever done heretofore." A week later, the *Detroit Inquirer* reported that the slaves, most of whom were from the St. Louis, Missouri, area, had crossed into Canada.[13]

Throughout his career as a newspaperman in Hannibal, Joseph Ament derided and ridiculed abolitionists. He reprinted the following humorous story from a racist northern paper just a few months after Sam went to work for his brother Orion.

AN ABOLITIONIST AT FAULT.
    "I had a brother-in-law," said Mose Parkins, "who was one of the ravenest-maddest, reddest-hottest abolitionist you ever see. I liked the pesky critter well enough, and should have been very glad to see him when cum to spend a day, fetchin my sister to see me and my wife, if he hadn't 'lowed his tongue to run on 'bout niggers, and slavery, and the equality of the races, and the duty of overthrown' the constitution of the United States, and a lot of other things some of which made me right mad, and the best part of 'em right sick. I puzzled my brains a good deal to think how I could make him shet up his noisy head 'bout abolition.

12. *MC*, June 19, 1852.
13. *PMW*, December 21, 1854.

"Wall, one time when brother-in-law come over to stay, an idea struck me.—I hired a nigger to help me haying time. He was the biggest, strongest, greasiest nigger you ever did see. Black! He was blacker than a streak of black cats, and jest as shiny as a new beaver hat. I spoke to him. 'Jake,' ses I, 'when you heer the breakfast bell sing, don't you say a word, but come into the parlor and set down right along the folks and eat your breakfast. The nigger's eyes stuck right out of his head about a foot!—'You're a jokin, massa,' ses he. 'Jokin!' ses I, 'I'm as sober as a deacon.' 'But,' ses he, 'I shan't have time to wash myself and change my shirt.' 'so much the better,' sez I. Wall—breakfast time cum—and so did Jake, and he set right down long side my brother-in-law. He started but he didn't say a word. There warn't no mistake about it. Shut your eyes and you'd known it, the odor was loud, I tell you. There was a fust-rate chance to talk abolitionism, but brother-in-law never opened his chowder head.

'Jake,' ses I, 'you be on hand at dinner time,' and he was. He had been working in the medder all the forenoon—it was hot as hickory and bilin pitch—and—but I leeve the rast to your imagination.

'Wall—in the arternoon—brother-in-law cum up to me, madder than a short-tailed bull in hornet time.

'Mose,' sed he, 'I want to speak to you.'

'Sing it out,' sez I.

'I hain't but a few words to say,' sez he, 'but if that ere confounded nigger comes to the table agin while I'm stopping here I'll clear out.'

"Jake ate his supper that night in the kitchen, but from that day to this, I never heard my brother-in-law open his head about abolitionism. When the Fugitive slave bill was passed, I thought he'd let out some but he didn't *for he knowed that Jake was still a workin' on the farm!*"

Hit him again, Mose.[14]

It is interesting that Ament did not catch on to the story's weakness as propaganda. For although Ament clearly thought the piece made fun of the abolitionist brother-in-law, it also can be read from the opposite perspective. Jake wishes to wash and change his shirt before coming to eat, thereby evidencing his manners and humanity. However, Mose prohibits him from doing so. The repulsive odor of Jake is a contrivance by the racist Mose. The real Jake wants to clean himself and assume a place at the table. However, this was not apparent to Ament.

Cases of abolition mobs liberating slaves never failed to receive special attention. One such case struck very close to home. In 1851, the Clemens

14. *MC*, June 12, 1851.

brothers covered the story of a slave named Jerry who ran away from his owner in Marion County and was living in Syracuse, New York.

> The slave rescued at Syracuse of which an account is given in the extract below, from the Buffalo *Commercial*, belonged to Mr. John McReynolds, of this county. "Jerry," or "Henry," as he now calls himself, ran away from his master, some eight or ten years ago. He was seen in Syracuse, working as a carpenter, and recognized, by a citizen of this State. Mr. McReynolds was informed of the fact, and prevailed on Mr. James Lear, who was going East to purchase goods, to act as his agent,—prepared, as he supposed, with proof of ownership and identity. The bill of sale, however, on which reliance was placed, to prove ownership, was found defective, from the fact that the signature of the witness, Mr. Sam. Smith, of New London, had not been attested before a magistrate. Keeping himself disguised when about the negro, and his movements and purpose secret, Mr. Lear sent for Mr. Smith, and upon his arrival the arrest was made, with the result as narrated by the *Commercial*. People should be more careful about making out such documents. This informality, which incurred the expense and delay of sending for Mr. Smith, might have caused trouble in this State.
>
> From the formidable number engaged in this mob, it is natural to infer that the sentiment in the region of Syracuse, is both bitter and unanimous against the Fugitive Slave Law, and that there is a disposition prevailing the entire community, hostile to extending to Southern men rights guarantied to them by the Constitution and laws of the land. It is true that everybody in Syracuse was not engaged in this mob of two or three thousand, so violent and determined, could be raised in a city no larger than Syracuse, if the respectable men who did not appear among the ruffians, had not patted them on the shoulder, and secretly winked at their proceedings. Another thing—the Marshal could not have been so blind as to be surprised by this outbreak, and we may well suppose the true reason why he had not a larger posse was, that he trembled for his popularity.
>
> Slaveholders may now set it down as an established fact, that their chance of recovering a fugitive slave is almost as good in Canada, a foreign country, as in the Northern States of this Union, though in the latter, the people call us brethren, in liberty religion and law. The slaveholder may calculate on recovering his lost property, in those States, if at all, at the imminent risk or failure, after incurring heavy expense, and at the hazard of his life.[15]

15. *Hannibal Journal and Union* (hereinafter *HJU*) October 16, 1851.

Sam Clemens would remember the case bitterly when he passed through New York two years later.

Joseph Ament edited the *Courier* into the fall of 1852, attacking abolitionists to the last. On November 30, he sold the paper to Josiah Hinton, a former correspondent for the *Tri-Weekly Messenger*. (Hinton had been a victim of young Sam's editorial derision and cartoons after Sam went to work for Orion. Hinton had retaliated by claiming Sam's writing abilities were "the feeble eminations [*sic*] of a puppy's brain.") The November 25 edition of the *Courier*, Ament's last, contained a story that ran two full columns on the front page about a British Navy vessel that spotted a Brazilian slave ship off the coast of Africa. The British gave chase, and the Brazilian ship grounded on rocks. The 630 slaves aboard drowned when the ship sank, dragged down by their chains. Ament's conclusion: "Surely this sad tale may at least be added to the catalogue of ills produced by England's 'good intentions' in striving to suppress the slave trade."[16]

A longtime Democrat, Ament was rewarded for his paper's loyal support of the party. President Pierce appointed him receiver in the land office in Palmyra. It is hard to gauge how much Ament may have influenced young Sam Clemens, who lived and worked with him from age twelve to age fifteen. Upon learning of Ament's appointment to the land office, the Clemenses commented in their paper, "As a clever man, and a man of strict integrity, the Whigs also were as much pleased with his appointment as any Democratic appointment that could have been made." Upon his departure from the Hannibal newspaper market, the Clemenses wished him well and complimented him on his "courtesy, and uniformly manly course" which "procured him many friends among his opponents."[17]

Josiah Hinton held the *Courier* to the course of battling abolitionism. In January 1853 Hinton wrote that the idea of immediate emancipation was a "a great moral evil" and warned of the "baneful consequences that would follow the freeing of slaves in the United States."[18] In September 1853, he wrote:

> No call is ever successfully made upon an abolitionist for any legal or wise assistance to the black man. Apply to him for aid in purchasing the fugitive's freedom; he never gives it. Ask him to do something toward

16. *MC*, November 25, 1852.

17. M. M. Brashear, *Mark Twain, Son of Missouri*, 100; *HJ*, April 28, 1852, November 25, 1852.

18. *MC*, January 13, 1853.

sending our colored population to Liberia, where alone they can enjoy independence and happiness, and he will answer you with insult. What does he attempt toward instructing and improving and elevating the condition of the swarms of blacks around him here at the North? What do you find him doing in his assumed character of the black man's friend, except venting, from the public platform, dogmas of impossible application and he, steeped in bitterness; casting disorganizing votes at the polls, and violating the laws of the land concerning runaway slaves whenever he has an opportunity. His philanthropy goes just far enough to gratify his spite, and there stops short. He reasons just enough to curdle nature's milk of human kindness into intensest [sic] gall and then is content to judge and labor with the cold indignity of an evil spirit.[19]

Sam and Orion joined other editors in Marion County in ridiculing the abolitionists. They copied the following from the *Memphis Eagle and Enquirer,* claiming it was a true account of an incident that took place aboard a steamboat on the Hudson River.

Our Southern friend discovered a disposition in a very genteel looking man on board the boat to open a chat with him, and nothing loth [sic] to hear what his friend wished to say, indicated by his manner that he was approachable, whereupon the following dialogue ensued:

Yankee—"Well, sir, I wish to ask you a question; I hope it will be no offence."

Southerner—"Certainly not; I will listen with pleasure."

Y.—"Well, sir, is it true that they work negroes in the plough at the South?"

S.—"I will answer you in the favorite method of your countrymen—by asking you a question or two."

Y.—"I admit the right, sir."

S.—"How many negro fellows do you suppose it would require to draw a good large one-horse plough?"

Y.—"Well, I suppose six or seven—say seven."

S.—"Well, sir, and what are they worth per head?"

Y.—"Well, I suppose $800."

S.—"That would be $5,600. Now, what would one large strong horse cost?"

Y.—"I guess about $100."

Upon this the Southerner looked a little quizically at his neighbor, who, without waiting to hear the conclusion, stuttered and stammered:

"Well, I—I—I knew it was a d—d lie!"[20]

19. Ibid., September 29, 1853.
20. *HJ,* April 27, 1853.

At the same time, slave culture enjoyed poking fun at what was perceived as the stupidity of abolitionists. Harriet Beecher Stowe's book *Uncle Tom's Cabin* was hated in Hannibal. William League, who had worked under Joseph Ament with Sam, reprinted in his *Tri-Weekly Messenger* the story of an abolitionist living in Paris who had fallen under the spell of the book and had become a friend of the African.

Blackmanity.—The Paris correspondent of the Philadelphia Register gives us the following:

"A morning paper relates a funny little anecdote about an old man in Paris who lived very happily until Mrs. Stowe's novel put into his head all kinds of colored manias. The old man, rich as a Southern planter, had from that time but one fixed idea—to make a black man happy. Therefore he dismissed his white domestic, and went to the Intelligence Office to procure a black one. They gave him one as dark as Eerebus [*sic*]. The old man received him with the affability of an American Senator, and introduced him into his house rather on the footing of a friend than a servant. This state of things lasted a week, when the old man received an anonymous letter saying.

"Sir, you have in your service a dyed negro. Your servant is a white of the lowest species. You are the dupe of a pot of blacking." Indignant at this revelation, the old man conducted his man into a closet.

"Wretch," said he. "I know all. There is soap, water, and a towel; I give you an hour to wash yourself and pack up your clothes."

At the end of an hour he returned and found his man as black as ever. "What?" he cried, "you are not washed yet?" But I am black," returned the other; "I can't wash myself white." "I tell you, rascal, that I know all. Wash yourself."

At the end of two hours there was a new visit to the closet; the black was still black, and there were reasons for it which belonged to the cost [*sic*] of Guinea. Irritated by what he took to be obstancy [*sic*], the old man conducted his demestic [*sic*] to the commissary of police; the magistrate proved him fast color, his master took him back and redoubled his kindness toward him.[21]

Missouri had long cast a wary eye on Illinois, but there were many racists in the free state who could give the most ardent slaveholder a run for his money. In 1853, newly revised Illinois Black Laws prohibited free blacks from immigrating to Illinois and required any who did to be sold by the sheriff into servitude. The law essentially returned all Negroes to a

21. *TWM*, May 14, 1853.

form of slavery. Quincy was home to both passionate abolitionists and ardent supporters of slavery. The *Quincy Herald*, a Democratic paper, spoke for the latter group and could be as inflammatory as any paper in a slave state.

The *Herald* denounced the Underground Railroad consistently and argued that money contributed by abolitionists to aid runaways was wasted. The *Herald* stated that the same amount of money spent "stealing" slaves would have purchased twice the number and sent them "home to Africa."[22] The paper sought to reassure Illinois's slaveholding neighbors:

> An impression prevails among our neighbors on the other side of the river that there is a formidable organization in and near Quincy engaged in no higher and no better business than stealing away and running off their slaves. This impression is not founded in truth. The people of Quincy are above all such little business, nor do they in any way give countenance to the acts of others in any such behalf. Whenever the Negroes of our Missouri neighbors run off and they have any reason to believe they have come this way, they have never failed yet, and probably never will, to get abundant assistance among our citizens in hunting them up.[23]

Missouri editors frequently reprinted articles from the pages of the *Quincy Herald*. A venomous parody of an abolitionist's prayer was reprinted by the *Whig Messenger* in 1855. The *Herald* had first observed, "It is not to be presumed that an abolitionist prays very often or very long at a time":

> Within the last week we have had an abolition preacher in town, one Ichabod Codding who trampled the American flag under his feet.
>
> This is a prayer he supposedly delivered:
>
> "O, Lord, whatever is, is wrong. Thou hast established or permitted Slavery on earth, yea, even the Bible sanctions distinctions among men. Thou has permitted the strong to rule the weak, the intelligent to govern the ignorant. Thou has created big fishes and allowed them to eat up the smaller ones. Thou dost allow the lion and the tiger to feed on smaller animals, and the eagles and the hawks to devour little innocent birds. Also, thou hast sent death into the world, and suffereth little babes and the innocent young to die, and permitteth the old and sinful

22. *Quincy Herald*, quoted in *WM*, April 19, 1853.
23. *MC*, November 17, 1853.

to live to old age. O, Lord, Thou art a Master; Thou hast created fire, water, the whirlwind, and thunder and lightning, that destroyeth the great and the small. There is nothing good, nothing perfect on earth, (save us Abolitionists.) All is wrong—all imperfection—all evil—all confusion. O, Lord, wilt thou, by special providence, create all things over again, that all things may be made aright—that we may be pleased—that uniformity may be the order and genius of the world, that all may be equal, all be free; for none can be blest until all are equal; none can be happy until all are happy.

"O, Lord, aid us by thy power to agitate the abolition question, which is the great question of the day. Aid us to establish Abolition presses and underground Railroads without number, that the minds of men may, by such means, become excited to action—without action nothing can be accomplished—aid us then, O, Lord, in accomplishing the great and good work, although it may lead to revolution and the trampling under foot the flag of the country and the laws and Constitution of the land.— Let sudden and immediate emancipation take place, let the results be what they may—be it treason and the shedding of blood, let it be done, for the curse of Slavery is the cause of all the sin and evil in the world.

"O, Lord, we do not desire Thee to remember the sins that are against us, but we desire to draw thy special attention to the sins of the Slaveholders. We desire the sins of ourselves and others of like faith, put off until the final day, when all will be fully judged and awarded according to their merits; but, O, Lord, for our sake do not put off the punishment due to the Slaveholders—if their sins are not punished promptly they might escape thy remembrance altogether.

"In conclusion, wilt Thou hear our prayers, and as we are opposed to all distinctions, and to all rulers and Kings, and as thou art the greatest of all Kings, and far above us, wilt Thou,—for the sake of there being no distinctions,—make us equal to Thyself, in wisdom, in power, and in glory. These things we modestly ask for ourselves that we may have cause to praise Thee and honor Thy name—Amen."[24]

Orion Clemens reprinted an article that the *Quincy Whig* had copied from a paper in Charleston, Illinois. The *Whig*, while not as avidly proslavery as the *Herald*, was opposed to the settlement of free blacks in Illinois. Orion added his own commentary to the Illinois articles:

B. Bird, (colored) was found dead on the highway, east of town, a day or two ago. He had evidently been shot by some persons unknown. He was on a collecting tour, presenting bills, and securing produce. Bird had a large circle of relatives in this county.—[*Charleston Courier*]

24. *Quincy Herald*, quoted in *WM*, August 8, 1855.

And All over this State too. We noticed the arrival of many of the family [sic], last spring, at this point, where they have remained in spite of the "Stringent Black law," although they have been a nuisance to many localities [sic] in which they have settled.—[*Quincy Whig*]

A good many of the same family were "spotted" as dangerous characters in this part of our State, last year. Since then they have either learned to behave themselves better, or have concluded to remove to some other locality. If they have gone to Illinois, we assure our neighbors that no excitement need be apprehended on account of attempts by Missourians to arrest and bring back such "fugitives."[25]

The dangerous characters referred to were free Blacks.

The Price of Vigilance

Constant vigilance came at a cost. The wary eye cast on the stranger looked at the friend as well. As the 1850s progressed, the solid front of Missouri slavery began to crack. German immigrants fleeing the failed revolutions in Europe began arriving in St. Louis. They brought with them republican ideas. Tired of repression and militarism, they were eager to breathe the air of democracy. And while the native sons of slave culture saw nothing hypocritical in whipping a slave on the Fourth of July, the "peculiar institution" did not sit well with these new citizens.

A German newspaper, the *Anzeiger*, was founded in St. Louis and began openly questioning the institution of slavery.[26] The Germans organized clubs and societies. They debated and discussed all the political reforms and ideas that had been verboten in the repressive microstates they had fled. The good people of slave culture looked on in horror as these "Dutch" people moved in and began challenging a society that declared all men to be created equal yet accepted slavery.

Remembering the Glory of Thompson, Work, and Burr

Back in Marion County, the struggle between the forces of slavery and abolition intensified. In 1858, J. P. Rutter of Palmyra took pen in hand and composed a letter to the *Hannibal Southern Sentinel*.[27] In his letter he

25. *HJ*, July 13, 1853.
26. Ironically, Sam Clemens would later set type at the *Anzeiger*.
27. Rutter may have been related to Richard Rutter, Sam Clemens's fellow apprentice at *Missouri Courier*.

recounted the depredations of the abolitionists and painted a vivid picture of the impact runaway slaves and the abolitionists were having on Marion County.

[A]t different times, often repeated, have the slaves of our citizens been run off to Illinois, thro' the instigation of those pious thieves, who fancy they have a special mission from heaven to steal. Many slaves have succeeded with the assistance of their white conductors, in reaching Canada, where they are lost to their owners, and equally lost to themselves, lingering out a living death in penury and suffering—others have been pursued and captured, after reaching Illinois, and several, before they had reached the river. On some of them forged papers have been found, purporting to be from their masters or former masters, being passes, or what purported to be papers of emancipation—showing conclusively that there are, and have been persons residing amongst us, who are disposed to counsel and assist slaves to make their escape— perhaps under pay of the abolition societies, and sent here for that express purpose,—at other times, strangers under suspicious circumstances have been seen passing through the country, on some shallow pretext, such as professing to be hunting stray horses—or hunting work, etc., and who have, in several instances, been detected in tampering with slaves—some of the slaves giving information to that effect. . . .

This state of things has produced a high degree of insubordination in the Negroes of this county—they have become insolent and disobedient—no doubt from a feeling of independence, induced by a belief, that if chastised, they can effect their escape through the aid of abolitionists. The result is that they have become comparatively worthless, and are still becoming more and more so. Their owners from fear of their running off, are deterred or restrained from exercising as strict a control over them, as is necessary, either to their profit, or the good of the slaves themselves. This indulgence is not appreciated, or perhaps being attributed by them to the real cause, tends to encourage them in insubordination, and leads to further acts of rebellion.[28]

Rutter then recalled for his readers the entire story of Thompson, Work, and Burr. He told how they had approached the slaves, who had reported the men to their masters. He recounted how the slaves "with an intense ardor of affection" helped their masters capture the abolitionists. He wrote that though the abolitionists tried to persuade the slaves, "the devoted

28. *SS*, February 10, 1858.

affection of the African gentlemen appeared to increase in exact proportion to the waning of that of their Northern brethren." He recalled the twelve-year sentences and resolve of the people.

He took Thompson, Work, and Burr to task for breaking their word to the governor of Missouri, saying they had lied when they promised, upon being paroled, to return to private life. They had continued abolitionist activities. Rutter wrote, "by downright misrepresentations and perversion of facts" they demonstrate they did not deserve the clemency they received.[29] The story is nostalgic. The author longs for a simpler time—when men like John Marshall Clemens oversaw a neatly ordered world of slavery. Much had changed since 1841.

29. Ibid.

Chapter 17

Dehumanizing the Slave in the Press

you's a nigger!—bawn a nigger en a slave!—en you's a nigger en a slave dis minute

Mark Twain, *Pudd'nhead Wilson*

In addition to maintaining a constant defense against slavery's enemies, Missouri newspapers bolstered the institution from within. Just as Sam was exposed to dialect stories that mocked slaves' speech—from which he learned to write in dialect to the great enrichment of American literature—he was also familiar with a type of humorous story that reinforced racist stereotypes.

The psychological burden of treating slaves like animals necessitated a system that classified African Americans as subhuman. The Bible justification of slavery served this purpose and was complemented by other pseudoscientific theories on the nature of Africans. Then-popular racist theories held that people descended from Ham were physiologically adapted to the conditions of slavery. Stories illustrating these adaptations ran regularly in the newspapers. Some of the "inferior" attributes ascribed to Africans were, of course, conditions imposed on slaves by their masters. Cleanliness, for example, was considered to be the sole domain of European Americans. Lice and insects were considered natural to the African—rather than the result of his being deprived of clean living quarters, adequate clothing, and washing facilities. The following story illustrates the point. The passengers referred to are lice and other insects.

AX YOU A CIRCUMSTANCE.—"Pete, I want to ax you a circumstance?"
"Make a break, nigger."

"Why is a nigger's head like a U.S. omnibus? Does you guv him up up?"

"Wouldn't do nothing else."

"'Cause dey carry passengers outside."

"Mr. Nigger, dis will 'mortalize you."[1]

The "otherness" of African Americans was also reflected in references to their being "greasy." Sam or Orion Clemens wrote a description of a hot spell in 1853: "The weather is rather warm—ladies have commenced the usual amusements of the season, viz: fainting, fanning, slopping about in the mud, &c.,—fat lazy "niggers" begin to sweat and look greasy—chills no longer considered an affliction."[2] The characterization of "niggers" as fat and lazy was also common. Without the benefit of the master class's work ethic, they would surely perish, the reasoning went.

Some of the dehumanizing notions about people of African descent sound very peculiar to the modern ear, their purpose being solely to set the slave apart. One popular theory about people of African descent was that they had a very long heel:

"An', Cuff, will ye be afther tipping us a little bit of a song this cold mornin?" exclaimed a son of the Emerald Isle to a brother of the sable race, a co-laborer in the division and sub-division of wood.

"Golly, massa, I can't sing!"

"Can't sing! An' what's yer leg stuck in the middle of yer fut for, like a bird's, if ye can't sing!"[3]

Note the use of Irish dialect and the reference to the Irishman as a "co-laborer"—perhaps a reflection of the low standing of that immigrant group.

A more easily understood stereotype was the portrayal of African Americans as insensitive to pain.

A Darkie's Heel.—There is a capital anecdote of "Kentuck" in the "Spirit of the Times," illustrating the thickness and insensibility of a negro's heel. Ten or twelve colored pussons' were snoozing in one of their cabins with their feet to the fire, when one of them suddenly exclaimed: "I smell foot a-burnin!" Presently he added, anxiously, "Who foot dat a-burnin?" Receiving no answer, he reiterated the question with still

1. *PMW*, July 16, 1845.
2. *HJ*, May 23, 1853.
3. *PMW*, December 18, 1845.

more emphasis: "Who foot dat a-burnin' I say? Dat your'n Cuff?" Still no answer; when, drawing himself up he reached his hand toward his feet, and exclaimed: "My foot burnin', by Golly," and quietly stretched himself out to sleep again.[4]

As previous stories have shown, racist notions of the time also considered African Americans to be endowed with unusually thick skulls. A story in the *Palmyra Missouri Whig* said that a Negro in New Orleans had fallen from the top of a four-story house into the street. Jacob Sosey reported, "Happily he alighted on his head and sustained no injury."[5] Of course, the notion that African Americans did not experience pain in the same fashion as other human beings was used to justify their cruel treatment. A child who might question the beating of a slave could be told that it was okay because the slave did not feel pain "like us."

The Human Zoo

One aspect in the dehumanization of slaves was a fascination with physical oddities among African Americans. Like livestock breeders, slave owners closely examined their holdings. Particularly well built slaves could bring a premium on the market. The rare multiple birth rated a notice in the paper. The following was recorded by Joseph Ament after Sam had gone to work for his brother Orion: "A Negro woman belonging to Capt. John D. Moss, of Grand Pass, in Saline county, was delivered of three fine healthy children at a single birth. They are all boys, and are likely to live and do well."[6]

Beyond the general fascination with slave breeding, oddities and freaks of nature were a frequent topic of conversation. The science of genetics was unknown, and medicine was still very crude—the germ theory of disease had not yet been discovered—and the occurrence of birth defects and abnormalities fascinated people. Throughout Sam Clemens's youth he was exposed to these stories.

A SECOND ESAU.—We saw, the other day, a well formed male child, born of negro parents, covered completely with a coat of hair: the shoulders, back and extremities thickly covered; the head and forehead down

4. Ibid., May 6, 1847.
5. Ibid., April 20, 1844.
6. *MC*, April 15, 1852.

to the eyes, were covered with a long straight, black coat of hair. The child has since died.

More "Siamese" twins.
    Two negro children are exhibiting in Wilmington, who are a match for the Siamese twins. They are connected by the vertebra.[7]

Slave culture persisted in its fascination with unusual physical conditions among slaves. Sam may have set the following articles after he went to work for his brother.

CURIOSITIES.—Yesterday we were told by an old man named Tyler, living in S. Louis County, that he has in his possession a negro girl about six years old, whose body, legs and arms, are marked like a spotted horse. She is very black, with kinky hair, except where these spots are, some of which are very large. These spots present the appearance of healthy skin, but very fair—as much so as that of white persons of the fairest complexion. On her forehead is a white blaze, extending from between her eyebrows some distance under hair. All the hair on her head is very black except that which grows over this blaze, and that is in color like the whitest wool.
    It is a pretty hard story; but we don't like, unless we know the man better, to say right down that we don't believe it. He talks about exhibiting her.

ANOTHER.—A bystander stated that there is in Monroe County a white boy who has a black spot covering the back of his neck, extending half way down his back, and covering both shoulders.[8]

Interest in Negro oddities was not limited to Missouri. An Illinois newspaper responded to the story about the spotted Negro with an article about a similar man their editor had seen in St. Louis. Orion liked the article and reprinted it.

The Lewistown [Ill.] Republican copies our statements about two spotted negroes—one in St. Louis county and one in Monroe county, and adds:
    Now, Mr. Journal man, we don't know about the white wool! But last winter, in St. Louis, we saw a negro man, who up to his nineteenth year, was as "black as any nigger," after which time he began to turn white,

7. *HJ*, July 29, 1847; *MC*, July 1, 1852.
8. *HJ*, April 30, 1853.

in spots. His face and shoulder, are now almost white. He was raised in Kentucky. If the editor of the Journal will call at Dobyns & Spaulding's daguerean rooms, corner of Fourth and Olive streets, St. Louis, he can see a splendid miniature picture of the "animal," which if not as large as life, is "twice as natural."[9]

In a society where the dark color of African skin was taken as a sign of God's disapproval, people were very interested in slaves with white skin. Skin conditions that lightened an African American's complexion particularly fascinated the members of slave culture. One of the earliest preserved papers from Marion County, from the year the Clemens family arrived in Hannibal, contains the following story picked up from a New Orleans paper:

> A gentleman of our city owned or owns a negro woman in whom the process of absorption in the coloring matter which tinges the skin of the "African black," has been going on for several years.—The removal of the colouring matter is, however, imperfect and irregular; it takes place in patches, giving to portions of her arms and legs a pure white appearance, which contrast unnaturally and disagreeably with the jetty hue of the surrounding surface. We presume the slave in question will never become entirely white—but the case is spurious as being illustrative of the mode in which nature performs this singular freak—viz; by absorption of the black pigment from which the skin of the negro derives its color.[10]

The woman described appears to have suffered from vitiligo, an autoimmune disorder in which melanocytes, the pigment-producing cells, are destroyed by the immune cells. White patches of skin then appear on different parts of the body.

Eleven years later, Sam may have set the following story in Joseph Ament's *Courier*: "A White Negro.—The North Carolinian tells a story of a slave who has gradually become white. The change is supposed to have been caused by the bite of a rattle-snake which occurred some ten or a dozen years since. He was formerly as black as any African and now shows no sign of the negro except the kinks in his hair."[11]

The fascination with race and black skin was perhaps natural in a society in which one group of people exploited another on racial grounds.

9. Ibid., May 21, 1853.
10. *PMW*, November 2, 1839.
11. *MC*, February 14, 1850.

Racial equality was inconceivable to members of slave culture, and the slightest taint of African blood was like a curse. The writer Alexander Dumas was at the height of his popularity when the following was printed in Hannibal:

ALEXANDER DUMAS.—The annexed anecdote is from the May No. of Blackwood. It is well known that the celebrated romancer has a slight tinge of black in his blood:

A person more remarkable for inquisitiveness than for correct breeding—one of those who, devoid of delicacy and reckless of rebuff, pry into everything—took the liberty to question M. Dumas rather closely concerning his genealogical tree.

"You are a quadroon, Mr. Dumas," he began.

"I am, sir." Quietly replied Dumas, who has sense enough not to be ashamed of a descent he cannot conceal.

"And your father?"

"Was a mulatto."

"And your grandfather?"

"A negro," hastily answered the dramatist whose patience was wanting.

"And may I inquire who your great grandfather was?"

"An ape, sir," thundered Dumas, with fierceness that made his impertinent interrogator shrink into the smallest possible compass. "An ape, sir,—my pedigree commences where yours terminates."

The father of Alexander Dumas, the republican general of the same name, was a mulatto, born in St. Domingo, the son of a negress and of the white Marquis de la Pailleterie. By what legitimatizing process the sinister was erased, and the marquisate preserved, we have hitherto been unable to ascertain.[12]

The African ancestry of Dumas is characterized as "sinister," as was everything associated with Africans. Joseph Ament's attitude toward African Americans can clearly be discerned from this article.

The Negro Race.

Bayard Taylor, writing from Nubia, in Upper Egypt, says: Those friends of the African race, who point to Egypt as a proof of what that race has accomplished, are wholly mistaken. The only negro features represented in Egyptian sculpture, are those of slaves and captives taken in the Ethiopian wars of the Pharaohs. "The temples and pyramids throughout Nubia, as far as the Dafur and Abyssinia, all bear the

12. *HJ*, June 24, 1847.

hieroglyphy of the monarchs, and there is no evidence in all the valley of the Niles that the Negro race ever attained a higher degree of civilization than is at present exhibited in Congo and Ashantee. I mention this, not from any feeling hostile to that race, but simply to controvert an opinion very prevalent in some parts of the United States."[13]

In the slave culture of Hannibal, anything African was inferior. While a mulatto would be "elevated" by the white "blood" he possessed, a white person would be dragged down by breeding with African Americans. Amalgamation was one of the greatest fears of slave culture. The press effectively used this fear against the abolitionists. Whites socializing with blacks was considered disgusting.

Matters of Taste

The ultimate fear of slave culture was sexual relations between white women and black men. Real or imagined, stories of these relationships inspired horror within Hannibal slave culture. The myth of white superiority required absolute segregation in this delicate area. The following was probably set by Sam Clemens while he worked for Joseph Ament:

A Negro Man with a White Wife.
The Legislature of Connecticut recently divorced a young white woman from a big black negro man, with whom, while in a partial state of lunacy, she had been deluded into a marriage contract. On recovering her faculties she was horrified at her condition, and on application to the Legislature, a divorce was immediately granted. The Connecticut *Courant* describes the feeling among the people there as one of great indignation at the outrage.
Such disgusting amalgamation of races, it seems will not be tolerated-even in Connecticut, the hot-bed of Abolitionism. How, then, can it be expected that citizens of a slave State will sanction any thing of the kind in their midst?[14]

Orion Clemens published this next account in his *Hannibal Journal* in May, 1850. Though Sam was not working for his brother at the time, he undoubtedly read his brother's newspaper. Under the headline "Amalgamation" ran this story. "The *Cincinnati Dispatch* says there are in that city,

13. *MC*, May 6, 1852.
14. Ibid., August 1, 1850.

two really handsome white women living as wives with two darkies so black that a candle would go out within forty feet of their fathers. They belong to the "Free Soil Menegerie" [*sic*] of Messrs. Seward & Douglass."[15]

For years Jacob Sosey and his *Palmyra Missouri Whig* had been attacking the abolition movement by playing on white slaveholders' fear of intermarriage. He reported mixed marriages, and the movements to abolish state laws forbidding such unions, with comments upon the "taste" of the abolitionists and those who married across the color line.

Every One to her Taste.—A petition was lately presented in the Massachusetts Legislature, by Mr. Adams, of Boston, from Emeline Hollis, and 42 other females of Baintree, praying for the repeal of the law forbidding intermarriage between persons of different color.

Every one to their fancy.—We find the following singular advertisement in the New York Tribune:

Matrimony.—A white gentleman wishes to marry a *colored lady* of education, of religious principles, and who is willing to reside in a country where the accident of complexion will not debar her from the worship of God in any church or cathedral with the fairest of her sex, and where character, not color, is the passport to society. The advertiser is unacquainted with the colored ladies of this city; he therefore requests that any lady answering this advertisement will be candid and explicit in stating age, pecuniary circumstances, &c. The greatest honor may be relied on. Address Q.Z. Any white lady who detests slavery and is free from prejudice against color, who may please to answer, will be attended to.

Taste.—A young girl of New Haven, Con., recently ran away with a negro.[16]

Ament repeated the notion in the headline "A Matter of Taste" for the following article, which was probably set by Sam Clemens while he was at the *Missouri Courier.* "Two abolition editors contending about the amount of humility which they possess, the one boasts that he never passes a colored man without speaking to him; while the other claims precedence on the ground that he not only speaks to every negro that he meets, but he absolutely kissed a colored lady at a camp meeting!"[17]

15. *HJ*, May 9, 1850.
16. *PMW*, February 11, 1843, July 16, 1845, and February 19, 1846.
17. *MC*, July 25, 1850.

Ament again commented on "taste" in a story published a year after Clemens left the *Courier*.

Colored Lawyers
    The Boston *Commonwealth* says that Messrs. Morris and Allen, a couple of "young and talented colored members of the Suffolk bar," during the recent services in relation to Mr. Webster, in the United States Circuit Court in that city, occupied seats inside the arena appropriated to members of the bar, "in close proximity to such men as Judges Parsons, Warren and Rogers, and the Hon. Messrs. Winthrop, Choate and Loring, and a long train of other nobles in the law," and that said "gentlemen" were "regarded with as much deference as any in the assembly."
    Surely, "there's no accounting for tastes!"[18]

While it was perfectly permissible for white men to have sex with slave or free black women—as even Sam Clemens noted in his story about the apprentice who tormented Ament's slave girl—they could not marry African Americans. In Missouri it was illegal. White male/black female sex was an unspoken fact of life. The practice was so common that in 1860, 16 percent of Hannibal's slaves were identified as mulatto in the census. Marriage would have elevated the African American to a status equal to that of the white person and so could not be allowed. Therefore, the following, true or not, made for effective propaganda.

A Matrimonial Speculation.
    Mr. Lemuel Shane, lately made a journey out South for the purpose of improving his condition by an eligible match.—he met "a young lady of fortune" at a moonlight pic-nic—was introduced, proposed and was accepted. They were married the next evening by lamp light; Lemuel was the happiest of mortals, having received an assurance that his bride was the owner of forty slaves; but his felicity was a little dashed by the discovery he made next morning; for the lady, besides having three or four dozen niggers of her own, proved on examination by daylight to be at least sixty per cent nigger herself.[19]

Of course, some stereotypes are familiar to modern readers. African Americans were frequently portrayed in both fiction and nonfiction as thieves. A propensity to steal was considered a character trait of African Americans. The following story was written either by Orion or Sam

18. Ibid., November 18, 1852.
19. *HWGM*, October 27, 1852.

Clemens, who managed to portray the Negro as a scheming thief and, at the same time, attack abolitionists.

Cunn'ng Negro.—On Monday a small boy was going to Selmes' store with a $3 bill in his hand to get it changed, when he was accosted by an ebony son of Africa, who informed him that he was engaged in the exchange business, and would give him silver for the bill, and not charge any discount, if he (the lad) would go with him to a house up town. The boy, thinking it all right, gave the negro the bill and followed him to the house. The negro went in, but returned in a few moments, looking haggard and pale as a sheet, and told the boy he must wait awhile, as he had a child which had just died, and he must run immediately for somebody to help him bury the sweet innocent. The boy, thinking this a case of actual necessity, waited a long time, and then waited no longer! But hours rolled on, and he saw neither Cuffy nor the money. The lad then informed Marshall Dudding of the facts, and the negro was arrested and brought before Recorder Hold, and sentenced to receive ten lashes. This is one of the Free Soilers you read about, and we think Seward would find it a good speculation to get this colored member of the "higher law party," to act as his private secretary.[20]

Consistent with their father's thinking on the dangerous influence of free Negroes upon slaves, Orion or Sam also selected the following story from the *Louisville Courier* for publication in the *Western Union:*

By referring to our police report it will be seen that a couple of free negroes were on trial for robbing the store of A. Bacon, on Market street.

Since the examination, a more thorough investigation has been instituted, which resulted in the arrest of no less than thirteen negroes, several of whom are slaves. It appears that these fellows have been depredating upon the store for nearly two years, and about $2,000 worth of goods have been abstracted. False keys were made to the door and drawers, and the robberies were made at will. Goods were missed from time to time but it was impossible to detect the robbers, as the negro boys belonging to Mr. Bacon were concerned in the thefts, and knew all the movements of Mr. Bacon and his clerks.

The police yesterday found a large quantity of goods at several negro houses, including the house of a negro preacher by the name of Henderson, where was found upwards of $300 worth of fine goods. Henderson escaped detection. In his house was found the regalia and emblems of a secret society of which he was the leader. The free negroes are to be

20. *WU,* January 16, 1851.

tried before the Police Court this morning, when no doubt, further developments will be made.[21]

Of course, African Americans were expected to adhere to strict rules
in their dealings with whites. Disrespect by African Americans triggered
violent reactions by whites, which received the approval of local editors.

> A Spunk Lad.—A few days since as a beautiful and respectable lady was
> passing near the corner of Price and Fourth, she was grossly insulted by
> one of three colored men, a boy of about 15 or 16, an entire stranger to
> her, happening to hear the insulting words, at once undertook to avenge
> her wrong. Stepping into the street, he picked up several good sized
> stones, and hurled them at the negro's head so accurately as to put his
> best dodging abilities to full exercise. Not hitting with a stone, the boy
> determined to try another weapon, and drawing a good sized knife, was
> making rapidly toward his object, when he was arrested by the hand of
> an elderly man, to whom he seemed to yield a ready obedience. We love
> peace and good order, but it is impossible not to admire the spirit of such
> a youth.[22]

Another story in the *Hannibal Journal* told of a St. Charles, Missouri, Negro
who was not as lucky as the fellow in the story above. In November of the
same year there was no calming hand to stop the knife blade.

> The Republican of the 28th contains an account of a murder recently
> committed in St. Charles. It originated in the impudence of some ne-
> groes, who were standing upon the street talking. Mr. Culver came
> along, and asked what they were talking about.—One of the negroes
> replied *it is none of your business,* upon which Culver struck him with a
> bowie-knife, inflicting a mortal wound.—Mr. Lackland, the son of the
> owner of the negro, then came up, and a difficulty ensued between him
> and Culver, which resulted in Lackland's death.
>   Culver was committed to jail.[23]

In the first story, the *Journal* editor was barely able to control his admiration for the young man. In the other, he lay responsibility on the "impu-
dence" of the Negroes. Perhaps slave masters read these stories to slaves
as lessons about the consequences of "uppity" behavior.

21. Ibid., August 21, 1851.
22. *HJ*, August 12, 1847 (reprinted from the *Cincinnati Atlas*).
23. Ibid., November 4, 1847.

The world of slave culture divided sharply into white and black. This duality was represented in nearly every aspect of life. The two castes existed side by side. Consider for example the article written by one of the Clemens boys in July 1851 when the radical new Bloomer style arrived in town. Invented by the early feminist Amelia Jenkins Bloomer to free women from skirts, a pair of Bloomers consisted of a short skirt and loose trousers gathered at the ankles. They were controversial attire.

THE NEW COSTUME.

It had been previously heralded that Miss Jemima would appear in the new costume, and accordingly, as if to fulfill the prophecy, Miss Jemima did make her appearance, last Sunday, at precisely five minutes and three-quarters past 3 o'clock, P.M.

On the landing of the Bon Accord, she attracted the special attention of everybody on board; particularly the pilot, who became so abstracted as to run the bow of his boat on a raft, and nearly put out the eyes of the passengers by the abrupt introduction on the middle deck of an overhanging tree top.

The pilot of the Wyoming, still more infatuated, actually attempted to steer his boat up the hill, and was only brought to recollection by being thrown on his back by the shock, when the boat ran square into the bank.

The negroes took this innovation upon the established fashions of their woolly headed ancestors, in extreme dudgeon. We noticed about a dozen colored women in full chase after the wonderful dress. Some of them, affected with an overplus of modesty, hid their blushes behind their white cambric handkerchiefs. Higgins (everybody knows HIGGINS,) plied his single leg with amazing industry and perseverance, keeping up a running fire of comment not calculated to initiate him in the good graces of the person addressed. When the leg became tired, its owner would seat himself and recover a little breath, after which, the indomitable leg would drag off the persevering Higgins at an accelerated pace. John (the drayman) was coming up street, the dress was going down street. When John beheld the latter, he brought himself up against an awning post, and opened his eyes very wide. When the apparition had approached within a few steps, John made a sudden detour into the middle of the street, and fairly cut the fair Jemima's acquaintance.

Seriously, there was not so much ridicule of the style of dress from the white lookers on, as might have been expected. All thought there should be a reform, but most persons were in favor of a compromise between the extreme fashions. The question of dress, however, is one which the ladies alone are competent to settle themselves. Whatever course they may take, will, in time, if not immediately, be considered the most sensible and the most appropriate. The notion that all should wear identically the same style, is becoming unsettled, old as that notion is, and firmly fixed as it has been. We name the Home Journal, the Louisville Journal, and the Quincy Whig, among papers advocating the reasonable doctrine that each individual should wear that form of dress which best becomes him or her.

We understand that several young ladies have dresses at home, made in the new style; have appeared in their parlors in them, and have even ventured on an evening visit so attired.

The Canton Reporter says that several ladies of Canton intend soon to don the Bloomer costume.[24]

The different reactions of blacks and whites are interesting. The man Higgins mentioned in the article is a one-legged mulatto. When Sam was younger, Higgins was one of his playmates.

Although the two castes occupied common physical ground in Hannibal, any deviation from the neat hierarchical relationship was considered threatening. Thus, when Dartmouth College announced that it would begin admitting students without distinction to color, the story was reported in Marion County with the familiar lead, "Every one to his Taste." When a judge in Toronto, Canada, ruled that he had no authority to remove a Negro from the jury, "the white portion of the jury became highly indignant at the association, and presented a protest to the Judge, demanding the darkey's dismissal." Joseph Ament reported in the *Missouri Courier* that "the jury were compelled to endure the fragrant companionship of the black—a just punishment to them for the mock sympathy and protection they give the 'poor enslaved negro.' "[25]

A Strong Liking for the Race?

The other side of the demeaning representations of African Americans was a genuine affection for African Americans, slave songs, and the white imitations they fostered. Later in life, Sam Clemens would fondly recall minstrel shows and slave songs. He became a great fan of the Fisk Jubilee Singers. Speaking of the American Negro, Clemens would proclaim in his old age to have possessed a lifelong "strong liking for his race."[26]

24. *WU*, July 10, 1851.
25. *PMW*, November 27, 1845; *MC*, June 12, 1851.
26. Neider, *Autobiography of Mark Twain*, 6.

Clemens expressed one of the great ironies of slave culture. Whites were attracted yet repulsed by the slaves' own culture. His former employer, Joseph Ament, wrote a story in 1852 on the feelings of many slaveholding whites about the uniquely American slave music.

Negro Minstrelsy.

We confess to a fondness for negro minstrelsy. There is something in the plaintive wail of "Dearest May"—in the affectionate remembrance of "Lucy Neal,"—and in the melodious moaning of "Uncle Ned," that goes directly to the heart, and makes Italian trills seem tame. It is like Ossian's music of memory "pleasant and mournful to the soul." "Dearest May" has become classic—a sort of Venus Africanus, with

"Her eyes so bright they shine at night
When the moon has gone away."

And "poor Lucy Neal," the Heloise of darkies, her very name has become the synonym of pathos, poetry and love.—The whole world is redolent of the sweet and plaintive air in which her charms are chanted; and the beauty of her sining form often comes over us like a pleasant shadow from an angel's wing.

"Oh, if I had her by my side
How happy I would feel."

And as for poor "Uncle Ned," so sadly denuded of his wool, God bless that fine old colored gentleman, who we have been so often assured, has

"Gone where the good niggers go."[27]

Ament does not comment on why people who could feel such fondness for this music could be so cruel to the people who originated it. It was an unexamined contradiction of slave culture. Another contradiction with which Hannibal had to contend was runaway slaves. It did so through another device—the loyal slave.

The Loyal Slave

While the slave culture of Sam Clemens's youth believed that slavery was ordained by God and the natural condition of the African American, people apparently also needed to believe that their slaves were contented and loyal. Therefore, they treated themselves to a constant stream of stories about loyal, hardworking slaves. While they perceived their world as

27. *MC*, May 13, 1852.

being threatened and nearly surrounded by abolitionists, they took comfort in the support of their slaves. The good slave knew and enjoyed his place in the structure of society. In appreciation for food and shelter, he provided his master with hard work and loyalty. Like a faithful dog, the good slave would selflessly serve his white superiors.

Affecting Incident—A Master's Life Saved by his Slave

On Sunday last, Mr. G. McCann, while crossing the Mississippi river alone in a canoe, from Battle Island to his plantation, whither he had been on a visit to his friend and neighbor on the island. Ben Hardin, Esq., was upset in the middle of the river; he clung to the canoe until he had floated opposite to the wood-yard on his farm, when his cries attracted the mention of one of his negro men; the boy immediately put off in a skiff, to the rescue of his master; before the negro arrived, Mr. McCann had become exhausted, and sunk. The faithful negro succeed[ed], however, at the imminent peril of his own life, in reaching his master, which he did by seizing him by the hair, and took him in the skiff. Mr. McCann was in an insensible state, and life was nearly extinct. By the assiduous attentions of the servant, and the application of such restoratives as were at hand, he was restored to consciousness. On Wednesday, when the John Simonds passed his plantation, he was slowly recovering. This is another fact to illustrate the truth of history touching the social and moral condition of the master and slave.[28]

The Clemens brothers published this homage to an old, hardworking, crippled black man:

This morning we noticed a black man fifty or sixty years old on his knees grubbing up a garden. "Old Jack" as he is called, is crippled, but is independent enough to labor to the best of his ability for a support. His conduct in this respect will bear favorable comparison with that of some "mean white folks" in town, who drink up all they earn, beat their wives, and send their children out to beg. Yet these men are healthy and strong, and in the prime of life.

Look at "Old Jack," you rascals, and imitate his better example.[29]

Constantly challenging the notion of the contented and loyal slave was the runaway. Slave culture responded with countless stories of loyal slaves who returned to slavery after experiencing the rigors of life in

28. Ibid., March 17, 1853 (reprinted from the *Republican*).
29. *HJ*, April 7, 1853.

hiding in a free state or in the unknowns of Canada. Invariably, return-ing runaways were portrayed as having been duped by the abolitionists. While these stories may have been read to slaves as moral lessons, they were ultimately ineffective. Missourians were no doubt frustrated that while slaveholders in other states were enjoying a decline in runaways from 1850 to 1860, they were experiencing an increase in the number of slaves escaping. Those slaves, unlike the Hannibal slaves in the following story, were not anxious to return.

RUNAWAY COME BACK.
Mr. Thos. K. Collins, one of our citizens, says the Hannibal Journal of the 3d instant, returned home on Wednesday from Canada, bringing with him his servant David, who ran off last fall or winter. The boy had been but a short time in Canada, when he found that he had gained nothing by running off. He found that he had to work harder than at home, and only got the *Promise* of five or six dollars per month—less than he could earn here for "pocket money," and then had great trou-ble by sueing, &c., to get what he earned. The snow, too, and cold of that bleak northern climate, appalled him, and made him wish himself at home, where there was sun enough to grow tobacco. He wrote re-peatedly to his master to come for him, promising most solemnly, if he would just bring him back, to be one of the most faithful servants living in future. Mr. C. at last took pity on him and brought him home.

David says that Capt. Barnett's man, Charles, and several others be-longing to Messrs. Glascock, Garrard, Beebe, Rackliffe, and others, are at or near where he was, and are all anxious to return. In fact they would return in spite of the efforts of the abolitionists to detain them, if they had the assurance that their masters would not "send them down the river."[30]

It appears that the actual number of Hannibal slaves who did return willingly was small. To fill the gap and perpetuate the illusion that slaves wished to remain in slavery, stories from other parts of Missouri and the nation were printed. Sam Clemens probably set the following story for Joseph Ament at the *Missouri Courier.*

NEGRO WOMAN FOUND.—Some three years since the family of Mr. W. I. Stratton of this place, was on a visit to Virginia, and while at Cincin-nati, on their way a negro girl mysteriously disappeared, and no trace of her was ever discovered until within a few weeks past. Mr. S. Learned

30. *PMW*, November 11, 1843.

she was in Cincinnati, to which place he went, succeeded in getting the negro; and returned home with her Monday evening.—The girl states she was pursuaded [sic] from her mistress by a whiteman [sic], and has been in Cincinnati, and immediate vicinity ever since. She was gotten possession of by stratagem, but appeared anxious and willing to come home.[31]

One cannot help wondering if the story the Negro girl told the Strattons was true or was some maneuvering on her part to avoid punishment. If she was the "victim" of a kidnapping, the girl could not be guilty of running away. By telling her masters this story, she might have hoped to avoid being whipped or sold in punishment. Many of the stories emphasized that the abolitionist was no friend of the slave, but an enemy. Whether they were intended for the instruction of whites or slaves, the message was the same, as is illustrated by the following story.

A negro man belonging to Mr. John H. Gay of this city [St. Louis], left his master in August last, and nothing was heard from him until yesterday, when to the surprise of Mr. Gay, he returned home. The negro states that the man who decoyed him off, promised to take him to Buffalo. But having taken him as far as Scott county, in Illinois, he left him at the house of an abolitionist, promising to return in a few days and proceed with him. The negro being dissatisfied with the perfidy of the man, and from other causes, concluded, like the prodigal son, to return. He started for home, but being overtaken by a snow storm—having but indifferent shoes and being thinly clad—he was not able to prosecute his journey. He stopped at the house of an acquaintance of Mr. Gay, who kindly consented to return him to his master. Mr. Gay presented the man with the very generous sum of one hundred dollars. The negro is now perfectly satisfied with the abolitionists.[32]

Likewise, the stories of loyal slaves returning to their masters were used to demonstrate that the courts of free states and free Negroes were no friends of the slave. "A telegraphic despatch [sic] from Albany, published in the New York Herald, says: 'A planter arrived here from New Orleans last evening, with 2 slaves who were arrested & brought before a Judge of the County Court. The court set them at liberty, and told them that they were free. They escaped from the colored mob, and returned to their master, who left for New York this evening.' "[33]

31. *MC*, November 15, 1849 (reprinted from the *Glasgow [Mo.] Banner*).
32. *HG* (reprinted from the *American*).
33. *HJ*, June 24, 1847.

When the California gold rush lured men to the West Coast, many took along slaves. In the fields of California, masters and slaves became separated. A common story of the early 1850s was of the return of the loyal slave. Often in these stories, the slave returned with a bulging bag of gold.

Who does not remember Capt. Bondurant's faithful old slave Peter, of Saline county [Missouri]? Well, Peter was dreadfully smitten with the California fever some two or three years ago, and his master outfitted him "for the golden country" on shares, sending him in company with a former overseer. Along the way Peter had a falling out with the overseer, and they separated. The abolitionists next got into Peter's good graces, and took care of him while his money and health lasted in the mines.—He was finally glad to fall in with Kentuckians and Missourians, who gave him a home welcome, and a chance to make something by his industry.

To make the story short, old Peter has arrived back in Saline again, "of his own accord," safe and sound, bringing for his master and himself a "right smart pile." His experience among the abolitionists has led him to prefer southern servitude to northern sympathy; his best friends he has found to be those who were legally so.[34]

We cannot know, of course, whether the stories of returning slaves were true. Life in California or Canada for uneducated and unskilled people would have been rough. Some slaves may have been lonesome for family and friends. Some may have preferred slavery to the ordeal of the cold winters of Canada or upstate New York—common destinations of runaways. The fact is that increasing numbers of slaves ran away as the 1850s progressed. Regardless of the truth, there is no doubting the propaganda value of the items. In some instances, the articles themselves were addressed directly to the abolitionists, as is the following piece from spring of 1853 printed in Joseph Ament's *Missouri Courier.*

AN ITEM FOR MRS. STOWE.—We noticed several weeks ago that a slave of Mr. Clarkson, of Charleston, Virginia, had been allowed to pay a visit here, but taking advantage of his master's confidence in his fidelity, put for Canada, where his wife and children escaped. A few days ago his master received a letter from him, dated at Detroit, in which he complains that he can't find his family, and the people don't suit his taste; *he's sick* of liberty and starvation. He says people there think more of a cent than he did, when in Virginia, of a dollar. He is anxious to

34. *MC,* July 8, 1852 (reprinted from the *Brunswick [Mo.] Brunswicker*).

return to Kanawha, but his money is gone—he asks his master to send him money. Mr. Clarkson will do so, and in a few weeks we may expect Simon to be regularly reinstalled in his barber-shop, where he will shave much better than ever, and *cuss* the Abolitionists to his colored brethren most heartily.[35]

35. Ibid., October 13, 1853 (reprinted from the *Brunswick [Mo.] Brunswicker*).

Chapter 18

The Slave Trade in Hannibal

I have no recollection of ever seeing a slave auction in that town;
but I am suspicious that that is because the thing was a common
and commonplace spectacle, not an uncommon and impressive
one.

The Autobiography of Mark Twain

In his position as apprentice at the *Missouri Courier,* and later as assistant at the *Hannibal Journal,* Sam Clemens was ideally situated to monitor the economics of slavery. Between 1848 and the summer of 1853, Sam set type for sale advertisements and auction announcements. The prices of slaves were closely watched. However, Clemens was not a very good chronicler of slave sales in Hannibal. The explanation for this is easy: The very ordinariness of slavery in the Hannibal of his youth made it difficult for the old Mark Twain to recall. As one northern observer noted, "[T]he planters used to bring in their niggers to sell same as we would up North bring horses or cattle into town for sale."[1]

The memories of Sam Clemens are like the ambiguous prophecies of the oracle of Delphi—subject to interpretation. Slave auctions were rare in Hannibal, but the slave trade flourished nonetheless. The modern mind, like Sam's, has been conditioned—from the woodcut illustrations of abolitionist literature to the familiar scenes of Hollywood television and films, we have been bombarded with visions of slaves standing on boxes or stumps, leered at by anxious buyers while fast-talking auctioneers sell them. The slave auction block has become a cultural icon. But slaves

1. "Memoir of Franklin Harriman."

changed hands in several other ways, including private sales to commercial brokers or individuals and being hired out for a period of time.

Commercial Slave Buyers

Hannibal was part of a large and thriving national slave-trading network. Riverboats frequently left the city and headed south with groups of slaves chained together on their decks. While Sam Clemens was working at the newspapers, the area was a net exporter of slaves.[2] Key members of this local slave trade were the professional slave traders.

Slave-owning members of Hannibal and Marion County society could easily convert their valuable human property into cash through several slave merchants in Hannibal and Palmyra during the time Sam Clemens was growing up. The biggest advantage to sellers in dealing with professionals was that dealers paid cash. Buyers at auction usually put down half the purchase price and paid the balance over time. This exposed the seller to the risk of nonpayment. Dealers purchased slaves outright—singly or by the lot—and shipped them to the larger slave markets in St. Louis, Memphis, and New Orleans.

The earliest surviving Hannibal newspapers carry advertisements from nine local slave dealers and one St. Louis dealer wishing to buy. They were probably only a portion of those involved in the trade. A study of slave dealers in South Carolina found that fewer than one in three advertised in a newspaper. How many slave dealers operated in Hannibal and relied on word of mouth or circulars for advertising will never be known. The partnership of Blakey and McAfee ran weekly advertisements throughout 1848 and 1849. Though their office was in Palmyra, they maintained associations with local men, first two named Shoot and Orr, and after April 1848, "Mr. Gridley Pratte, at the Brady House, Hannibal."[3]

In 1850, Joseph Dudding began advertising in the *Missouri Courier* while Sam Clemens was working there as an apprentice:

50 Negroes wanted.
The subscriber will at all times pay the highest prices in CASH for likely negroes. He may at all times be found in the City of Hannibal.
                    JOSEPH DUDDING[4]

2. Tadman, *Speculators and Slaves*, 7.
3. Ibid., 34; *MC*, April 13, 1848.
4. *MC*, December 12, 1850.

Francis Davis was another slave dealer in Hannibal. He began advertising in the newspapers on August 14, 1851. Davis had a horse stable in partnership with William Shoot near the river on the north side of Hannibal. He first advertised in the newspaper of Orion Clemens while Sam was working there. His advertisement stated:

> Cash for Negroes!
> I TAKE this method of informing the people that I am prepared at all times to pay the highest cash prices for NEGROES, and can at all times be found at the stable of Shoot and Davis.
>   FRANCIS DAVIS.[5]

The slave market appears to have heated up in 1852. Thomas D. Reed joined those seeking slaves through the newspapers that year. Reed began advertising in August in the *Weekly Messenger:*

> Negroes Wanted!
> T H O M A S D. R E E D
> (Of the late firm of Reed & Rutherford,)
> will continue to purchase Negroes, always paying the highest cash price. He can be found in the city of Hannibal.[6]

Reed and Rutherford had been in business some time before August and had apparently not relied on advertising in the newspapers, but once on his own Reed ran a separate advertisement announcing the breakup of the partnership and also began to solicit business.

The firm of Blakey and McAffee also split in 1852, and Granville Blakey began advertising individually for slaves. However by the summer of 1852, Blakey had stopped using a local agent and was advising Hannibal sellers, "Letters addressed to me at Palmyra giving a description of negroes offered for sale will receive attention."[7] William Perry Owsley entered the market and began running ads in September.

> W A N T E D !
> Twenty-five or Thirty young Negros for which the highest prices in cash will be paid, apply to W. P. Owsley.[8]

5. *HJU*, October 19, 1851.
6. *HWM*, September 15, 1852.
7. *MC*, June 10, 1852.
8. *HWM*, September 15, 1852.

Owsley played a very important role in Sam Clemens's life and was the inspiration for a character in *Adventures of Huckleberry Finn*. In 1845, Owsley shot and killed Sam Smarr at the corner of Hill and Main Streets just a few yards from the Clemens's house. Smarr was carried into Grant's Drug Store and laid on the floor. Sam Clemens joined the small crowd in the drugstore who watched Smarr die.

Smarr believed that Owsley had stolen money from a friend and had been loudly and publicly denouncing Owsley on the streets of Hannibal for weeks. At a time when a man's reputation was taken very seriously, Smarr's behavior was risky. Finally, Owsley reached his limit, and encountering Smarr on the street, he pulled a pistol and shot him down in cold blood. Owsley was arrested and tried for murder, but with Samuel T. Glover as his attorney he received an acquittal. Glover convinced the jury that Smarr had provoked Owsley. Sam Clemens used Owsley and the killing as the basis for Colonel Sherburn and the murder of old Boggs. However, Clemens never referred to Owsley's slave trading.

Another memoir records the practices of slave dealer Owsley. It provides some insight into the commercial slave trade in Hannibal. Franklin Harriman was a young man from Michigan who was on his way to Pike's Peak to prospect for gold. He stopped in Hannibal in the spring of 1859 and found work in the livery stable of Jourdan and Fuqua. Years later he recorded his recollection of prewar Hannibal.

> While working in Hannibal, Jourdan & Fuquays [Fuqua] Livery Barn was the headquarters for the slave trade in that city. The principal operator [or buyer] was a man by the name of Owsley. He used to sit around the office and always had an unlited cigar in his mouth and the planters used to bring in their niggers to sell same as we would up North bring horses or cattle into town for sale. Old Owsley would look them over and examine them & generaly [sic] bought for I don't recalled that he had much if any opposition. The calliboos [jail] was on the levie only a ½ block from the barn & when he bot [sic] a nigger, he put him in the calliboos and kept them there ntil [sic] he got from 6 to 8 or ten, then he would put handcuffs on them or chain them together and put them on board a boat going south & go down to some southern state and dispose of them & would soon be seen out in front of the barn waiting for more niggers which were sure to come in.[9]

Unlike Sam Clemens, who was accustomed to slavery and the brutality it required, Harriman was from a free state. He blanched at the treatment

9. "Memoir of Franklin Harriman."

of slaves in Owsley's hands. "It was a very hard thing for me to do to stand and see such work goin on and not dare to say a word. Although sometimes I felt like trying to help the poor things to their liberty, but it would likely have been sure death to me if I undertook it as the feeling at the time was very bitter against a northern man that would let a word drop against the slave trade."

Business must have been substantial to maintain so many commercial buyers in a town of fewer than six thousand souls in the 1860 census.[10] Of course, being on the Mississippi, the only means of north-south transport in antebellum Missouri, buyers could expect sellers from nearby counties as well as those from farther west.

The slaves were held in the jail until their number warranted transporting them south. When it came time to move them, the slaves were chained together in a coffle and moved as a group. It was such a coffle that Clemens recalled in his autobiography, "I vividly remember seeing a dozen black men and women chained to one another, once, and lying in a group on the pavement, awaiting shipment to the Southern slave market. Those were the saddest faces I have ever seen." Clemens tried to minimize the numbers of slaves transported in this fashion. He wrote, "Chained slaves could not have been a common sight or this picture would not have made so strong and lasting an impression upon me." However, other observers recorded sighting groups of slaves being transported. William Wells Brown, a slave working for a dealer, recalled, "[A] few weeks after, on our downward passage, the boat took on board, at Hannibal, a drove of slaves, bound for the New Orleans market. They numbered from fifty to sixty, consisting of men and women from eighteen to forty years of age. A drove of slaves on a southern steamboat, bound for the cotton or sugar regions, is an occurrence so common, that no one, not even the passengers, appear to notice it, though they clank their chains at every step."[11]

In 1853, a change took place in the Hannibal slave market. Owsley began selling slaves as well. He advertised a Negro woman and child for sale that April. Thomas D. Reed began advertising in June 1853 in Orion Clemens's paper: "He will always keep on hand a lot of Negroes which he will sell on accommodating terms."[12] It appears that Reed ran the only "yard" where slaves could be purchased in Marion County. If others existed, they have left no evidence behind. The sales by Reed were evidently

10. *HDM*, December 22, 1860.

11. Neider, *Autobiography of Mark Twain*, 30; Brown, *Narrative of William W. Brown*, 32.

12. *HDJ*, July 26, 1853.

one-on-one transactions with buyers. There is no record of Reed having conducted auctions at the stables. Auctions in Hannibal generally fell into three categories: estate auctions, sales of people moving on to different parts of the country, and court-ordered sales.

Prospects were bright enough in 1856 that a St. Louis dealer began advertising in Hannibal papers to both buy and sell slaves. Corbin Thompson claimed that he "had a good and safe yard to board and keep negroes" and would buy and sell on commission as low as any other dealer in St. Louis.[13] Thompson continued to advertise through 1859. It appears he did not use an agent in town but required buyers to come to him in St. Louis.

The Status of the Slave Trader

Sam Clemens and others have written that slave trading was not considered a respectable business. Clemens said, "The 'nigger trader' was loathed by everybody. He was regarded as a sort of human devil who bought and conveyed poor helpless creatures to hell—for to our whites and blacks alike the Southern plantation was simply hell; no milder name could describe it. If the threat to sell an incorrigible slave 'down the river' would not reform him, nothing would—his case was past cure."[14] However, here, as in other aspects of slave culture, society's vision of itself was at odds with reality. Respectable people gladly sold slaves. Just as John Marshall Clemens sold slaves when he needed money, other members of slave culture treated their slaves as they would any other investment or commodity. The slave trader was an important and accepted part of slave culture. Slaves' value to their owners came from the price they could bring at sale or lease.

Slaveholders took comfort from myths and religion that allowed them to view themselves as benign parents exercising a God-given duty to their childlike slaves—but the reality was often frighteningly different. A study of slave marriages in Boone County, Missouri, between 1830 and 1864 found that twenty-seven of thirty-four marriages were ended by sale.[15] The story of the sale of the Clemens's slave, Jennie, is another example.

John Marshall Clemens sold Jennie to businessman William B. Beebe in late 1842 or early 1843. Sam Clemens recalled that Beebe was a slave dealer. He may have been, but there is no evidence to support this claim. It

13. *HDM*, September 11, 1856.
14. Neider, *Autobiography of Mark Twain*, 30.
15. R. Douglas Hurt, *Agriculture and Slavery in Missouri's Little Dixie*, 232.

is impossible to estimate the number of people like John Marshall Clemens who engaged in occasional slave trading or who did not advertise or leave other records of their business.

Jennie was undoubtedly sold because the family needed money, and she was their one liquid asset. She may have been sold by creditors on an order of a court along with other property of the Clemens family. However, it is interesting to note what Sam Clemens believed about the sale of Jennie: he left notes in his personal papers indicating that Jennie was responsible for her own sale. Clemens wrote: "Had but one slave—she wanted to be sold to Beebe, and was. He sold her down the river. Was seen, years later, ch[ambermaid] on a steamboat. Cried and Lamented." He also wrote that "she pleaded hard—for that man had been beguiling her with all sorts of fine and alluring promises—and my mother yielded, and also persuaded my father." Of course, Clemens is writing about an event that occurred when he was seven years old. The Clemens children were very fond of Jennie. It was, Clemens wrote, "a sore trial, for the woman was almost like one of the family."[16]

It is highly unlikely that Jennie engineered her own sale. More likely that was a comforting story parents would tell children to keep them from being upset. "We don't want to sell her, but she insists," would have made home life easier for John Marshall and Jane Clemens. As Sam Clemens properly noted, being sold downriver was the terror of slaves—they were constantly told that to be sold downriver was a terrible fate. The threat was used by whites to manipulate slaves in Missouri. Whether slavery was actually any worse in Mississippi or Louisiana than it was in Missouri is impossible to determine—and is offensive to debate. People were routinely raped, beaten, separated from family, and subjected to daily dehumanizing treatment throughout the slave states. Perhaps working in the fields on a cotton or sugarcane plantation was more taxing—perhaps not. There is more than a little sexism behind the notion that "domestic slavery" was easier. The house slave was the first up, the last to bed. The slave was often the only person of color in the household. How is loneliness quantified? The slave in the household worked all his or her waking hours, and the work was very hard. A remnant of slave culture among whites in northeast Missouri is the use of the term *nigger work* to describe any hard, dirty, labor-intensive activity. Finally, the domestic slave was very vulnerable to sexual attack from members of the household.

The threat of sale "downriver" was maintained by slaveholders and

16. Armon, *Huck Finn and Tom Sawyer among the Indians*, 104; Wecter, *Sam Clemens of Hannibal*, 72.

evidently whites as well as blacks believed that the only thing worse than death to a slave was being sold downriver. Sam Clemens obviously believed it. It is unlikely that Jennie would have brought this on herself. It also seems very unlikely Beebe would have had the opportunity to talk to Jennie without the consent of John Marshall Clemens. The more plausible version is that, despite the feelings of the Clemens children, Jennie was just another piece of property at a time when the family was flat broke. The story has all the trappings of a comforting lie slaveholders told themselves about slavery.

Another root of the story may lie in the falling-out between John Marshall Clemens and Beebe. Clemens had sued Beebe and won a judgment against him in 1844. It was on that occasion that John Marshall Clemens had a nine-year-old slave girl seized and sold at public auction to satisfy the debt. How easy to blame Beebe and Jennie when the children would ask Jane Clemens "whatever happened to Jennie?" It is also possible that when Sam Clemens reflects upon the disrespect the community had for slave traders, he is unconsciously expressing his disgust for his father and his slave-trading activities. Sam recalled his father participating in another bit of slave trading on the unsuccessful 1842 downriver trip. John Marshall attempted to sell Charley in New Orleans, where he was offered fifty dollars, and again in Natchez where he was offered forty dollars. He ultimately ended up trading Charley for ten barrels of tar. Some scholars, reading a letter from John Marshall Clemens dated January 5, 1842, have suggested that Charley was a horse.[17] However, Sam recalled the incident involving the sale of a man.

Auctions

Slave auctions did take place in Marion County, and Sam Clemens is correct when he recalls there were few of them in Hannibal. Of the 137 county auctions advertised in surviving newspapers between 1839 and

17. Armon, *Huck Finn and Tom Sawyer among the Indians*, 277–78. The editors base much of their argument upon the low amounts of money offered for Charley. However, if Charley was an aged slave, he might have had some residual value in the southern slave markets—but none in Missouri. In fact, unscrupulous slave owners frequently set old slaves free rather than care for them. In the Mark Twain Boyhood Home's collection is just such a manumission paper for an old, sick slave. If, as the editors argue, Charley was a horse, that raises the question of why John Marshall Clemens would have attempted to sell him in New Orleans and Natchez if he had brought him along to ride in Tennessee.

1861, only three were held in Hannibal while Sam Clemens lived there: one in 1842, one in 1847 and one in 1851. The reason for this scarcity of auctions in Hannibal is simple—the custom and practice in northeast Missouri was to hold the sale at the courthouse in the county seat. This was true for both court-ordered and private sales. In Marion County the vast majority of slave auctions were held at the county courthouse in Palmyra.

In the years between the death of John Marshall Clemens and Sam Clemens's leaving home, the number of slave auctions in Marion County varied greatly. In 1847, eight auctions were advertised. In 1848, there were ten, and in 1849, there were twelve. But there were only eight in 1850, four in 1851, and none in 1852. There were two in 1853, the year Clemens left Hannibal to go to New York and Philadelphia. The drop reflects the development of the southern slave market and sales to slave dealers. The following year saw the peak of slave auctions in the county with eighteen advertised.

The most common type of slave auction was the estate sale. The death of a master frequently resulted in a sale. Of the 137 auctions for which advertisements survive in Marion County newspapers between 1839 and 1861, there were 57 estate sales with slaves. Almost all of these sales were held at the courthouse door. One auction, perhaps to take advantage of the large crowd of people attending, was held at the fairgrounds during the county fair of 1858. Other than the unusual location, the advertisement is typical of those for estate auctions.

> For sale—A Likely Negro Girl
> BY VIRTUE of an order of the County Court of Marion county, Mo., to me directed as administrator of the estate of W.R. Burch, dec'd, I will sell at public sale at the Fair Grounds, near Palmyra on Friday the 15th day of October, 1858, at 1 o'clock of that day a likely mulato girl, aged about 15 or 16 years named Rebecca. Said girl is of a fine disposition, good house keeper, cook and washer, and in all respects a number one servant. Terms, Cash
> W.S. Cobbs, Adm'r[18]

Emigrating and Quitting Business

The nineteenth century was characterized by a restless shifting of people westward. Eighteen public auctions were advertised between 1839 and 1861 by individuals moving on, giving up farming, or quitting business. A typical advertisement from 1855 read:

18. *SS*, September 15, 1858.

Valuable Farm, Negroes, Stock, Crops, &tc For Sale.

INTENDING to discontinue farming, I shall offer at public auction on the premises on Thursday the 1st of Nov. next, the tract of land on which I now reside, three miles east of Florida, and about thirty miles south west from Hannibal, containing six hundred and thirty-seven acres, well calculated for stock raising, or for the production of hemp, tobacco and all kinds of grain and grass. The buildings are partly new and sufficiently spacious for a large family, with necessary stables and out buildings. There is also another dwelling house on the premises sufficient for a small family. A liberal credit will be allowed for the principal part of the purchases [two or three words obliterated by tear] the stock of horses, cattle, and crops. The negroes consist of a woman 20 years old, with a child one year old, (a good plain cook,) a girl 10 years old and a boy 9 years old. For these cash or negotiable paper at 4 months will be required. About 50 fat hogs and 45 sheep will be sold for cash.

For further information, apply on the premises or to D. J. Garth, Hannibal[19]

Garth was Sam Clemens's Sunday school teacher at First Presbyterian Church.[20]

Public Sale

The subscriber will offer at Public sale on Thursday, the 22d instant, at his residence 4 miles west of Palmyra, on the Monticello road, his entire Stock and Farming Utensils, consisting of Nine head of Horses & Colts, 38 head of Cattle, among which are 4 yoke of well broke Oxen, a number of Milch Cows, and 12 head of fatted Cattle, 60 head of fatted Hogs, 13 stacks of Hay, a quantity of Corn, Hemp-Seed, Buckwheat, &tc

Terms—All sums of five dollars and under, cash: all over five dollars, twelve months' credit, with approved security. I will also offer for sale at the same time, for one half cash in hand, the balance in four and eight months, with bond and approved security, FIVE LIKELY NEGROES; three of them boys, one 19, one 14 , and one 4 years old, one girl 13, and one woman 46 years old.

I will also at the same time offer my FARM for rent or sale on accommodating terms. Sale to commence at 10 o'clock, and continue from day to day until finished.

THOS. TAYLOR[21]

19. *HWM*, October 18, 1855.
20. Armon, *Huck Finn and Tom Sawyer among the Indians*, 320.
21. *PMW*, December 10, 1842.

Trust Sales

Another common type of auction was the execution of a deed of trust. A deed of trust creates a security interest in a piece of property. Under Missouri law, for instance, there are no mortgages. When a person borrows money from a bank to purchase a house, he or she gets a deed from the seller to themselves and, at the same time, executes a deed of trust to a trustee for the bank. If the buyer meets all the terms of their note and makes the payments, when the loan is paid, the deed of trust is released. If the purchaser fails to make payments, the trustee for the bank sells the property by virtue of the deed of trust. In Missouri between 1839 and 1861, people often used slaves as collateral for loans and gave deeds of trust to lenders. It was another means by which slaveholders could extract value from their slaves.

The sale of slaves in foreclosure was just like the foreclosure sale of a house in Missouri today. Public notice of the sale was placed in the newspaper giving the time, date, and location of the auction. Thirteen such auctions took place in Palmyra at the Marion County courthouse, and one was held on the square in Palmyra.

> By virtue of a deed of trust executed by Jacob Sodowsky to me, on the 10th day of February, A.D. 1840, for the benefit of Henry Goodno and others, I shall sell for cash in hand, to the highest bidder, on Tuesday the 25th of August, inst. On the public square in the town of Palmyra, in the county of Marion, Mo., the following property, to wit:
>
> One Negro Boy named Lindsay, alias Jesse, about 16 years old. Also a lot of Hogs, Cattle, Farming Utensils, & Household and Kitchen Furniture.
>
> Sale to commence between the hours of 12 and 2 o'clock
> Thos. L. Anderson, Trustee.
> August 15, 1840.[22]

Two such auctions were held in Hannibal while Sam Clemens was growing up, the first in 1842.

> NOTICE
> BY virtue of a deed of trust made to me by David O. Glascock, in favour of creditors, I shall, on Saturday the 5th of March next, in the town of Hannibal, offer to the highest bidder, for cash, the following property:
> Lots 8 and 9 in Block 33, in said town—and the following slaves:—

22. Ibid., August 15, 1840.

John, a negro man aged about 22 years; Alfred, aged about 18 years, and Priscilla, a negro woman, aged about 41 years.
RICHARD J. WRIGHT, Trustee[23]

The second was held on June 21, 1851, in front of the Brady House Hotel in Hannibal. The sale was advertised in Orion Clemens's newspaper while Sam was working there. In that auction, the hotel itself was being auctioned. But among the items secured by the deed of trust and being sold were "one negro woman named Hagar, then aged 36 years; one girl named Henrietta then aged 12 years, one girl named Rosette then aged 8 years; and one boy named George, then aged 10 years."[24]

Judicial Sale of an Unclaimed Runaway Slave

Another type of auction took place in Marion County. The law provided that an unclaimed runaway slave could be sold by the state to recover the costs of housing the runaway in the public jail. Such an auction was held in 1843.

Sale of a runaway Slave
Notice is hereby given to all persons interested, that I shall sell in the town of Palmyra, county of Marion, State of Missouri, at the door of the courthouse of said county, on the 12th day of August next, for cash in hand, a certain Negro Woman who calls herself Lavinia McLikewise, of dark complexion, aged about 36 or 38 years. Said girl was committed to the jail of Marion county aforesaid on the 3d day of July, 1842, as a runaway, and not having been claimed, will be sold to pay expenses, agreeably to the statute in such cases made and provided.
J. J. MONTGOMERY,
Sheriff of Marion county aforesaid[25]

The balance of advertisements until 1861 consisted of forty-three auctions in counties adjoining Marion County.

Results of Slave Auctions

People were interested in the results of slave sales, whether they were local or outside the area. Newspapers regularly reported the results of dis-

23. Ibid., February 26, 1842.
24. *HJU*, June 25, 1851.
25. *PMW*, July 8, 1843.

tant slave sales. Market results, particularly from around the state and in the important slave markets of Memphis, Vicksburg, and New Orleans, were frequently communicated by correspondents. There are fifty-four surviving articles from Marion County newspapers relating slave prices from other parts of Missouri or other slave states until 1861. This example is typical: "A lot of negroes were sold at Fayette [Missouri] the other day, at higher figures than any lot of negroes ever bought in that market. One man sold for within a fraction of $1,200; a boy, 17 years old, brought $1,400; one woman and child brought near $1,300, children from 5 to 8 years of age brought from $500 to $700."[26]

Thus, slaveholders were able to keep track of the value of their slaves. A story, perhaps typeset by Sam Clemens in his brother's *Hannibal Daily Journal*, reported on April 4, 1853, "GOOD PRICE FOR NEGROES.— A private letter says that at Shreveport, La., common field hands bring from nine to twelve hundred dollars." The price of slaves was ultimately geared to the price achieved in New Orleans. The year 1854 saw the greatest number of advertisements regarding the sale, lease, and auctioning of slaves. A local newspaper offered the following observation on the boom in the market and accurately predicted a decline in slave sales.

STAND FROM UNDER.—A friend informs us that there are at this time over five thousand Negroes in New Orleans, in the hands of traders, for sale; and that prices are declining. It is an unusual circumstance, we believe, for any considerable number of negroes to remain on hands at New Orleans at this period of the season. The general scarcity of money, if no other cause, will soon reduce slave property to its true value. The exorbitant prices of the past year will be a source of wonderment a year or two hence.[27]

With slaves being such a valuable investment, they were also insured. Slave owners could purchase insurance policies to indemnify them if their slaves should die or become injured. James Clemens, Jr., a distant cousin in St. Louis who frequently loaned the Hannibal branch of the family money, was a director of the Phoenix Insurance Company, which ran regular advertisements in the *Missouri Courier* while Sam was apprenticed there: "Risks will be taken on persons going to California, and on slaves employed on land or on boats, on favorable terms." In 1851, Joseph Ament advertised in his own *Missouri Courier* that he was the agent for Boston

26. *HWM*, October 28, 1858.
27. *TWM*, April 13, 1854.

Union Mutual Insurance Company. In bold print, his small advertisement announced, "Insurance on Negroes."[28]

Private Sales

Slaves were also commonly transferred by private sale between individuals. The surviving newspapers of Marion County through 1861 contain sixty-six ads seeking to buy or sell slaves. Frequently, the editor of the newspaper served as a broker for these transactions. Joseph Ament performed this function, as did Jacob Sosey, and William League. Would-be buyers or sellers called at the newspaper office, and the editor forwarded their names to the other parties. In this fashion, persons placing the advertisements could shield themselves from unwanted contacts. Modern newspapers still perform this function for employers seeking workers. An advertisement is run, and respondents send applications and resumes to a "box" at the newspaper. Those responses are forwarded to the employer.

No doubt, the vast majority of private sales were never advertised. Today, slave bills of sale are common in the antiques market, evidencing the pervasive nature of the practice. Sam Clemens took little note of these sales. Raised amidst slavery, he found them no more unusual than later generations would a car sales lot. There is no evidence that he ever questioned any aspect of slavery while a young man in Hannibal. It is small wonder he did not recall the slave dealing of his youth.

28. *MC*, June 14, 1849, December 18, 1851.

Chapter 19

Leaving Hannibal and Taking
a Swipe at the Abolitionists

Neighbors, I don't know whether the new couple is frauds or not;
but if *these* two ain't frauds, I am an idiot, that's all. I think it's our
duty to see that they don't get away from here till we've looked
into this thing.

Mark Twain, *Adventures of Huckleberry Finn*

In the summer of 1853, Sam Clemens left Hannibal. He was seventeen
years old and ready to expand his horizons. He was fortunate to possess
a skill that would virtually guarantee him employment. His apprenticeship behind him, he was now a journeyman printer. In a country that was
hungry for news and one of the few places where the press was unhindered by government interference, Clemens left the small town confine-
ment of Hannibal and went out into the world. He started in St. Louis,
where he probably stayed with his older sister, Pamela. She had married
William A. Moffett, a commission merchant. Clemens worked for the *St.
Louis Evening News* and possibly several other weeklies.[1]

Like thousands of young men before and since, Sam Clemens decided
to try his luck in New York. He returned home to Hannibal to prepare
for the trip. Jane Clemens extracted one pledge from Sam before he left
home. He promised not to drink alcohol while away from Hannibal. He
apparently kept the promise.[2]

Travel in those early years was time-consuming and, for a seventeen-
year-old with an active mind and keen eye, exciting. His excursion took

1. Branch, *Mark Twain's Letters, 1853–1866*, 2.
2. Ibid., 5.

him for the first time into the heart of abolition country. On the first day of his trip he experienced three modes of transportation. He took the steamboat *Cornelia* from St. Louis to Alton, Illinois, on August 19. The two-year-old sidewheeler belched wood smoke as she plowed the water to Alton. (The boat would survive only another four months on the Mississippi. A week before Christmas 1853 she was destroyed on the Chain of Rocks, lower rapids above St. Louis.[3] Travel was not without risk in Clemens's world.) That same day, Sam caught the train at Alton. He rode along the partially completed Chicago and Mississippi Railroad to Springfield, the state capital. The train station was just a few blocks from the law office of Abraham Lincoln. Clemens carried his luggage to the offices of Frink's Stagecoach Service, where he boarded the stage for Bloomington.

Saturday, August 20, Sam rode another train, the Illinois Central line, to LaSalle, then caught the Chicago and Rock Island into Chicago, the booming metropolis of the prairies. He arrived at 7:00 P.M. He spent the next twenty-six hours exploring the city. Sunday, August 21, Sam took the 9:00 P.M. Michigan Central line to Toledo, Ohio. He slept on the uncomfortable wooden seats of the car as it jostled eastward. He continued on from Toledo to Monroe, Michigan, riding the Northern Indiana and Michigan Southern railroads.

The next morning found Sam Clemens on the shores of Lake Erie. The huge expanse of water must have been a strange sight to the boy from Hannibal. The Mississippi was the largest body of water he had ever seen. He traveled to Buffalo, New York, aboard the steamer *Southern Michigan*. The next morning he took the 8:00 A.M. New York *Lightening Express* from Buffalo to Albany. The train passed through Rochester and Syracuse. At 7:00 P.M. on August 23, he once again took to the river. He boarded the Hudson River steamer *Isaac Newton* for the last leg of his journey.

Sam Clemens arrived in New York as the city was waking at 5:00 A.M. on August 24.[4] Five days of travel separated him from his home in the familiar slave culture of northeast Missouri. Slavery did not exist in the hustle and bustle of the freewheeling city of free enterprise in which he had landed. Laborers were paid by the hour. It was a shocking new world. Gone were the familiar social roles and expectations. Gone were the hierarchies. The civic religion of slavery that had sustained him was of no use here. Though New York in 1853 harbored racists and proslavery zealots, it was also home to thousands of abolitionists. Adapting to the social real-

---

3. Frederick Way, *Way's Packet Directory 1848–1894: Passenger Steamboats of the Mississippi River System*, 111.

4. *HJ*, September 5, 1853; Branch, *Mark Twain's Letters, 1853–1866*, 5.

ities of this world would be difficult for Clemens. He would find himself homesick for the old, safe order of Hannibal.

That he carried his culture's racism with him to the East is clear in his first letter home. In an August 24 letter that Orion Clemens published in his *Hannibal Journal,* Sam told his mother that he had seen the courthouse in Syracuse, New York, made famous in 1851. A runaway slave named Jerry, from Clemens's own Marion County, had been captured there and held by the authorities under the Fugitive Slave Act. Orion's paper had published the story that year, and Sam may have set the type. Jerry was legally the property of a McReynolds, who lived near Hannibal. When New York abolitionists had heard that the slave was going to be returned to Missouri, they had organized a rescue. On October 1, 1851, an abolitionist mob had stormed the courthouse in broad daylight and carried Jerry away to freedom. Even two years later, Clemens was still bitter about the insult to Hannibal slave culture. Sam wrote in the published letter to his mother, "I reckon I had better black my face, for in these Eastern States niggers are considerably better than white people."[5]

Abolitionists also remembered the events of October 1851. Little more than a month after Clemens wrote to his mother, abolitionists held a state convention in Syracuse. On October 1, 1853, the Liberty Party convened. Speakers included Lucy Stone, Gerrit Smith, and Frederick Douglass. The event was reported in the Hannibal newspapers.[6] Sam Clemens remembered the event as a great defeat and insult, but the abolitionists commemorated the liberation of Jerry as a great victory.

In a letter dated August 31, 1853, Sam Clemens informed his mother about the job he had found as a printer and told her of the boardinghouse where he was staying. Orion published this letter in the *Hannibal Journal* as well. Once again, Sam Clemens expressed his distaste for the egalitarianism of New York streets. His racism was reflected in his comments on the children he encountered in New York.

Of all the commodities, manufactures—or whatever you please to call it—in New York trundle-bed trash—children I mean—take the lead. Why, from Cliff street, up Frankfort to Nassau street, six or seven squares—my road to dinner—I think I could count two hundred brats. Niggers, mulattoes, quadroons, Chinese, and some the Lord no doubt originally intended to be white, but the dirt on whose faces leaves one uncertain as to that fact, block up the little, narrow street; and to wade

5. Branch, *Mark Twain's Letters, 1853–1866,* 4.
6. *WM,* October 22, 1853.

through this mass of human vermin, would raise the ire of the most patient person that ever lived.[7]

The use of the term *trundle-bed trash* anticipates the later term *trailer trash* by a century and a quarter. It is obvious that Clemens was troubled by the race mixing that he saw in New York. He missed the subservience of Hannibal's Negroes. By November, Clemens had tired of New York and moved on to Philadelphia.

Back in Hannibal, brother Orion did some moving of his own. He gave up on the *Journal* and moved to Muscatine, in the free state of Iowa. Curious as to how his brother liked living in a slavefree environment, Sam wrote to him on November 28 and inquired "How do you like 'free-soil?' " Sam indicated his own distaste for the free states in the next sentence, "I would like amazingly to see a good, old-fashioned negro."[8]

Clemens spent the winter of 1853–1854 on the East Coast working for different papers and printers in Philadelphia. But in March, it appears he returned to New York. This time he was unable to find employment. He came back to what is now the Midwest in the spring of 1854. After that little is known of him until February 1855. He was vague about this period himself, and no letters from the period survived. He went to Muscatine and was reunited with his family, but he left for St. Louis after only a few months. He recalled setting type for newspapers in St. Louis, but there is no record of his being permanently employed anywhere.

It was during this time that a most curious event occurred, one familiar to everyone who knows of Clemens's love for the trickster. From Tom Sawyer's tricking his friends into whitewashing the fence to the Duke and the Dauphin duping everyone in their path, the works of Mark Twain are peppered with people pretending to be what they are not. Samuel Clemens tricked the abolitionists out of $24.50.

Sam Clemens Tricks the Abolitionists

Some frauds take longer than others to unravel. In the quotation from *Huckleberry Finn* that opens this chapter, the real brothers of the dead Wilks have just arrived on the scene, and the Duke and Dauphin's plot to steal the brothers' inheritance is about to be exposed. It appears that Clemens participated in a little fraud of his own with the abolitionists.

7. *HJ*, September 10, 1853; Branch, *Mark Twain's Letters, 1853–1866*, 10.
8. Branch, *Mark Twain's Letters, 1853–1866*, 29.

Just as his father had struck a blow against the abolitionists in the case of Thompson, Work, and Burr, Sam took a swipe at them as well in a characteristically Twain fashion. His trick would go undetected for more than 140 years.

On October 21, 1850, a public meeting was held in Boston at venerable Faneuil Hall. The purpose was to aid runaway slaves who were living in communities in the Northeast and in Canada. The meeting was one of hundreds of public meetings that were taking place across the free states. The abolition movement was gaining momentum. In Boston, Francis Jackson was elected to serve as treasurer of the organization. Jackson was a prominent New England abolitionist. He was active in the Massachusetts Anti-Slavery Society and was a colleague of William Lloyd Garrison and Wendell Phillips.[9]

Jackson took his duties seriously and kept a very neat and tidy record book. He recorded each donation and expenditure in a clear script. He had a very steady hand. There was certainly nothing special about the records at the time. Jackson served faithfully until December of 1861, when the last entries were made. The events of the Civil War overtook the little committee, and the book was put away without fanfare and rested unnoticed for sixty-three years.

The book was a family memento until March 1924 when Mrs. Henry H. Edes of Cambridge donated the book to the Bostonian Society. She recognized the ledger as an important document relating to the Underground Railroad in New England. The Bostonian Society preserved it and has lovingly reproduced it in exact handwritten form. However, it was another seventy years before anyone turned to page thirty and read the first entry for September 1854. Robert Sattelmeyer, an English professor at Georgia State University, was researching Henry David Thoreau. In 1851 Thoreau had helped a fugitive slave escape to Canada. Sattelmeyer was quietly reading through such entries as "July Robt. F. Wallcut for Mrs. Catherine E Greeinge & her chil.. Jas." and "Henry, Elijah, Paul & Geo W. to Canada . . . $20."

Imagine Sattelmeyer's surprise when he read: "Samuel Clemens passage from Missouri Penetentiary [sic] to Boston—he having been imprisoned there two years for aiding fugitives to escape . . . $24.50."[10] Sattelmeyer notes mildly that he was "intrigued" by the entry.

9. Robert Sattelmeyer, "Did Sam Clemens Take the Abolitionists for a Ride?" 294–99.

10. Francis Jackson, *Account Book of Francis Jackson, Treasurer, the Vigilance Committee of Boston*, 30.

Sattelmeyer, a former professor of English at the University of Missouri and a devoted Twain fan and scholar, set about doing research. He went to the 1850 federal census for the state of Missouri and determined that there was only one Samuel Clemens in the state. Then he searched the Missouri archives and learned that there had never been a Samuel Clemens incarcerated in the state penitentiary. A William Clemens had been sentenced to life in prison in 1849, but he could not have been paroled by 1854.

Sattelmeyer told other scholars of the discovery, which was met with considerable skepticism. The first reaction of nearly everyone was to suggest that it "had to be another Clemens." However, it appears obvious that it was indeed Sam Clemens formerly of Hannibal. Tricking abolitionists had long been a favorite joke in Hannibal. The following article offers a sense of the contempt with which slave culture regarded abolitionists.

> "DOG EAT DOG."—A few days ago a free negro barber was discharged from a steamboat at the city of Quincy, Ill., for the grave offence of travelling without money. Being anxious to get to Galena, he applied to a brother chip of the same ebon hue, to "aid and comfort" him by advancing the "bogus" necessary to take him to his place of destination. The darkie refused to fork up the "rinctum" himself, but referred him with a knowing grin to a benevolent old gentleman in the neighborhood, and told him if he would represent himself as a runaway slave from Missouri, he could easily "diddle" the old fool out of his travelling expenses. Accordingly down went the colored gentleman to the Abolitionist, reported himself as a runaway, and was received with open arms. Upon stating his penniless condition and his desire to proceed to Galena, the old ass forthwith hitched up his buggy, and offering his worthy companion a seat by his side, conveyed him to that city free of charge. We have the above from undoubted authority, and believe every word of it. The chagrin of the old rascal upon hearing that he was duped, was excessive.[11]

The abolitionists themselves frequently taunted slave culture in the press. The jibes that were hurled back and forth were printed on both sides of the free/slave divide. They provoked hard feelings. The following was printed in Hannibal in May of 1853:

UNDERGROUND RAILROADS.—The following paragraph from the Detroit Tribune shows how some editors relish the joke of theft and stirring up ill-blood between sections of the country.

11. *HJ*, June 24, 1847.

The under ground railroad is in active operation running its trains regularly nearly every night About three o'clock this morning a train arrived here with twentyeight [sic] goods and chattles [sic] in the shape of men and women and children. It not being safe for them to remain in the city until daylight, in consequence of the great rewards offered for their capture (about $9,500) means were taken at once to place them in safety in the free land of Canada.—They were fugitives from slavery from the chivalric State of Kentucky. It is needless to say perhaps, that the *down trains* of this road always go empty.[12]

It is easy to understand how a hotheaded young man could decide to retaliate against the abolitionists. The Boston Vigilance Committee had been in the St. Louis news over the summer of 1854. The nation was in an uproar over the Nebraska Bill. Then on May 26, 1854, the Vigilance Committee attempted to rescue a runaway slave named Anthony Burns. In the ensuing violence, one man was killed. To quell the rioting, the state militia was called out in Boston to escort the runaway and his master to the ship that would take them back to the South. The committee would have been a prime target for a spirited defender of slave culture. Sam, a keen reader, was doubtless aware of these events. How easy to concoct the story, and what a coup to fleece the enemy without running any risk.

Abolitionist activities were illegal in Missouri. Any friends of abolition kept their own counsel. Samuel Clemens could very well use his real name to have money sent to him in St. Louis. Not only would the joke have been a very good way of getting some much-needed money, there was virtually no risk of prosecution. No prosecuting attorney would have brought charges against him—it would have been political suicide. No grand jury would have returned a warrant. If they had, no jury would have convicted Sam. In fact the abolitionist who had the audacity to show his face and make the claim for the money could have been arrested himself. If Samuel Clemens risked anything, it was the possibility of being proclaimed a public hero.

As Tom Sawyer reflected as he watched the boys painting the fence, Tom gave up the brush with reluctance in his face, but alacrity in his heart. And while the late steamer Big Missouri worked and sweated in the sun, the retired artist sat on a barrel in the shade close by, dangled his legs, munched his apple, and planned the slaughter of more innocents. There was no lack of material; boys happened along every little while; they came to jeer, but remained to whitewash. By the time Ben was fagged

12. *MC*, May 12, 1853.

out, Tom had traded the next chance to Billy Fisher for a kite, in good repair; and when he played out, Johnny Miller bought in for a dead rat and a string to swing it with—and so on, and so on, hour after hour. And when the middle of the afternoon came, from being a poor poverty-stricken boy in the morning, Tom was literally rolling in wealth. He had besides the things before mentioned, twelve marbles, part of a jew's-harp, a piece of blue bottle glass to look through, a spool cannon, a key that wouldn't unlock anything, a fragment of chalk, a glass stopper of a decanter, a tin soldier, a couple of tadpoles, six firecrackers, a kitten with only one eye, a brass doorknob, a dog collar—but no dog—the handle of a knife, four pieces of orange peel, and a dilapidated old window sash.[13]

And Sam had $24.50 belonging to the Boston Vigilance Committee.

13. Mark Twain, *The Adventures of Tom Sawyer*, 31.

Chapter 20

The Great Change

The Railroad

The building of the Hannibal and St. Joseph Railroad will bring about such a revolution in the destinies of this State, as to surprise even the most sanguine.

Orion Clemens, *Western Union*, July 10, 1851

If Orion and Sam inherited anything from their father it was a love for internal improvements. A Whig to his dying day, John Marshall Clemens had dreamed and schemed of railroads and canals throughout his sojourn in Missouri. He had believed that the government best served the public by building the means to facilitate migration, commerce, and manufacturing. Like so many dreamers, he could not see the consequences of the changes he sought, for the revolution brought about by the railroad would devour the slave culture the Clemenses knew. It would utterly change the patterns of social and economic intercourse. Hannibal would no longer face south. With the arrival of the railroad, the town would look to the northeast.

There is a popular story that the idea for the Hannibal and St. Joseph Railroad was born in John Marshall Clemens's office. It is not implausible. Clemens had a track record of advocating public transportation projects. In Florida, Missouri, he had attempted to get the state to construct dams and locks to make the Salt River navigable. He was chairman of Hannibal's Committee on Roads and joined with attorney Robert F. Lakenan, his future son-in-law William A. Moffett, and his close friend Zachariah G. Draper to try to get the National Road extended to Springfield, Illinois, and then west to the Mississippi River across from Hannibal. The National Road was a federally funded highway. It was a twenty-foot-wide gravel road that by 1841 extended from Cumberland, Maryland, to Vandalia, Illinois. The booming progress of railroads in the East soon caused the committee to shift their attention to a railroad. However, it appears that St. Joseph, Missouri, on the western side of the state, spearheaded the movement to build a railroad across the prairies of northern Missouri.[1]

Regardless of where the idea first originated, the Hannibal and St. Joseph Railroad had many parents in many places. Discussions were held in parlors and offices across the northern part of the state on ways to open the fertile prairies of northern Missouri to immigration. By the fall of 1846, leading citizens of Hannibal and St. Joseph were mobilizing the public in favor of construction of the railroad. The leader of the emerging movement was a man named Robert Stewart of St. Joseph. He would serve as governor of Missouri from 1857 to 1861.

Railroads were inevitable. The Mississippi River was fairly reliable for north-south transportation, even with its shifting channels, but the need for east-west transportation spurred development of the rail system. The Missouri River, which cut across Missouri from Kansas City to St. Louis, was far more treacherous than the Mississippi. The dangers of traveling on the Missouri were reflected both in the rates charged by riverboats and in the insurance rates for boats and cargo. The *Hannibal Gazette* of November 5, 1846, reported that insurance rates on the Hannibal to St. Louis run were 0.3 to 0.5 percent of the insured value, while the rate to make the run from St. Louis to Weston (a town just a few miles above present-day Kansas City) was up to 1.5 percent. Freight rates were proportionately high and particularly affected agriculture. The *Gazette* reprinted a report from a Chillicothe, Missouri, paper stating that it cost the price of two bushels of corn to ship one bushel to St. Louis.[2]

It frustrated Missouri farmers to know that they could not get their products to a ready market in the settled areas of the East. Though there was some market for grain, flour, and livestock in the Deep South, freight rates made it virtually prohibitive to ship there. The idea of shipping to New Orleans by riverboat and then transferring the crop to a coaster for the trip to the Northeast was out of the question.[3] So the notion of railroads was welcome in Missouri. Rail would provide inexpensive, reliable transportation for agricultural products being sent east.

The first real step toward a trans-Missouri line was taken in February

1. Bennett, *Hannibal and St. Joseph Railroad*, 24, 32.
2. *HG*, January 28, 1847.
3. Ibid., December 10, 1846, quoted in Bennett, *Hannibal and St. Joseph Railroad*, 29.

1847 when the Missouri Legislature chartered the Hannibal and St. Joseph Railroad. A special act created the entity to build the railroad, but little was done during the next two years. Then in 1849, Robert Stewart organized a preliminary survey of the route. Money was raised to pay for the survey from the counties along the proposed line and from private individuals who hoped to profit from the railroad. The road would be easy to build. The survey found that the relatively flat land of northern Missouri presented no major engineering challenges. The real problem was money. Local communities did not have the resources to pay for the railroad.

The banking interests in the United States at this time were concentrated in Boston and New York. While railroad projects were booming in the eastern states, eastern investors were hesitant to put money into a project in Missouri with its sparse population. It was a problem common to areas in the West.[4] Congress came to the rescue with a plan that made the development of railroads like the Hannibal and St. Joseph practical. The federal government had been helping turnpike and canal companies in sparsely settled portions of the country by offering federal lands as an inducement to build since 1822. In September 1850, Senator Stephen Douglas of Illinois rammed through a bill granting similar benefits to a railroad connecting Chicago with southern Illinois. This precedent spurred developers in northern Missouri. They lobbied Congress, and finally on June 10, 1852, Congress authorized a land grant to the Hannibal and St. Joseph Railroad.

The grant gave the state of Missouri every other section of public domain land for six miles on each side of the track. A section of land is one square mile, or 640 acres. In those places where land along the railroad was already claimed or settled, the plan gave the state authority to select equivalent acreage from a strip of land six to fifteen miles from the railroad. To visualize the plan, think of a six-mile checkerboard made up of one-square-mile squares along the railroad. Every black square belonged to Missouri. When the railroad line completed a specified length of track, the state was authorized to give the lands to the railroad. The railroad in turn could sell the land to immigrants, thereby paying for its construction costs. In return for the land grants, the railroad was obliged to carry the mails at a price set by Congress and to transport troops and government property free of charge. Once the 207-mile line between Hannibal and St. Joseph was plotted, the grant of land amounted to 600,000 acres. It was a boon to development.

4. Richard Overton, *Burlington Route: A History of the Burlington Lines*, 19–21.

The state legislature also took steps to aid the building of the road. After Congress passed the Illinois legislation in 1850, a railroad convention was called in St. Joseph for October 7, 1850. Each county along the route sent representatives to the meeting. The convention lobbied the Missouri Legislature to take steps to help fund the project. On February 22, 1851, the State of Missouri authorized the issuing of bonds for the Hannibal and St. Joseph Railroad. Ultimately $3 million worth of bonds were issued at 6 percent interest. In 1851, $1.5 million in bonds were issued to be redeemed in twenty years. In 1855, the remaining $1.5 million were issued at the same rate for thirty years.[5]

The financing of the railroad was followed closely in Hannibal. Sam Clemens was an enthusiastic booster of the project. On March 25, 1852, he sent a letter promoting immigration to Hannibal to the eastern newspaper the *Philadelphia American Courier.* He was working with Orion at the time. The *American Courier* published the article on May 8, 1852, under the title "Original Correspondence" in its regular column "The Topographist." Regarding Hannibal and the financing of the railroad, Sam wrote:

> This town is situated on the Mississippi river, about one hundred and thirty miles above St. Louis, and contains a population of about three thousand. A charter has been granted by the State for a railroad, to commence at Hannibal, and terminate at St. Joseph, on the western border of Missouri. The State takes $1,500,000 of stock in the road; the counties along the route have also subscribed liberally, and already more than one-third the amount requisite for its construction has been subscribed. The manner in which the State takes stock is this: for every $50,000 that the company spends in the construction of the road, the State gives her bonds for that amount, until the $ 1,500,000 is paid.[6]

This investment by the state and federal governments uncorked the bottle, and initial work began on the railroad.[7] However, it was slow going through the early 1850s. Initially the line was locally controlled, but financing was always a problem. With Robert Stewart as president of the railroad, the company went east to find investors. Finally, in January 1854 Stewart secured solid financial backing with a syndicate of Boston financiers. They restructured the railroad.

5. Perkins, *History of Marion County,* 80.

6. *American Courier,* May 8, 1852, reprinted in Branch, *Early Tales and Sketches, 1851–1864,* 67–68.

7. Overton, *Burlington Route,* 19–21.

The majority of stockholders in the new company were all from the East. In November 1854 at the annual meeting of stockholders, Bostonians John Murray Forbes and his brother Robert Bennet Forbes, John Thayer, and H. H. Hunnewell were elected to the board of directors along with Stewart. With Stewart the lone Missourian, control had passed from Missouri to the group of Boston financiers.

The railroad spent most of 1855 acquiring rights of way and depot grounds. Terminal arrangements were made in Hannibal and St. Joseph and rather primitive facilities constructed. Grading began on the line. The construction of the railroad took eight long years. Much of the hard labor was performed by slaves who were hired from local slave owners. The railroad sold the land early through a scheme using bonds, which would be redeemed when construction was completed and the state had turned the land over to the railroad. A large portion of the market for these bonds was in Europe. Cheap land was very popular in Europe. It could be sold to the thousands of Europeans who wished to emigrate.

These immigrants to Missouri would bring great social change. As early as 1851, Orion and Sam Clemens noted the shift in the pattern of immigration to Missouri. "We observed also the other day, a large company of German Emigrants landing at our wharf, destined for West Ely Prairie. Their friends say they bring with them industry and wealth. Such, from whatever clime or country is what Missouri wants."

Of course, the Clemens brothers did not take note of what the Germans did *not* bring with them: slaves. They saw in the influx of newcomers nothing but good news for their area. The West Ely Prairie they mentioned in the article had been considered bad farmland just a few years before— in part because of the distance to the river and the inconvenience of transporting crops to market. "But contemplate the 'highland navigation' of a Rail Road stretching through a country now vacant and unimproved, of 40, 60, 100 and 200 miles, all brought into cultivation while the R. R. is building! Who will or can oppose?"[8]

There were countless construction delays. Many of these were due to national and international events. In 1855, the Crimean War unsettled the money market, and the flow of capital slowed to a trickle. However, early in 1856, conditions improved, and the Boston syndicate was able to purchase 13,500 tons of rail and 16 locomotives. This brought about a spurt of construction activity and, with it, one very noteworthy observer of Hannibal slave culture.

8. *Hannibal Western Union,* July 10, 1851.

In addition to the immigrants who would settle along the railroad lines, the building of the Hannibal and St. Joseph Railroad also brought to Hannibal laborers, mechanics, and engineers. These were men from New England and immigrants from Germany and Ireland. Many of the German immigrants had fled after failed revolutions in Europe. They brought with them strong notions of social justice and republican ideals, and they forever changed northern Missouri. The new arrivals were different from the aspiring patricians who had come in earlier decades from the Carolinas, Virginia, Tennessee, and Kentucky. They were industrious and self-sufficient. They were educated. Among these men was a young master mechanic from the Boston area named John Rogers.

John Rogers

Born in Salem, Massachusetts, in 1829, Rogers was one of the most popular and successful sculptors of his day. He mastered the techniques necessary to produce large quantities of sculptures in inexpensive media—plaster. He produced and manufactured his statuary groupings throughout the late nineteenth century. Because his works could be sold profitably at reasonable prices, his statues were common fixtures in middle-class American Victorian parlors. But in April 1856, John Rogers's art career lay in the future. The Hannibal and St. Joseph Railroad hired Rogers that year as a mechanic and engineer. He arrived in Hannibal on April 2 and was put in charge of the construction.

Rogers arrived to find a dismal scene. Though the project was five years old, fewer than ten miles of track climbed up from Bear Creek valley to the prairies to the west. The machine shop of the fledgling railroad was in a converted pork shed in the river bottoms just underneath Lover's Leap. Working conditions were less than ideal. The shed roof was made of cottonwood shingles, which easily caught fire. At a time when all steam engines were powered by—and all buildings heated with—wood or coal, the roof was very dangerous. Within the first two weeks, John Rogers reported to his father, four or five fires sent everyone scrambling to the roof to put out the blazes.[9]

Building a railroad in the 1850s in the wilds of Missouri was quite an enterprise. Not only did Rogers's men prepare the roadbed and lay the ties and tracks, but the workmen in the machine shop also constructed the cars that would run on the line. Rogers performed a valuable service

9. David Wallace, *John Rogers: The People's Sculptor*, 46.

besides building the Hannibal and St. Joseph Railroad. While the industrious Yankee put his prodigious energy and mind into constructing the
railroad, he also took the time to observe the slave culture that surrounded
him. His correspondence home to his abolitionist-leaning family is an invaluable chronicle.

In his very first letters to his family, Rogers recorded his reaction to
human bondage. In contrast to the industrious Northeast, he found the
patriarchal slave culture of Hannibal repugnant. Raised with the New
England values of hard work, discipline, and industry, he was appalled
by a system in which work was delegated to slaves and personal responsibility shrugged off.

> The curse of slavery is dreadfully apparent here. There is no enterprise
> at all. Although the road will be running for twelve miles within a
> month there is scarcely a new building going up in the town. There is
> a grand opening for an enterprising yankee to put up a first class hotel.
> I don't see how travellers are to be accommodated. Some of the con-
> tractors wives who live along the line of the road in the interior of this
> state say that we have a small idea of what slavery really is here. They
> never have anything on hand at the taverns there. Every morning the
> slaves have to split the wood before breakfast to cook it by. If breakfast
> is late—why, the darky didn't get up in time to split the wood. Unless
> they import some yankees I am afraid they will never make much of a
> place of Hannibal.[10]

Rogers found much to be unhappy about in Hannibal. His boardinghouse was filthy, and he lamented the education level of the town's residents. He found Hannibal a cultural wasteland. He observed that there
was not a single public school in Hannibal. There were no concerts or
lectures—only the occasional lowly circus or minstrel show. It was a dramatic change from the East.

Rogers corresponded with his sister Clara, who had very strong abolitionist opinions. While he was in Hannibal, the Kansas troubles were
in full swing as the forces of slavery and free soil fought it out on the
plains. Rogers's family back East was concerned for his safety. Like the
Easterners of today, Bostonians had little knowledge of the geography
of the Midwest. Kansas was two days' travel from Hannibal before the
railroad was completed. Rogers would have had to take the boat to St.
Louis, then take a Missouri River boat for the slow upstream ride across

10. John Rogers, Jr., to John Rogers, Sr., Sunday [April 27], 1856, Rogers
Papers.

the state. He sought to calm his family's fears. "You ask in your letters if there is no disturbance on account of Kansas here—I think there is less here than with you—I am not much of a politician you know, but there seems to be little said about it. The most I hear is in the papers I get from Boston."[11]

The Kansas troubles were far away, but there was no mistaking where Hannibal sympathies were. While there was no shooting going on in 1856, Hannibal slave culture had been battling the abolitionists to the east and north for a decade and a half. Rogers had a sense of humor. He constructed a handcar to use on the line and named it the "Border Ruffian." The term *border ruffian* was used by people opposed to the expansion of slavery into Kansas. It referred to Missourians who aided proslavery forces. Rogers's playfulness belied the true danger of even being suspected of abolitionism in northeast Missouri. In June 1856 he wrote playfully to his abolitionist sister about one of her letters.

> Dear Clara
> I rec'd your letter today written last Sunday which so emphatically denounces F. Pierce. I beg you won't use such inflammatory language. Remember that I am in a slave state & if any of these Border Ruffians knew that I corresponded with such an abolitionist as you are the consequences might be very sad. I shall be careful & let no one see your letter. President Pierce might send Sheriff Jones to arrest me. I am not much of a politician. I never was. You are much more of a one. But I begin to see how things really are now. They are much worse than I supposed them, before I read your letter. The car is a little dangerous. I begin to feel afraid. I don't know what to do. The people take it as a compliment to have the car called the Border Ruffian that I am afraid they will feel slighted if I change it. Please advise me *what* to do.[12]

However, a little over a month later he wrote a more somber letter. Being perceived as an abolitionist could have dire, and very real, consequences.

> Dear Clara
> It is fortunate that such a rank abolitionist as you are not here. A meeting was held last week in one of the towns on the line & fifty people appointed to tar & feather Mr Sickels (a brother to the one I was with) when he should return there from Hannibal because someone had some

11. John Rogers, Jr., to Martha Rogers, August 12, 1856, Rogers Papers.
12. John Rogers, Jr., to Clara Rogers, June 7, 1856, Rogers Papers.

spite against him & gave out he was an abolitionist though he has said as little on such subjects as I ever did. Just imagine what a gay looking bird I would make with a coat of tar & feathers.[13]

Rogers grew comfortable with life in Hannibal, though never with slavery. Many of his observations about Hannibal are punctuated with his observations about slaves. In a public relations gesture, the railroad organized a Fourth of July celebration ten miles out in the country. John Rogers fitted twenty-five open railcars with seats and rigged them with arbors for shade. The railroad roasted a beef at a barbecue for the people of Hannibal. The picnic was the first "barbecue" Rogers had ever attended. He did not enjoy the food or the company of the white citizens. But the slaves who prepared the feast for the white folks caught his attention.

> The "glorious Fourth" is over and I am glad of it. I worked hard fitting up about my 25 open cars with seats and bushes for shade. I went out about ten miles on the road to a "barbecue" which signifies nothing more than a great picnic where a dinner is furnished for everybody. I thought it a rather stupid affair. They had nothing to eat but dry bread and meat and no music or anything going on but some speaking. I was principally amused in watching the cooking and the negroes who appeared to enjoy themselves better than anyone else.[14]

Rogers regularly reported on the activities of the slaves. He went to a church revival in the woods called a "basket meeting," after the baskets of food attendees brought to share. Rogers noted that the slaves had a portion of the woods where the meeting was held to themselves. He noted that the slaves seemed to enjoy themselves highly as "I have always found they do on such gatherings." He also attended a dance where a slave fiddler provided the music. However, the repertoire of the black musician did not rise to his expectations. "We had a black fiddler who called just two figures all the evening first one then the other & there was nothing but cotillons danced it was very tedious particularly when it get towards three o'clock."[15]

Although Rogers stayed for a year and a half in Hannibal, he never came to accept slavery. Despite the risk, he bought and read Harriet Beecher Stowe's book *Dred*. The novel dealt with a failed slave rebellion.

13. Ibid., July 19, 1856.
14. John Rogers, Jr., to Ellen Rogers, July 6, 1856, Rogers Papers.
15. John Rogers, Jr., to Sara Ellen Derby Rogers, October 5, 1856, Rogers Papers.

Rogers liked the book. Nothing in his Hannibal experiences contradicted the antislavery book. "She takes a strong common sense view of the subject. It seems perfectly convincing to me." Rogers had earlier reported to his family about the treasurer of the railroad whose wife had thrown a bowl of scalding hot preserves into the face of their female slave. As the slave writhed in agony, the treasurer and his wife took turns beating her. "As this was done by people I have always considered respectable it shows how mistaken we may sometimes be by a decent exterior."[16]

John Rogers was a fascinating individual. He moved from the Hannibal boardinghouse to a small house of his own, which he constructed himself, paying five hundred dollars for the lot and materials. There, more than a hundred years before they were fashionable, he built himself a waterbed. He constructed a large tank to hold a six-inch pool of water and fitted the top with a waterproof cover. He slept floating on the water. And he demonstrated the fondness for art that would later be the key to his success. He had always aspired to be an artist, but his Yankee practicality overcame his aspirations. Rogers constantly sketched and modeled small sculptures in clay. The New-York Historical Society in New York City currently owns a drawing he made as he sat on Lover's Leap overlooking Hannibal. Complete with his feet dangling over the edge, he recorded the machine shed and yard of the new railroad terminal as well as the little town nestled in Bear Creek Valley.

However, it was Rogers's work with clay that would prove to be important. He had been making small figurines for years. While he was in Hannibal, he made a very fanciful tiny sculpture of a nightmare. It featured a man in bed being tormented by demons and skeletons. But these endeavors took a backseat to the serious work of constructing the railroad. Then came the national financial crisis of 1857. Money for construction of the railroad completely dried up. Rogers was notified by the bosses in Boston to close down the shop and lay off the men. He lost his job as well. With his practical plans crushed, he decided to turn to his dreams of art. He returned to Boston and then set sail for France in the fall of 1858. He studied sculpture in the Paris studio of Antoine Laurant Dantan, and he took French lessons.[17]

After a few months, he moved to Rome and studied in the studio of the English sculptor Benjamin E. Spence. However, he was not happy under the tutelage of Spence. Spence was a rigid man who believed in definite

16. Ibid., October 19, 1856; John Rogers, Jr., to John Rogers, Sr., August 17, 1856, Rogers Papers.
17. Wallace, *John Rogers*, 66.

rules of art and aesthetics. Rogers did not like the inflexibility of the Englishman. Further, he thought the marble craftsmen of Italy were hidebound by tradition. Disappointed, he returned to America in April 1859 intending to give up art and return to the business of building railroads.[18]

However, the United States had recovered from the economic crisis of 1857, and construction had gone very quickly on the Hannibal and St. Joseph Railroad. The railroad was completed in February 1859. On St. Valentine's Day the first passenger train arrived in Hannibal from St. Joseph. On Washington's birthday, there was an official grand opening celebration of the line in St. Joseph. A special car carried a delegation of local dignitaries from Hannibal. The ceremony was hosted by the popular mayor of St. Joseph, Jeff Thompson.

Like Hannibal, St. Joseph was a river town, a jumping-off place for westward migration. Immigrants could take boats up the Missouri River and then cross the plains in the wagon trains that organized in St. Joe. Also like Hannibal, St. Joseph had suffered greatly from the abolitionists. Across the river lay Bloody Kansas. If anything, the depredations along the western border were worse. Since 1856, civil war had reigned. St. Joseph, too, had been socially and culturally linked with the South. Prior to the railroad, northern Missouri had felt more kinship with St. Louis, Memphis, and New Orleans than with the Northeast. Some would resist change fiercely. Thompson would go on to distinguished service in the Civil War as a Confederate general. He would be known as the Missouri Swamp Fox.[19]

The speakers at the ceremony in St. Joseph on that blustery winter day illustrate the changes that were to come. There was not a person there from south of Missouri. Among the speakers were Deacon Bross, of Chicago, Nehimiah Bushnell, of Quincy, Illinois, John I. Campbell of Hannibal, and, of course, Thompson.

Just as the boosters of the railroad could not see the devastating effect the train would have on slave culture, they could not see that the train would also forever alter river, coastal, and Great Lake navigation. Along with the band music and speeches, a special "mingling of the waters" was performed. During the ceremony water from the Atlantic Ocean, the Great Lakes, the Mississippi River, and the Missouri River were poured together symbolizing their being linked by the new line.[20] In a few short

18. Ibid., 72–73.
19. Jay Monaghan, *Civil War on the Western Border, 1854–1865*, 133, 185, 233, 347.
20. Perkins, *History of Marion County*, 337.

years people and freight would move across the continent without ever having been on a watercraft. The age of the railroad was dawning.

In April 1859, John Rogers returned to Hannibal hoping to find a job with his old employer. However, the new railroad had no engineering positions open. The best the line could offer was a job as a draftsman. Unwilling to take the job and feeling dejected, Rogers took the train to Chicago, and it was there the idea hit him. He had a dream of creating art that could be enjoyed by everyone. The art world to which he had been exposed in Europe was an elitist one dominated by upper classes. Rogers wanted to produce art for ordinary people.

Rogers came up with the idea of mass-producing his sculptures. He would create original works, then cast them in plaster and sell them at affordable prices. He took art from the ethereal world of European salons to the democratic American market. He would select as his subjects not idealized classical themes from Greek and Roman antiquity but images from the world around him. He made his fortune with statues of checker games, Abraham Lincoln, Union soldiers, and scenes from American life. But the idea for his very first commercial piece came from the Hannibal he had just left in 1859: It was a slave auction.

Chapter 21

Steamboating Days

A pilot, in those days, was the only unfettered and entirely independent human being that lived in the earth.

Mark Twain, *Life on the Mississippi*

In the four years following his departure from Hannibal, Sam Clemens worked in St. Louis as a journeyman printer and in Keokuk with his brothers, Henry and Orion, at the Ben Franklin Book and Job Office. Ever-dissatisfied, he dreamed of bigger things. The year 1857 found him in Cincinnati, where he worked several months for the printing establishment Wrightson and Company. Then with a young man's flair for adventure, he decided to go to Brazil to get into the coca trade. "I had been reading Lieutenant Herndon's account of his explorations of the Amazon and had been mightily attracted by what he said of coca. I made up my mind that I would go to the head waters of the Amazon and collect coca and trade in it and make a fortune."[1]

The coca plant is best known today for the cocaine processed from its leaves. But Clemens never entered the coca trade. Instead, the trip to New Orleans on the steamer *Paul Jones* provided him with a different opportunity, one that would change his life. Somewhere on the Ohio and Mississippi Rivers Sam Clemens befriended steamboat pilot Horace Bixby. By the time they reached New Orleans, the experienced Bixby had agreed to teach Sam Clemens the skill of piloting steamboats.

Though Sam Clemens would love his time as a river pilot, it was to be a short-lived career. In fact, had he read the *Cincinnati Daily Gazette* on the

1. Neider, *Autobiography of Mark Twain*, 98.

day of his departure, he would have seen the following: "Passengers by river are rather scarce at present, nearly all the emigrants, as well as other passengers, now go by railroad hence. The passage by river, in a fine boat, is certainly equally desirable, but people seem to prefer a speedy trip in a crowded car."[2] The dominance of the railroad and the looming Civil War would cut short Clemens's river career just as they would destroy Hannibal's slave culture.

In the twilight of the steamboat's era, Clemens served as an apprenticed "cub pilot" under Horace Bixby and learned the lower Mississippi from St. Louis to New Orleans. On April 9, 1859, he received his pilot's license.[3] He loved the ever-changing Mississippi, but it was not a time of uninterrupted pleasure. In 1858 tragedy struck. Sam had managed to get his younger brother, Henry, a job as an unpaid "mud clerk" on the *Pennsylvania*, where Sam was the cub pilot. Although mud clerks received no compensation, they were in line for promotions to positions that did pay. Just before an upriver run, Sam got into a fight with the pilot of the *Pennsylvania*, William Brown, and was put off the boat. Henry continued on the *Pennsylvania* while Sam was to follow upriver on another boat. At Memphis, a boiler on the *Pennsylvania* exploded, burning Henry Clemens badly. Sam rushed to Memphis. There he found his brother in the hospital. A Memphis reporter recorded the moving scene.

> We witnessed one of the most affecting scenes at the Exchange yesterday that has ever been seen. The brother of Mr. Henry Clemens, second clerk of the Pennsylvania, who now lies dangerously ill from the injuries received by the explosion of that boat, arrived in the city yesterday afternoon, on the steamer A.T. LACY. He hurried to the Exchange to see his brother, and on approaching the bedside of the wounded man, his feelings so much overcame him, at the scalded and emaciated form before him, that he sunk to the floor overpowered.
>
> There was scarcely a dry eye in the house; the poor sufferers shed tears at the sight. This brother had been pilot on the Pennsylvania, but fortunately for him, had remained in New Orleans when the boat started up.[4]

Henry Clemens lingered and suffered from his burns for a week, then died on June 21, 1858. Sam notified his mother and sister, who were stay-

2. *Cincinnati Daily Gazette*, April 15, 1857, quoted in Raymond Ewing, *Mark Twain's Steamboat Years: The Years of Command*, 2.
3. Ewing, *Mark Twain's Steamboat Years*, 61.
4. *Memphis Eagle and Enquirer*, June 16, 1858.

ing in St. Louis. He had the sad duty of escorting the body back to Hannibal, where Henry was buried in the Baptist Cemetery alongside John Marshall Clemens. Sam continued as a pilot until the Civil War began. He piloted sidewheeler steamboats exclusively. In addition to the *Paul Jones* and *Pennsylvania,* evidence indicates he was a cub pilot on the boats *Colonel Crossman, Crescent City, Rufus J. Lackland,* and *John J. Roe.* After he obtained his license, he piloted the *Alfred T. Lacey, J. C. Swon, Edward J. Gay, A. B. Chambers, City of Memphis, Arago,* and *Alonzo Child.* There were good times on the river. For the first time, Clemens had a job that brought him respect and a good income. In a June 1860 letter he bragged to Orion about his status:

> This is the luckiest circumstance that ever befell me. Not on account of the wages—for that is a secondary consideration—but from the fact that the CITY OF MEMPHIS is the largest boat in the trade and the hardest to pilot, and consequently I can get a reputation on her, which is a thing I never could accomplish on a transient boat. I can "bank" in the neighborhood of $100 a month on her, and that will satisfy me for the present (principally because the other youngsters are sucking their fingers.) Bless me! what a pleasure there is in revenge! and what vast respect Prosperity commands! Why, six months ago, I could enter the "Rooms," and receive only a customary fraternal greeting—but now they say, 'Why, how are you, old fellow—when did you get in?'[5]

Sam had friends among the other river pilots. Four of them—the Bowen brothers, Bart, Sam, and Will, and Absalom Grimes—were from Hannibal. Even at this early stage of his life, Sam could spin a tale that kept the attention of an audience. A comrade recalled an incident in which Clemens's storytelling resulted in the grounding of a steamboat.

> He [Sam] had a reputation then, though the boy of the crowd, for telling good stories, and he always had one ready to fill in. One of the best stories which I ever remember of Sam telling was when we were on the EDWARD J. GAY crossing from Goose Island to the Missouri shore, a very shoal place. A number of pilots were in the pilothouse. They were on a surveying tour to Cairo. Squire Bell was at the wheel, and ran the boat out of the channel 25 or 30 yards and grounded her. She was aground for 30 minutes, and Bell made the air blue with all the swear words in his vocabulary in declaring that, if it hadn't been for Sam Clemens's story, he would have kept the boat in good water. I could repeat the story, but

5. Branch, *Mark Twain's Letters, 1853–1866,* 97.

it's entirely too long. However, we were all convulsed with laughter, particularly as we did not see the point nor the real gist of it until it had been told for quite a few minutes.[6]

Sam Clemens, son of the man who had failed at every business enterprise he had attempted, must have enjoyed greatly taking his mother on a steamboat trip in the late winter of 1861, just before the war cut short his career. He wrote playfully to Orion:

Ma was delighted with her trip, but she was disgusted with the girls for allowing me to embrace and kiss them—and she was horrified at the Schottische as performed by Miss Castle and me. She was perfectly willing for me to dance until 12 o'clock at the imminent peril of my going to sleep on the after watch—but then she would top off with a very inconsistent sermon on dancing in general; ending with a terrific broadside aimed at the heresy of heresies, the Schottische.[7]

Sam Clemens was a successful man. He could afford to take his mother to New Orleans. He was a hit with the ladies. But the good times were drawing to a close. War loomed ahead. Sam made the last trip north on the *Nebraska* as a passenger on May 14, 1861. Sam's friend Zebulon Leavenworth was serving as pilot, and Sam helped him stand his watch. Even as the steamboat made its way upriver, traffic on the Mississippi River was grinding to a halt as the new Confederacy braced for war with the old Union.

As the boat approached Jefferson Barracks, on St. Louis's south side, nervous troops fired a shot across her bow. Not realizing they were being ordered to stop, the *Nebraska* continued upriver. The artillerists then placed a shell into the smokestacks of the vessel.[8] As Sam later recounted the experience to his biographer, "Less than a minute later there was another boom, and a shell exploded directly in front of the pilot-house, breaking a lot of glass and destroying a good deal of the upper decoration. Zeb Leavenworth fell back into a corner with a yell.

"Good Lord Almighty! Sam," he said, "what do they mean by that?" Clemens stepped to the wheel and brought the boat around. "I guess they

6. *Cincinnati Enquirer*, September 12, 1909.
7. Branch, *Mark Twain's Letters, 1853–1866*, 117–18.
8. Neider, *Autobiography of Mark Twain*, 102.

want us to wait a minute, Zeb," he said.[9] Soldiers boarded the *Nebraska* and examined the boat before allowing her to proceed to St. Louis. The river was closed. The country was descending into the chaos of civil war. Like thousands of other young men, twenty-five-year-old Sam Clemens had a decision to make.

9. Albert Bigelow Paine, *Mark Twain: A Biography*, 162.

Chapter 22

Sam Clemens Comes Back to Fight

You have heard from a great many people who did something in the war; is it not fair and right that you listen a little moment to one who started out to do something in it, but didn't?

Mark Twain, "A Private History of a Campaign That Failed"

Few presidential elections have been more confusing than that of 1860. The Republican Party was a young, relatively unknown quantity that year. The party had fielded John Charles Frémont as its first presidential candidate four years earlier. Frémont had made his reputation as a western explorer and had the catchy nickname "The Pathfinder." He had strong connections with Missouri. He had married Jesse Benton, daughter of Thomas Hart Benton, who served Missouri as both a U.S. senator and a congressman. (His grandson, an artist, would share his name.) Frémont was trounced by Democrat James Buchanan in 1856, garnering only 38.5 percent of the electoral votes.[1]

There were five serious contenders for the Republican nomination in 1860. The four losers, William H. Seward, Simon Cameron, Salmon Chase, and Edward Bates of Missouri all later served in the Lincoln administration. The Republican convention was held in Chicago, in the log hall called "The Wigwam," where, after several votes, delegates nominated Kentucky-born Abraham Lincoln of Illinois. Despite a raucous

1. Scott G. Thomas, *The Pursuit of the White House: A Handbook of Presidential Statistics and History*, 63.

convention, the party emerged united by U.S. standards, and the Republicans entered the fray.[2]

The Democrats were another story. By 1860 the Democrats were the only other political party left in Missouri. The American Party and the Whigs had died in the preceding decade. The Whigs had been born as the anti-Jackson party and never formed a clear identity of their own. They petered out with losses to the American Party and the new Republican Party. The American Party was called the "Know-nothings." This disparaging name reflected their bigoted, racist, and religiously intolerant anti-immigrant, anti-Catholic platform. Shared intolerance was not enough to sustain a political party. In the election of 1856, the American Party nominated former president Millard Fillmore. What remained of the Whigs endorsed him. He won only 2.7 percent of the electoral vote.[3] Thus, by 1860, one could be a Republican or a Democrat. The modern political parties had emerged.

But the Democrats were unable to exploit their majority position. Instead, they split into three groups, each with a different candidate. Stephen Douglas of Illinois was the candidate of pro-Union Democrats. John Bell of Tennessee was the candidate of a group calling itself the Constitutional Unionists. Both Douglas and Bell were opposed to secession. John C. Breckenridge of Kentucky was the candidate of the Southern Democrats, who advocated secession. His heart was in Dixie. The platform of his group called for the creation of a slave code for the entire country. Otherwise, they argued, enough free states would eventually enter the Union and abolition would become law.

It is important to remember that not one of the four presidential candidates advocated ending slavery in the states where it then existed. Many people feared that Lincoln secretly planned to abolish slavery. There were certainly abolitionists who supported him, but he carefully distanced himself from that position. Lincoln would be a good friend of Missouri slaveholders throughout his presidency.

In the election of 1860, a whopping 81 percent of the eligible voters turned out. Lincoln took 40 percent of the popular vote and carried all the northern states (but lost three of seven New Jersey electors, who went to Douglas) and the West Coast states. Douglas garnered 30 percent of the vote but only carried one state outright—Missouri. Breckenridge had 18 percent of the vote and carried most of the southern states. Bell received

2. Congressional Quarterly's *Guide to U.S. Elections*, 45–47.
3. Thomas, *Pursuit of the White House*, 63.

only 12 percent of the vote, carrying Kentucky, Tennessee, and Virginia. He ran a very close second in Missouri. When it became known that Lincoln won, states in the Deep South began seceding. South Carolina led the way. Though President-elect Lincoln made conciliatory speeches and gestures toward Southerners, nothing he did calmed their fears.[4]

The vote in Hannibal actually reflected the state's overall results. In Hannibal, Douglas received 623 votes, Bell, 574 votes, and Lincoln, 227 votes. Breckenridge, the secessionist candidate, came in dead last with 121 votes. It was a dismal showing for the secessionists. The town was solidly pro-Union.

The outcome for Marion County, including Hannibal, was slightly different. John Bell won the most votes—1,385. Douglas received 1,239. Lincoln received only 235 votes—nearly all of them coming from Hannibal. There were a few more pro-Breckenridge voters in rural Marion County. The secessionist candidate got 432 votes countywide. But still, the secessionists were a very tiny minority, mustering only 13 percent of the votes cast.[5]

The people of Marion County simply did not want to leave the Union. Secession had very little support in the community. When a secession rally was held at the county seat in Palmyra on November 14, 1861, only a dozen people attended.[6] By comparison, between five and ten thousand people were estimated to have attended Marion County's first public execution in 1850. But in the same election in which they rejected the radicalism of Breckenridge and Lincoln, the voters of Missouri sent a Southerner to the governor's mansion who would do his best to take the state out of the Union.

The new governor of Missouri was a fine Southern gentleman by the name of Claiborne Fox Jackson. Jackson was from a prosperous Kentucky family of tobacco farmers and slaveholders. In 1826, he came to Missouri—where he married well. His bride was the daughter of a wealthy slave owner named John S. Sappington. Sappington was a doctor who made one fortune speculating in land and selling goods to immigrants headed west at Arrow Rock, Missouri. He made another fortune by inventing, manufacturing, and selling a pill containing quinine for the treatment of malaria. Through his father-in-law, Jackson had contact with

4. For an explanation of New Jersey's split of electors, see Congressional Quarterly's *Guide to U.S. Elections*, 282, 258; Thomas, *Pursuit of the White House*, 64.

5. *HDM*, November 8, 1860.

6. Ibid., November 14, 1860.

the most powerful and important men of the state. He became active in politics and lived a life of luxury.[7]

Jackson knew on which side his bread was buttered. When his fortunes were threatened by the death of his first wife, he married another of Sappington's daughters. When she died, he married a third. A popular joke made the rounds of Missouri that if Jackson's third wife died, "he'd be coming for old lady Sappington next." When Sappington died in 1856, Jackson inherited the bulk of his estate. By 1860 Jackson owned a considerable amount of real estate and twenty slaves. His three marriages had been very profitable.

Jackson had a reputation as a strongly proslavery politician in the tumultuous 1850s. During the 1860 campaign for governor, he kept his presidential politics ambiguous. He claimed to personally support Breckenridge but argued that Douglas had the best shot at winning the White House for the Democrats. The people of Missouri should have listened more closely to what he said about Breckenridge. Following the election he felt free to indulge his personal preferences and fought hard to get Missouri to secede.

Jackson wanted badly to take Missouri out of the Union, but the voters would not agree. Frustrated by Lincoln's victory in the November election, he called a special convention to be held in St. Louis, hoping to persuade Missourians to secede. Delegates to the secession convention were elected by the people of each county. The election was held on February 18, 1861. Despite Jackson's best efforts, the secessionists took it on the nose again in February. The results were solidly in favor of staying in the Union. Statewide, 75 percent of the people voted for pro-Union candidates.[8] In Marion County, three of four candidates for the office of delegate to the convention were pro-Union. The secessionist candidate received only 1,651 votes out of 5,701 cast.[9] Seventy-two percent of the voters of Marion County voted for pro-Union candidates. The issue of secession was dead in Missouri. It would not be revitalized when the shooting started.

Why did Missourians not join the secessionist parade? The reasons are many and complex. It is true that Marion County in particular was solidly proslavery, but despite modern perceptions of that era, slavery had little to do with the issue of secession in Missouri. Geography, on the other

7. Lawrence O. Christensen et al., eds., *Dictionary of Missouri Biography*, 423.

8. Meyer, *Heritage of Missouri*, 350.

9. *HDM*, February 21, 1861.

hand, was very important. Had Missouri seceded, it would have been nearly surrounded by a foreign country. Slavery was actually a reason for staying in the Union. Missourians argued that by remaining part of the United States, they would benefit from the Fugitive Slave Laws. Illinois, Iowa, Kansas, and Nebraska would be compelled to return runaway slaves to a federal Missouri. If the United States was a foreign, nonslave country, that would not happen.[10]

This may sound ridiculous to the modern American who has the benefit of knowing what would soon be happening. But in 1861 it was a very popular argument in the newspapers and political speeches in Hannibal and Marion County. Lincoln did nothing to dissuade patriotic slaveholders. In the war to come, Missouri Union officers often took slaves as personal servants on their campaigns. When Frémont, the military commander in charge of the state, issued a proclamation freeing slaves on August 30, 1861, Lincoln fired him and withdrew the proclamation. Slaves in Missouri were freed not by the Emancipation Proclamation on January 1, 1863, but by the Missouri Legislature on January 11, 1865.[11]

While it is true that some out-of-state Union troops turned a blind eye to escaping slaves, troops in Missouri often captured runaways and returned them to their owners. As late as July 1863, a grand jury in Marion County returned an indictment against William R. Strachan for enticing a slave to run away from his master.[12] This was six months after slaves in the Confederate states were freed "on paper" by President Lincoln.

A compelling argument keeping northeast Missouri loyal to the Union was economic. It was true that the majority lifestyle of the region was Southern. It was also true that many Missourians had family ties in the Carolinas, Virginia, Kentucky, and Tennessee. For the first four decades of the state's existence the Mississippi River had connected Missouri economically and socially with Memphis, Natchez, and New Orleans. But things had changed by 1860. The railroad had replaced the river as the American highway. The new ties that bound Hannibal to the northeast held strong throughout the Civil War.

Hannibal, then the third-largest town in Missouri, was the prospering railhead of the new Hannibal and St. Joseph Railroad. Plans were already on the books to extend the railroad all the way to the Pacific. Whatever their cultural identities, most Missourians realized exactly where

10. Ibid., February 26, 1861, May 17, 1861.
11. James M. McPherson, *Battle Cry of Freedom: The Civil War Era*, 352–54; Meyer, *Heritage of Missouri*, 386.
12. Circuit Court records of Marion County, Missouri, July term, 1863.

their future lay. Besides connecting Missouri to the South, the river had also been an obstacle to east-west commerce and a formidable moat that protected slavery by hindering fleeing slaves. The same technology that made the railroad possible also brought about another great change in geography. It was now possible to bridge the Mississippi. By 1860 there were plans to span the tremendous river.

Missouri businessmen had connections with Chicago, New York, and Boston, and it was obvious that those relationships would grow and prosper. As the crisis was brewing in the spring of 1861, conferences were held by Illinois, Iowa, and Missouri commercial interests to maintain relations. The old river ties were becoming obsolete, and the new industrial, financial, and railroad bonds were strengthening. Josiah Hunt was the land agent in Hannibal for the Hannibal and St. Joseph Railroad. Eastern investors were worried about their railroad and the possibility of Missouri's leaving the union. Hunt wrote to his counterpart, the land agent in New York, in March of 1861:

The question whether Missouri will secede or not is best answered by the action of the State Convention which passed the . . . resolutions by a vote of more than three to one. I assure you Missouri will stay in the Union. She knows her own interest and is loyal to the Stars and Stripes. A few hot head fire eaters who loaf around the corner groceries, some broken down politicians whom the people have rejected (Jim Green for instance who has just been elected to stay at home from the U.S. Senate for the next six years) and some few others who have nothing to lose by a revolution and who have just sense enough to know that when the pot boils, the scum rises to the top, may talk disunion, but the bone & sinew of the State, the working men, the farmers, the land holders, and about all the slaveholders, have no such idea. As to people being driven away from the state for their opinion, I have read of such things in eastern papers, but never heard of any such case here. I find no difficulty in expressing my opinions with perfect freedom, and in the main they do not differ from yours. Although I do not call myself a [R]epublican, my platform being the Constitution (as our Judiciary interprets it), the *Union* (as it is) and the enforcement of the Laws as our legally constituted authority make them.

A person casually passing through Missouri might naturally be deceived as to the state of public opinion here. The Secession minority sometimes makes more show than the Union majority, on the same principle, that the less a bottle has it the more noise it makes in pouring it out.[13]

13. Bennett, *Hannibal and St. Joseph Railroad*, 278.

Citizen Soldiers

Every state in the Union had a militia in 1861. From the organization of the Missouri territorial government in 1807 until 1847, every able-bodied man in Missouri was required to serve in the militia. Prior to 1847 there had been musters four times a year. The citizen soldiers gathered by companies in April and September, by battalions in May, and by regiments or "extra battalions" in October.[14] But after 1847, the law was scrapped, and militia companies formed. Instead of all able-bodied men being required to be available for duty, each county became responsible for maintaining specific militia units. In other words, it was no longer a universal obligation. The militia companies armed and uniformed themselves—though uniforms were optional. The vast majority of militiamen drilled in their ordinary clothing. Uniforms were reserved for the well-to-do or those on fancy drill teams that competed against other militias in parade ground maneuvers.

Anticipating trouble, and hoping for the opportunity to take Missouri out of the Union, Governor Jackson reorganized the militias into the Missouri State Guard in early 1861. Former Missouri Governor Sterling Price commanded the guard. The state was divided into nine departments. State Guard members were sworn to protect the people's rights under the state and federal constitutions. Despite Jackson's hopes, the guard did not become a secessionist force. It was the legitimate militia of a state that acknowledged the sovereignty of the Union. Things stayed peaceful in Missouri during the first quarter of 1861. The secession convention met in St. Louis and, to the chagrin of Governor Jackson, decided by an overwhelming majority not to leave the Union.[15] However, Claiborne Fox Jackson was determined to find some way to help the new Confederacy. His opportunity came in April.

When Abraham Lincoln issued a call for 75,000 Union troops to put down the rebellion, the president requested that Missouri provide 3,213 men as its quota. Governor Jackson angrily refused. He replied on April 17, 1861, in a letter published throughout the state:

> To the Hon Simon Cameron, Secretary of War, Washington, D.C.:
> Sir—Your dispatch of the 14th inst., making a call on Missouri for four regiments of men, for immediate service, has been received. There can be, I apprehend, no doubt but these men are intended to form a part of

14. *Laws of Missouri*, 74–105.
15. *HDM*, March 24, 26, and 27, 1861.

the President's army to make war upon the people of the seceded States. Your requisition, in my judgment, is illegal, unconstitutional, and revolutionary, in its object, inhuman and diabolical, and cannot be complied with. Not one man will the State of Missouri furnish to carry on any such unholy crusade.

C. F. Jackson, Governor of Missouri.[16]

Needless to say, this did not sit well with the Lincoln administration. However, Governor Jackson went beyond baiting the president. He was not above playing political chess with his own state military force. Using his executive powers as governor, he called out the Missouri State Guard and ordered an encampment on the fringes of St. Louis, within striking distance of the U.S. arsenal. Seven hundred State Guard troops set up a tent city and drilled in new gray uniforms conspicuously like the uniforms of the new Confederacy. The soldiers named their camp after the governor: Camp Jackson.

To ratchet tensions even higher and to better arm his guard, Jackson sent a letter to Jefferson Davis asking for artillery. The wily president of the Confederacy responded in a bid to gain Missouri for his new nation. He realized that a Confederate Missouri could help keep the vast resources of the West from reaching the East. Davis promised to provide Jackson with artillery.[17] When Louisiana seceded, the Confederates had seized a federal arsenal in Baton Rouge and obtained a number of cannons. Davis believed they would be sufficient to seize the arsenal if placed on the nearby high ground, and he offered them to Jackson. He wrote:

> I have directed that Captains Greene and Duke should be furnished with two 12-pounder howitzers and two 32-pounder guns, with the proper ammunition for each. These, from the commanding hills, will be effective against the garrison and break the enclosing walls of the place.
>
> . . . We look anxiously and hopefully for the day when the star of Missouri shall be added to the constellation of the Confederate States of America. With best wishes, I am, very respectfully yours, Jefferson Davis.[18]

The Confederates packed the four cannons and a generous supply of ammunition in several large crates labeled "marble" and shipped them

---

16. *HDM*, April 19, 1861; Hans Christian Adamson, *Rebellion in Missouri: 1861*, 3.

17. Adamson, *Rebellion in Missouri*, 6, 34.

18. Ibid., 34.

upriver on a steamboat. The shipment also contained muskets and ammunition for the Missouri State Guard. On May 8, 1861, the crates were unloaded in St. Louis and delivered to Camp Jackson. Federal authorities knew what was going on at the guard camp. They knew the cannons had arrived. They were rightly nervous about the body of armed men so near the important city and the vital junction of the Missouri and Mississippi Rivers. The State Guard did little to allay those fears. They flew a secessionist flag along with the Missouri flag and named their streets after prominent Confederates. The heavy artillery shipped from Louisiana gave the state forces the firepower to blast into the St. Louis arsenal. Things were grim indeed. But the Union forces had a secret weapon in St. Louis—a young army captain named Nathaniel Lyon.[19]

Lyon was the hardheaded son of a farmer and lawyer from Connecticut. He had graduated from West Point in 1841. He had a bad reputation in the army as a disciplinarian fond of inflicting sadistic punishments on enlisted men. Like U. S. Grant, he was a lousy peacetime soldier, but he shone in wartime.

Stationed in Kansas during the late 1850s and appalled by the conduct of proslavery forces there, Lyon came to hate slaveholders as lawless aristocrats. He arrived in St. Louis on the eve of war determined to do everything in his power to undermine what he saw as a "slaveocracy." The polar opposite of Claiborne Fox Jackson, he was determined to keep Missouri in the Union. Lyon ousted Gen. William S. Harney, the moderate, mild-mannered commander of Union forces in St. Louis, and assumed command of the area. He armed loyal German units in St. Louis as Home Guard troops. When Jackson upped the ante by bringing in the cannons, Lyon was ready. Disguising himself as a woman, he reconnoitered the State Guard camp from a carriage.[20] Then on May 9, with a force of federal soldiers and loyal Home Guard troops, Lyon seized the seven hundred Missouri State Guardsmen in the camp.

As the state prisoners were marched by Lyon's men through the streets of St. Louis, angry crowds gathered and heckled the Union forces. Soon shots rang out, and in the confusion Union troops fired into the crowd.[21] Twenty-eight civilians and two soldiers were killed in the melee. One witness to the troubles in St. Louis would play a prominent role in the bitter war that was to follow. William Tecumseh Sherman was in St. Louis when the State Guardsmen were seized.

19. Ibid., 40–45; *HDM*, May 15, 1861.
20. Adamson, *Rebellion in Missouri*, 45.
21. *HDM*, May 15, 1861.

On May 15, Governor Jackson mobilized the State Guard through-out Missouri. The troops were instructed to "organize" and "hold . . . in readiness for active service, should the emergency arise to require it." He rammed a special bill through the Missouri legislature allocating money to the guard.[22]

As tensions mounted between Jackson in Jefferson City and Lyon in St. Louis, one final attempt was made for peace in Missouri. The governor and Sterling Price arranged a meeting with Nathaniel Lyon and Frank Blair at the Planter House Hotel in St. Louis on June 11. Governor Jackson was promised safe passage in and out of St. Louis. The seconds that Lyon and Jackson brought to the parley at the hotel were significant. Blair was a prominent Republican and strong Union supporter. He was a congressman from St. Louis elected with the help of German immigrants. His brother was Montgomery Blair, the postmaster in the Lincoln administration. Frank Blair spoke for the president. Price was a native Virginian and had served as governor of Missouri from 1853 to 1857. He was now commanding general of the Missouri State Guard. He had been president of the secession convention and had favored Missouri's remaining in the Union—until Lyon had seized Camp Jackson. He was very influential with Missourians.

Jackson and Price tried to obtain neutrality for Missouri. They offered to disband the Missouri State Guard and agree to keep Confederate troops out of Missouri if the federal government would keep Union troops out. Lyon would not yield an inch. He was in no mood for compromise. He would not consider a neutral Missouri. After a heated discussion, Lyon terminated the meeting abruptly with the words, "This means war."[23] Jackson and Price returned to Jefferson City by train. They took Lyon's declaration of war seriously. In Jefferson City, Price issued a call for fifty thousand Missouri troops to engage the Union forces.[24] As he wrote, State Guard members were already setting fire to the railroad bridges connecting the capital to St. Louis and cutting the telegraph wires.

Governor Jackson issued an order to the Missouri State Guard to do everything it could to resist the federal invaders. But even in this proclamation, the governor was careful to point out to Missourians that Missouri was still a member of the Union. "In issuing this Proclamation, I hold it to be my solemn duty to remind you that Missouri is still one of the United States, that the Executive Department of the State Government does not

22. Ibid., May 21, 1861; Thomas L. Snead, *The Fight for Missouri*, 180.
23. Snead, *Fight for Missouri*, 200; Adamson, *Rebellion in Missouri*, 113.
24. *HDM*, June 14, 1861.

arrogate to itself the power to disturb that relation; that that power has been wisely vested in a Convention which will, at the proper time, express your sovereign will; and that, meanwhile, it is your duty to obey all the *constitutional* requirements of the Federal Government."[25] Jackson still hoped the secession convention could be reconvened and an ordinance of secession lawfully passed.

The vast majority of men who responded to the governor's call were confused. Who was the enemy? To whom were they loyal? Missouri was legally in the Union, but the order of the governor was also lawful. The orders of Governor Jackson were printed in newspapers, even in strongly pro-Union newspapers. The contrary orders of federal commanders were also published. The men who had been sworn into the State Guard around Missouri were waiting with their squirrel rifles and shotguns for developments. They were sworn to uphold both the state and federal constitutions. They were not in any sense Confederate troops—though doubtless many had Confederate sympathies. It was a volatile time.

An order from Jefferson City was circulated in northeast Missouri: "Companies will be formed as rapidly as possible and await the arrival of the Brigadier Gen. for this district, who will perhaps be here in a day or two and receive them into service. Every man will provide himself with the best gun he can get which he will keep until replaced by a better gun from the State."[26]

Sam Clemens answered that call. Federal troops pursued Jackson and Price by steamboat up the Missouri River. It was at this crucial juncture that Clemens came on the scene. After returning by the steamboat *Nebraska* from New Orleans in May, he had been vacationing in Hannibal with his friends and fellow pilots Absalom Grimes and Sam Bowen. The peace conference at the Planter House was held on June 12. By June 15, the state government had taken flight from Jefferson City and federal troops transported by river occupied the capital. This event provides the date Sam Clemens took to the field with the Missouri State Guard.

Absalom Grimes recorded in his memoir that while he, Clemens, and Sam Bowen were in Hannibal, they were ordered to report to General Grey's office in St. Louis. They went downriver on the steamboat *Hannibal City* and reported as instructed. Grey told them, "I want to send a lot of boats [carrying soldiers] up to Boonville, on the Missouri River, the latter part of the week." He wanted the three men to pilot the boats on the

25. Ibid., June 15, 1861.
26. Ibid., June 18, 1861.

Missouri River. The men protested that they were Mississippi pilots, not Missouri River pilots, but all agreed that they could follow an experienced pilot up the river. It was clear, however, that the three did not wish to aid in the pursuit of Governor Jackson.[27]

According to Grimes, he, Clemens, and Bowen slipped out of the general's office while the Union officer was distracted by a pair of pretty women. The men made their way back to Hannibal. This event can be dated closely. It had to have occurred around June 15 when federal troops occupied Jefferson City, because Jackson had then moved to a place near Boonville, upstream from the capital. Federal troops overtook the governor and four to five hundred men near Boonville on June 17. The troops arrived by steamboat. A battle was fought, and Union forces were victorious. This was the operation to which General Grey referred.

After Clemens was back in Hannibal, he may have taken the time to report to a St. Louis newspaper on developments in Hannibal. A correspondent wrote:

To the Editor of the Daily Mo. State Journal:
Four of the Home Guards deserted Saturday night, and left for parts unknown. I heard from a very reliable source that there were seventeen bodies sent up the river this morning, killed in a skirmish up the railroad somewhere. It is not known where for the wires have been cut down. There are about 250 Home Guards here at present, and there is a requisition from General Scott here, for the troops that have been sent here.

The boys are responding bravely to the call of the Governor—about fifty have left already, and plenty left to strike when the proper time comes. Major T.A. Harris received his commission Friday night, (per courier) and has left for the seat of war. He is Brigadier General of this district. Our city is perfectly quiet at present.

Yours, in haste,
SAM.[28]

The letter was truly written in haste. The rumor about the bodies would prove untrue. However, the information about Thomas Harris was correct. It had just become known in northeast Missouri that Harris had been appointed commander of the Seventh District of the Missouri State

27. Absalom Grimes, *Absalom Grimes: Confederate Mail Runner,* 4; Monaghan, *Civil War on the Western Border,* 136–38.

28. *HDM,* June 20, 1861.

Guard. The authorship of the "Sam" letter is not definite. The writer of the letter could obviously write well like Clemens, and the timing fits like a glove.

Hannibal was full of Union troops. Steamboats arrived daily bearing troops from Iowa, Illinois, Wisconsin, and Ohio. Large numbers of loyal Missourians joined Home Guard groups in Marion County. Clemens, Grimes, and the Bowen brothers quickly made their way into the relative safety of the woods and hills of Ralls County to the southwest of Hannibal. Like all the units of the Missouri State Guard, they were unorganized. They were not uniformed and carried only the weapons they had brought from home. Grimes described Clemens as carrying a squirrel rifle and riding a mule.[29] They were also confused.

Clemens's actual experience with the Missouri State Guard was limited and was typical of many men in these very early days of the war. He rode to Col. John Ralls's house and took the oath of allegiance to the Missouri State Guard, in which he pledged to support both the state and federal constitutions. He did *not* swear allegiance to the Confederate government. Then he and his comrades drilled and camped. They were a ragged lot. They dressed in civilian clothing and slept wrapped up in blankets and quilts they brought from home. They had a motley collection of small-bore rifles and shotguns together with whatever ammunition they had brought along. They had nothing to do. The unit held a company election and picked Clemens for the post of second lieutenant. The ragtag amateurs were an officer-heavy group. After they had chosen a captain, first lieutenant, second lieutenant, and sergeant, there were only three or four privates in the group. They roamed about Ralls County and camped out where they could.

Despite electing officers, the men with Clemens did not take notions of military discipline seriously. Grimes reported that one day they encountered Gen. Thomas Harris and actually refused to follow his direct order. Clemens and the others had been camping in a very uncomfortable, wet location. They were on their way to a farmhouse that would offer more amenities. General Harris ordered them back to their waterlogged camp. According to Grimes, Clemens and his associates just laughed and continued on.

They also did not engage in any fighting. Grimes reports no violent encounters at all during this time. Hannibal newspapers confirm that no one was shot and killed in the manner described by Mark Twain in his "Private History of a Campaign That Failed"—a fictionalized account of

29. Grimes, *Confederate Mail Runner*, 6.

his service published in *Century Magazine* in 1885. The name "Marion Rangers" also appears to have been a creation of Mark Twain's. There is no record of it in Grimes's memoir or in any other source.

The only "wounds" Clemens suffered during his short time in the field were a painful boil and a sprained ankle. His little unit spent June and July hiding. Likely the men were bored. There was little military activity in that part of Missouri at that time. Jackson and the main body of the Missouri State Guard were hurrying toward southwest Missouri, where they hoped to find help from Confederate troops from Arkansas, Louisiana, and Texas.

Exactly how Clemens came in from the field is unclear. Amnesty was available to all who would lay down their weapons. Newly promoted Union General Lyon issued a proclamation stating, "All persons who . . . have taken up arms, or who are now preparing to do so, are invited to return to their homes, and relinquish their hostile attitude to the Federal government, and are assured they may do so without being molested for past occurrences." The local Union commander, Col. R. F. Smith of the Sixteenth Illinois, headquartered in Palmyra, issued another amnesty offer on July 3.[30]

Men took advantage of the amnesty offers in Marion County. The *Hannibal Daily Messenger* observed that "quite a number of the daring adventurers, and chivalrous, but duped and misguided young men of this and Ralls Co., who participated in the late action near Boonville, are returning perfectly satisfied with their brief campaign." Sam probably availed himself of the offer as well, and he must have done it early, too. By July 26, 1861, he and his brother Orion were on their way to Nevada. He arrived there on August 14 and went to work for the Lincoln administration as a secretary to his brother.[31]

He was not alone in abandoning the Missouri State Guard. His friend Sam Bowen also came in from the field. He was imprisoned for a while. Then he took the Union loyalty oath and went to work as a steamboat pilot for the government.[32] If Clemens took the loyalty oath, there is no record of it. He may have slipped out of the area unnoticed and quietly joined up with Orion.

Sam Clemens and the men who wilted away under Thomas Harris may unintentionally have served a very important purpose in the ultimate victory of the Union. The Twenty-first Illinois Volunteer Infantry was

30. *HDM,* June 22, 1861, July 7, 1861.
31. Ibid., June 23, 1861; R. Kent Rasmussen, *Mark Twain A to Z,* xiii.
32. Grimes, *Confederate Mail Runner,* 18.

dispatched on July 3, 1861, to Missouri to hunt Harris and his men down. The colonel of the unit was an rough-edged, underrated officer named Ulysses S. Grant.[33] As Sam Clemens was deciding to abandon arms, Grant was marching toward the rumored camp of his foe at Clemens's birthplace of Florida, Missouri. On the night before what he thought would be his first battle of the war, Grant learned a lesson that he carried throughout the long years of the contest. He wrote in his memoir,

> My sensations as we approached what I supposed might be "a field of battle" were anything but agreeable. I had been in all the engagements in Mexico that it was possible for one person to be in; but not in command. If some one else had been colonel and I had been lieutenant-colonel I do not think I would have felt any trepidation. . . . As we approached the brow of the hill from which it was expected we could see Harris' camp, and possibly find his men formed ready to meet us, my heart kept getting higher and higher until it felt to me as though it was in my throat.

Grant's men found Harris's camp abandoned. His men poorly supplied, disorganized, and deserting, Harris had stolen a march on the Union forces and gone to join up with other State Guard forces. Grant recorded his reaction a quarter century later.

> My heart resumed its place. It occurred to me at once that Harris had been as much afraid of me as I had been of him. This was a view of the question I had never taken before; but it was one I never forgot afterwards. From that event to the close of the war, I never experienced trepidation upon confronting an enemy, though I always felt more or less anxiety. I never forgot that he had as much reason to fear my forces as I had his. The lesson was valuable.[34]

Harris and the Missouri State Guard troops he maintained had fled and were forty miles away. Absalom Grimes was able to join up with a group and make his way south of the Missouri River. Small State Guard militias from across Missouri did manage to band together. About 5,200 finally rallied around the governor in Southwest Missouri. At Neosho, Missouri, after fighting battles at Wilson's Creek and Lexington, Missouri, with the

33. Actually, Grant was a general but was unaware of the promotion. He had been promoted effective May 21, 1861.
34. U. S. Grant, *Personal Memoirs of U. S. Grant*, 1:249–50.

help of Confederate troops from Arkansas, Louisiana, and Texas, Governor Jackson called a meeting of the legislature to consider a secession act. Estimates vary on the number of legislators who attended, but all agree that there was not a quorum present. This rump session passed a secession act on October 28, 1861. When the Missouri State Guard withdrew from Missouri into Arkansas, members who did not wish to leave the state were allowed to resign. The guard continued as an independent organization until after the Battle of Pea Ridge in 1862. Many were sworn into Confederate service. Many others went home.[35]

Many hundreds of people who had taken to the field in those first confusing days of the conflict with the Missouri State Guard did exactly what Sam Clemens did. They voted with their feet. It is hard to call what they did desertion. They went home the same way they had responded to the governor's call: one by one. They had sworn to support both the state and federal governments, and that proved impossible. Many of the early State Guard were loyal citizens for the rest of their lives. Some secretly aided the Confederacy when the chance arose. Some engaged in guerilla activities.

Sam Bowen was one of those who would turn a blind eye to rebel activity. His main assistance appears to have been not informing on people he knew had Confederate sympathies during the war, particularly passengers he transported up and down the river. No doubt a few smugglers and spies were able to get mail, medicine, or information through the lines through his silence. On the other hand, his piloting of steamboats laden with soldiers and cargo for the Union army did far more to aid the North than his discretion did to aid the Confederacy.

Absalom Grimes went on to an exciting career smuggling mail from Missouri families to soldiers fighting in the Confederate army. There were Missouri Confederates, but the fact is that nearly three-quarters of the Missourians who took up arms during the Civil War served with Union forces. Of the 139,000 men who enlisted in Missouri, 109,000 men joined Union units, while only 30,000 joined the Confederates.[36] In the early years of the twentieth century, a myth arose of a Confederate Missouri, which fit in well with the new racist realities of the Jim Crow era. Eventually this myth acquired the semiofficial recognition of state and local historians. It became as much a part of Missouri culture as slavery had been in that long-ago time. The Confederate flag was even waved at University of

35. Meyer, *Heritage of Missouri*, 379 et seq.; William E. Parrish, *A History of Missouri, Volume 3: 1860–1875*, 47.

36. Meyer, *Heritage of Missouri*, 400.

Missouri football games. The children and grandchildren of loyal Union men and women celebrated a Confederate past that had never existed.

The most that can be said of Sam Clemens's war record is that he was in the field for a few weeks with an amateurish group of Missouri State Guard. He never swore an oath to the Confederate government, but had to the Union when he joined the State Guard. He never deserted. The convention that Governor Jackson had legally called reconvened. Instead of passing an act of secession, it declared the office of governor vacant. The convention elected Hamilton Gamble to serve as governor until a free election could be held. The convention governed Missouri.[37] Men like Clemens were thus freed from any allegiance to Jackson.

Sam Clemens was probably, like many Missourians, ambivalent about the whole affair. To call him a Confederate in any sense is simply unsupportable. He must have been confused as he fled Missouri. The slave culture he had come home to protect was about to change beyond recognition. He could not serve the same cause his father had served as a member of the jury that tried Thompson, Work, and Burr and as a justice of the peace. The old Hannibal that looked south to Memphis, Vicksburg, and New Orleans was dying. By the summer of 1861 the community was more tied to the markets of Illinois and the East than ever before. For the four brutal years to come, the Mississippi River would be completely choked off south of Missouri. The Hannibal and St. Joseph Railroad would become a vital Union lifeline and steadily grow in importance. And the world of Sam Clemens's youth would disappear—but not without a struggle.

37. Ibid., 381–86.

Postscript

The Fighting in Northeast Missouri

As Sam Clemens arrived in Nevada, the war was heating up in northeast Missouri. Hotheaded young men with secessionist sympathies organized under the command of Thomas Harris, Martin Green, and Joseph Porter. After numerous skirmishes and a bloody defeat at the hands of Union forces in Athens, on the Iowa border, in August 1861, they turned to guerrilla raids. State Guard troops would go about their daily lives as farmers and merchants, banding together for missions, then dispersing as soon as they were able. They burned bridges, cut telegraph wires, ambushed and murdered opponents, and sniped at trains.

Events came to a climax on October 18, 1862. On September 12 of that year a group of four hundred troops under Joseph Porter struck Palmyra. No Missouri rebel unit ever managed to hold a northeast Missouri town, and this raid lasted just a few hours—long enough to free forty-five prisoners from the county jail. The raiders also took prisoner Andrew Allsman, a loyal Union man in his sixties. He was despised by the rebels and suspected of informing on his neighbors. Porter's men murdered him somewhere on the prairies west of town. His body was never located.[1]

The Union commander, John McNeil, unaware of Allsman's death, announced that if the old man was not returned he would order the execution of ten prisoners. He had in custody many rebels who had been arrested for sabotage and violating loyalty oaths. To the horror of the Lincoln administration, McNeil carried out his threat. On October 18, ten prisoners were transported by wagon to the Palmyra fairgrounds. During

---

1. Perkins, *History of Marion County*, 489–515. The skull of Andrew Allsman was reportedly found and was used in rituals by a medical fraternity in Kirksville. It is the possession of the descendants of Dr. John Bush in Marion County.

the trip, the men sat on their coffins. They were brutally executed by a nervous firing squad. Several victims were not killed outright. One man was not hit at all in the first volley. The North was shocked, and the South was outraged. Lincoln denounced the act in a cabinet meeting. The Union and Confederacy were barely able to stave off a round of tit-for-tat executions of prisoners.

Barbarous though the act was, it may have ultimately spared lives. It brought an end to most guerrilla activity in northeast Missouri. Though western Missouri would be plagued by the activities of William Quantrill and the band that rode with him, including "Bloody Bill" Anderson, Jesse and Frank James, and the Younger brothers, northeast Missouri would remain relatively calm for the rest of the war. Except for the activities of Confederate recruiters and mail-running by men like Absalom Grimes, partisan operations took place well to the south and west of Marion County.

Reverend William Caples

Reverend Caples did not live to see the demise of slave culture in Missouri. Like most Methodist ministers, he moved from congregation to congregation every few years. The outbreak of the Civil War found him in western Missouri. He joined up with Gen. Sterling Price as a State Guard chaplain after the Battle of Lexington and retreated to Arkansas. Being an excellent orator, he was sent back to northern Missouri to recruit a regiment of troops. He and his band of recruits were captured going south as they approached the Missouri River near the little town of Blackwater. After being imprisoned in St. Louis, Caples was paroled, but never exchanged. Stranded in Union Missouri with nothing to do, he finally took the Union loyalty oath—required if he wanted to preach again. He was assigned to a church in Glasgow, Missouri. He never stopped believing that God would lead the slave South to victory over the heathen, abolitionist North.

In 1864, during the last great Confederate raid into the state, Jo Shelby's Missouri troops besieged a small federal unit at Glasgow. Caples and his family were trapped between the armies and hid in their basement during the battle. When a lull in the fighting occurred, Caples emerged from his shelter to have a look. In one of history's little ironies, he was struck in the thigh by a Confederate twelve-pound cannon ball. It took him three excruciating days to die. He believed to his last breath in the divinity of slavery.[2]

2. Marvin, *Life of Rev. William Goff Caples*, 367–76.

Father Augustine Tolton

Augustine Tolton was seven years old when the war came to Missouri. He was already working in the fields and had felt the whip upon his back.[3] During the first year of the war, his father escaped to Illinois and joined the Union army. His mother remained with her three small children. Finally in 1862, she determined to make the run herself. Carrying her twenty-month-old and dragging along eight-year-old Charley and seven-year-old Augustine, the mother walked the two dozen miles to the Mississippi River. The four of them reached Hannibal only to be taken into custody by the local authorities. There were, however, out-of-state troops in town. They intervened and freed the small family. They placed them in a boat to row across the river. In later years, Father Tolton would recall the angry voices of Missourians jeering at them as his mother struggled with the oars. At one point someone in town opened fire on the fleeing slaves. Augustine's mother made the children lie flat as shots hit the water around the boat and the baby cried. The Toltons were lucky. They made it to Illinois alive.

Ever the faithful Catholic, Augustine Tolton joined the priesthood. Although some doors closed to him within the Church, he went to Rome and was ordained at St. Peter's in 1886. He was the first African American priest.

John Rogers

To Rogers's surprise, his statues of the slave auction never sold very well. However, other scenes proved very popular, and his mass-produced plaster statues were common in the Victorian parlors of middle-class America. His was a household name.

Samuel T. Glover

Samuel T. Glover left Hannibal after the trial of Ben the slave. He became a leading attorney in St. Louis. With the outbreak of the Civil War, Samuel T. Glover rose to prominence in the new Republican Party. He was a leader of the conservative branch and a darling of the Lincoln administration. Having never abandoned his emancipationist ideas, Glover reached his heyday during the first two years of the war. His speeches in support of Lincoln were reprinted as pamphlets. When Missouri's Radical

3. Hemesath, *From Slave to Priest*, 10.

Republicans attacked Lincoln for not immediately emancipating Missouri slaves and not being tough enough with Missouri rebels, Glover sprang to the president's defense.

He was proud of the gradual emancipation scheme the Missouri Legislature passed in 1863. Under the plan, slavery was to be ended in Missouri on July 4, 1876. Old slaves were to continue to serve for life, and all slaves under twelve were to serve until they were twenty-three. Thus over a twenty-five-year period slavery would gradually disappear in Missouri. Glover was the model of Missouri moderation. He was pro-Union and antislavery, but he had his eye toward easing loyal slaveholders out of slavery. However, just as the Marion County Colonization Society had been swamped by the hysteria following the Bright murders and spate of runaways, events soon outpaced Glover's emancipation dreams.

The End of Slavery

The last prosecution in Marion County for helping slaves escape occurred in 1863, after President Lincoln's Emancipation Proclamation freed the slaves in the Confederate states. As the war ground on and Union victories mounted, the need to placate loyal slaveholders in Missouri diminished. In October 1863 President Lincoln issued an order to General Schofield requiring federal troops in Missouri to neither return runaway slaves to their owners, nor encourage slaves to run away. In late 1864 it became obvious that the Thirteenth Amendment, ending slavery in the United States, would be approved by the required number of states. The Missouri Legislature abandoned the gradual emancipation scheme that had been so dear to Glover. However, a major obstacle to abolition existed: The Missouri Constitution specifically prohibited immediate emancipation. A new state constitutional convention was called to meet in St. Louis. On January 6, 1865, two full years after the Emancipation Proclamation, the convention adopted a constitution that permitted emancipation. Five days later the same convention passed an act forever abolishing slavery in Missouri. Freedom finally came for Missouri slaves on January 11, 1865.

After the war Missouri settled into a pattern of segregation—the systematic discrimination against blacks that would last for another century. The churches of Hannibal that had admitted slaves as members now excluded blacks from membership. The theology of slavery gave way to a theology of segregation. The myth of Ham was modified and used to explain why African Americans were at the bottom of the social ladder. The old Baptist Cemetery in Hannibal became a burying ground for blacks and very poor whites. Some white families who could afford to do so dug up their dead and reburied them in other cemeteries. The bodies of Henry and John Marshall Clemens were moved to Mt. Olivet Cemetery south of Hannibal, where only whites were buried. The old Baptist Cemetery fell into disrepair. Today, maintained by the city of Hannibal, it is a shamble of tumbled and broken headstones amid overgrown weeds and untrimmed trees.[4]

Sam Clemens and General Grant

Sam Clemens ended up writing for Nevada's *Territorial Enterprise* in 1862. In this return to the newspaper, he discovered his destiny as Mark Twain—a pen name he took from the steamboatman's term for "safe water." The culture that had produced him was gone forever. He would return to Hannibal only four times as an adult—for a brief visit in 1882, one night in 1885 while on a lecture tour, in 1890 for his mother's funeral, and in 1902, when traveling to the University of Missouri to receive an honorary degree. But in his mind, he returned to that world often. In middle age, he would produce his greatest work, *Adventures of Huckleberry Finn*. Not only would the novel's setting be the long-vanished world of Hannibal slave culture, but the language would echo the dialects he had learned while setting type for Joseph Ament and Orion Clemens. Sam Clemens would finally come home. All the themes of those stories, and his reactions to them, would be there: the violence, the slavery, the moral ambiguity, the inhumanity. . . .

U. S. Grant's career advanced steadily after the lesson he learned from General Harris's retreat. Grant's willingness to engage the enemy, his stubborn refusal to retreat, and his relentless pursuit of military objectives ultimately brought him to the attention of Abraham Lincoln, who was looking for a general to lead the star-crossed Army of the Potomac. Grant emerged from the Civil War a four-star general and a hero of the North.

In 1868, he was elected president and served two rocky terms. His administrations were marred by scandals. While he was personally uninvolved, many of his appointees used their offices to fleece the public and line their pockets. While Grant had been an outstanding soldier, he was a terrible judge of the character of businessmen. After he left the White

4. In 2002, restoration efforts began by Friends of Historic Hannibal, a not-for-profit group, and the Hannibal parks board to restore the cemetery. Included in the project is the resetting of the tombstone of Agness Flautleroy.

House, he lost all of his money in a Ponzi scheme operated by a man named Ferdinand Ward. When the enterprise collapsed, investors had lost $16 million, and President Grant had $180 to his name and was deeply in debt. To make matters worse, he was diagnosed with cancer.[5]

While their paths had never crossed in Missouri, Grant and Clemens became friends in New York and frequently met. Clemens admired Grant's plainspoken manner. Despite enjoying the admiration of the nation, the army commander and former president remained a humble and honest man. Grant enjoyed Clemens's company because, unlike so many others, Clemens sought nothing personally from him, but he did constantly urge the old soldier to write his memoirs.

When financial disaster struck, Grant took up the pen. He wrote some articles for *Century Magazine,* and Clemens was appalled when he learned that Grant was being paid only five hundred dollars for each piece. When he discovered that the magazine was offering Grant a royalty of 10 percent for a book-length memoir, Clemens was outraged. He offered to publish the book through Charles Webster, a company he had established to publish *Huckleberry Finn.* Clemens gave Grant 70 percent of the profits from the memoir.

As Grant lay dying of throat cancer at a summer cottage near Saratoga Springs, New York, he produced one of the finest military memoirs ever written. Subscription agents, mainly Union veterans, fanned out across the country to presell the two-volume work. Dressed in their old army uniforms, they would go door to door, asking if there was a Union veteran in the house. Shortly before Grant died, Clemens was able to visit him and inform the dying man that 150,000 copies had already been sold at $3.50 each—and that was just the beginning. Financial success was guaranteed.

Grant finished the memoir. Though at the end he was unable to speak and in great pain, he soldiered on. Then he died. His last great victory came because of his friendship with Sam Clemens. The one-time defender of slave culture had rescued from financial ruin the family of the man who had chased his friends from the field of battle in 1861. But Sam Clemens was not just being charitable. He was purging himself of ghosts.

Making Amends

Sam would marry into a family of abolitionists and have Harriet Beecher Stowe as a next-door neighbor. In a now-famous act of contri-

5. Geoffrey Perret, *Ulysses S. Grant, Soldier and President,* 468–69.

tion, he would help pay the way for black students through college. One of the students Clemens sponsored was a bright young law student at Yale named Warner McGuinn. McGuinn went on to become a prominent Baltimore civil rights lawyer and a mentor to Thurgood Marshall, the first black United States Supreme Court Justice. Clemens would refer to the financial aid as part of the reparation due from every white to every black man. As his friend and biographer William Dean Howells noted, "He held himself responsible for the wrong which the white race had done the black race in slavery."[6]

This was no abstract social debt. Clemens was making amends for specific wrongs. Perhaps as he wrote out the checks he thought of the six slaves inherited by his parents and sold, the little nine-year-old slave girl his father had seized and sold, Charley, and the slave Henry, who received the twenty lashes. He might have thought of the years Thompson, Work, and Burr spent in the Missouri State Penitentiary for doing what his character Huck safely did in a novel two decades after the Civil War. He might have considered the ads for human beings he set and sold. Perhaps he recalled the degrading stories. And there was the $24.50 from the Boston Vigilance Committee—money taken from people who were to become his friends. For a man with as big a conscience as Sam Clemens's, it must have been a terrible burden.

Jim

I have found Jim.

I realize now that I was never going to find him in the archives of newspapers. He isn't in the records at the courthouse and he isn't in the letters, diaries, or histories that have survived. Like an archaeologist sifting through soil for physical remnants of a culture, I am never going to find Jim in those places. I had hoped he might be in oral histories, but I repeatedly ran into a stone wall. Among people who had endured slavery, two topics were taboo: slave days and the white people to whom they were related. In my research I have been very fortunate to have met wonderful people whose ancestors labored as slaves in Marion County.

When researching the firm that employed John Marshall Clemens in 1845, I learned that the man who owned the Holliday and McCune Company was a direct ancestor of both Presidents Bush. I went and inter-

6. William Dean Howells, *My Mark Twain*, 40; Shelley Fisher Fishkin, *Lighting out for the Territory*, 101–7; Arthur G. Pettit, *Mark Twain and the South*, 9.

viewed descendants of the Holliday slaves, but again ran into a wall. They knew little about their ancestors—other than they could not read or write. One woman recalled a sadness about her grandfather who would sit quietly in the corner. She said that "he acted like a slave."

Researching and writing this book has been a wonderful, yet frustrating, experience. In Sam's world, the life of the slave was brutal and repressed. The histories and newspaper stories were written by white people who were, for the most part, blinded by the machineries of oppression.

I have read the theology of racial hatred and superiority as preached by Hannibal churches. This would have been the religion forced on Jim. I have seen the constant bombardment of racial propaganda in the press. I have been sickened by laws passed by the Missouri Legislature and Hannibal city council that attempted to regulate the life of Jim from cradle to grave. I understand he was denied the basic rights Americans now take for granted. He could not speak his mind freely. He could not assemble with others. He could not travel. He could not exercise religion as he wished.

Tragically, for my purposes, Jim could not read and write. It was illegal to teach him or his four million family members and friends. Ignorance was the foundation on which slavery stood. A slave who could read had power—the power to discover information and ideas that slaveholding society wished to keep from him. He also had the power to forge passes that would get him safely past the patrols, sheriffs, and constables. The goal of slaveholding society in banning reading was to control slaves, but the restriction had a far greater impact—it stilled Jim's historical voice.

Letters, diaries, ledgers, and notes are the things of historians' dreams. Through these the historian glimpses the unpolished ideas of the people he studies. Jim could write none of these. But Samuel Clemens could. It is ironic that I find myself back where I began this journey. I began looking for Jim by reading *Adventures of Huckleberry Finn*. In the end, that is where I find him, fully fitted with heart and soul. It is a wonder to me that Clemens was able to breathe life into him. If I have accomplished anything, it has been to show that Hannibal was never the white town drowsing in the sun of Clemens's childhood idyl, but instead a place of turmoil, which increased as the nation slid into civil war. Clemens was subjected to the same ideology of oppression that kept Jim a slave.

Samuel Clemens was able to overcome his upbringing and realize the full humanity of Jim. With his genius and empathy, Clemens has done the one thing no historian will ever be able to do—he has breathed life into a long-dead slave. Through the fictitious Jim, we can hear the real Jim speak.

I know that *Huckleberry Finn* is flawed. It must be. Clemens was white. He never suffered as a slave. He did not personally know the day-to-day, cradle-to-grave degradation experienced by the men, women, and children who made up one quarter of the population and labored for the other three quarters. But Clemens is one of the best we have. His gift is that he cared deeply and watched closely. He had a genius for nuance and language. At a time when most white people thought African Americans weren't quite as human as they, he knew better.

Appendix

An Ordinance Respecting Slaves, Free Negroes, and Mulattoes

Section 1 Be it ordained by the Board of Trustees of the Town of Hannibal that if any free negro or mulattoe shall commit any assault, or assault and battery, on any slave or free Negro, or Mulattoe, or any white person, or shall be concerned in any riot or unlawful assembly, he or she shall on conviction before any Justice of the Peace within said town, receive on his or her bare back, any number of lashes not exceeding thirty-nine, at the discretion of said Justice to be well laid on by the Town Constable.

Section 2 Be it further ordained that if any slave or slaves, or free negroes or mulattoes, shall menace, or abuse, or insult any white person, or shall use any insulting language or gestures, toward any white person within said town, he or she so offending shall, on conviction, thereof, before any Justice of the Peace in said town receive on his or her bare back any number of lashes not exceeding thirty-nine, at the discretion of said Justice, to be well laid on by the Town Constable.

Section 3rd Be it further ordained that, in any case arising under any of the provisions of any ordinance passed by said Board, respecting Slaves, that all costs that may be incurred in the apprehension, conviction or punishment of any such slave or slaves, shall be paid by the owner of such slave or slaves, and the Justice before whom the conviction is had, shall issue execution for the same, returnable as executions are returnable by law.

Section 4th Be it further ordained that if any slave, free negro or mulattoe, shall wantonly canter or gallop any horse, mare or gelding, or jack-ass or mule, within the town of Hannibal, he or she so offending, shall receive for every such offence, not less than ten nor more than twenty lashes on his or her bare back, at the discretion of the Justice before whom the conviction is had.

Section 5th Be it further ordained that not more than five slaves, free negroes, or mulattoes shall assemble at any one place at the same time within the Town of Hannibal, except in discharge of their duty to their master or owner or overseer, or unless they may have assembled at some place of worship, conducted by a white minister of the Gospel, or at some public place of worship conducted by a Negro minister, when such last named minister has previously obtained from one of the Trustees, permission to hold such meeting; and any slave or free negro or mulattoe who may offend against any provision of this section shall receive on his or her back, any number of lashes, not exceeding thirty-nine, at the discretion of the Justice before whom conviction is had.

Section 6th Be it further ordained that if any person shall, on the Sabbath Day give or sell any spiritous liquors to any slave, free negro or mulattoe, he or she offending shall be fined in any sum not exceeding twenty-five dollars for every such offence, recoverable as other fines, to the use of the Town of Hannibal.

Section 7th Be it further ordained that from and after the passage of this ordinance, no negro, mulattoe or slave, shall be permitted to hire his or her own time, or hire or contract with any person or persons, for work or labor, to be by him or her rendered or performed either directly, or indirectly, and any owner of a slave permitting such slaves to violate the provisions of this section, shall for every such offence, be fined in a sum not less than ten, nor more than one hundred dollars to be recovered before any Justice of the Peace in the Town of Hannibal for the use of the Town.

Section 8th Be it further ordained, that no slave or slaves shall be permitted to live, or keep a house or quarter of his or her Masters or owners, residing out of the limits of said Town of Hannibal; and any slave as aforesaid, who may transgress or violate the provisions of this ordinance, as contained in the 8th section hereof, he or she so offending, on conviction thereof before any Justice of the Peace within said Town shall receive on his or her bare back, not less than ten nor more than thirty-nine lashes, to be well laid on by the Town Constable.

(*Minute Book of Board of Trustees City of Hannibal 1839–1849*, Collection #1115, Manuscript Division, State Historical Society of Missouri, Columbia, Mo.)

"An act to prohibit the publication, circulation, or promulgation of the abolition doctrine."

If any person shall publish, circulate, or utter by writing, speaking or printing any facts, arguments, reasoning, or opinions, tending directly to excite any slave or slaves, or other persons of color, in this State, to rebellion, sedition, mutiny, insurrection, or murder, with intent to excite such slave or slaves, or other persons of color, to rebellion, sedition, mutiny, insurrection or murder, such person, upon conviction thereof, shall be fined in a sum not exceeding one thousand dollars, and be imprisoned in the State penitentiary for a term not exceeding two years; and for the second offence, being thereof convicted, he shall be imprisoned in the State penitentiary for a term not exceeding twenty years; and for the third offence, being thereof convicted, he shall be imprisoned in the State penitentiary during life.

(*Laws of the State of Missouri,* 2d ed. [St. Louis, Mo.: Chambers & Knapp, 1841], 3.)

Resolution of the Missouri Legislature, February 12, 1839

That whereas, the institution of domestic slavery, as it now exists in many of the States of this confederacy, whether or not a moral or political evil, was entailed on us by our ancestors, recognized by the constitution of the United States—the paramount law of the land,—and, by that same instrument, forming the solemn compact which binds these States together, entirely and alone left to be regulated by the domestic policy of the several States: and whereas the interference with that institution on the part of the citizens of other portions of the Union, among whom it may not be tolerated, is unconstitutional; a gross violation of the solemn compact subsisting between the States of the confederacy; officious, derogating from the dignity of the slave-holding States, and insulting to their sovereignty; well calculated to disturb their domestic peace, light up the torch, and plunge them amid the horrors of servile insurrection and war; disturb the friendly feeling and intercourse, which should ever subsist between the several States of the confederacy, and ultimately destroy their union, peace and happiness; and whereas we have long viewed with feelings of deep regret the disposition continually fostered and promoted by the citizens of many of the States of this Union, wantonly to intermeddle with such institution, as manifested by numerous disorganizing and insurrectionary movements; and have as fondly anticipated that the evil tendency of such a course of policy must long ere this have been seen and desisted from; but in these reasonable expectations, and calculations upon the sober sense and patriotism of our eastern brethren; we have been very disagreeably disappointed; therefore, the southern and southwestern States, in these numerous and continued acts of insult to their sovereignty, are admonished in language too plain to be misunderstood, that the dreadful crisis is actually approaching, when each of them must look out means adequate to its own protection, poise itself upon its reserved rights, and prepare for defending its domestic institutions from wanton invasion, whether from foreign or domestic enemies, "peaceably if they can, forcibly, if they must."

Resolved, That since the Constitution of the United States has no where deprived the States from regulating domestic slavery, that institution therefore is plainly and expressly left to the regulation and control of their domestic policy, and forms one among the most important features of their reserved rights.

Resolved, That the interference with such institution, on the part of citizens of other portions of the Union where it does not exist, is in direct contravention of the constitution of the United States and the solemn compact subsisting between the members of this confederacy, derogatory from the dignity of the slave holding States, grossly insulting to their sovereignty and ultimately tending to destroy the union, peace and happiness of these confederated States.

Resolved, That we approve the course of our Representatives in the Congress of the United States, for their able and manly defence of the domestic institutions of the Southern and Southwestern States, and for their uncompromising opposition to the wanton encroachments now attempting to be made upon them.

Resolved, That we view the active agents in this country in their nefarious schemes to subvert the fundamental principles of this government, in no other light than as the mere tools of a set of arch machinators, who envy the prosperity of these confederated States, and desire to effect by management, what they cannot do through force of arms—the destruction of our domestic peace and the reign of equal laws.

Resolved, That we can see in these numerous acts of aggression and interference with the domestic institutions of the southern and southwestern States, noting but wanton invasion of their reserved rights, and contemptuous insult to their dignity as sovereign and independent States; and that they have no other safe alternative left them but to adopt some efficient policy by which their domestic institutions may be protected and their peace, happiness and prosperity secured.

Resolved, That copies of this preamble and these resolutions be printed, and that the Governor be requested to transmit a copy of them to the governor of each of the States of this Unions, and one to each of the members in the Congress of the United States.

(*Laws of the State of Missouri,* 2d ed. [St. Louis, Mo.: Chambers & Knapp, 1841], 337.)

Jury Instructions Tendered by the Defense of Thompson, Work, and Burr

"That before they can find the Defendants guilty they must from the evidence in the cause—(and from no other source) find the following facts:

"1st That the defendants had possession of the slaves—(and to constitute a possession in them of said slaves, the jury must from the evidence in the Cause find that the Defendants exercised authority to restrain the movements of said slaves—or (the slaves being present—) claimed the right of control, dominion or authority over the will of the slaves.

"2nd That if they find that the Defendants were so possessed of said slaves, the jury must also find from the evidence in the Cause, that at the time of becoming so possessed of said slaves, it was the intention of said Defendants to convert the property in said slaves to their own use.

"They ask the Court further to instruct the jury—that whether Anthony met the Defendants with or without the consent of his master, still to constitute a taking of said slave by Defendants—the said slave must have been in the possession of said Defendants—as before explained—and that even such possession, cannot authorize the jury to find Defendants guilty of stealing—unless the jury also find from the evidence in the cause—that at the time, defendants had the intention to convert the property in said slaves to their own use.

"That a conversion to the use of said Defendants cannot be made out by merely showing that the Defendants were willing and desirous to give aid and assistance to said slave or slaves, in crossing the Mississippi River and in pursuing their journey to Canada—but that there must be an intention to sell or hire, or retain said slaves for their service—or otherwise to exercise acts of ownership over said slaves."

Jury Instructions Tendered by the State
(author's note: *There was no jury instruction number 5.*)

"1st That if they believe from the Evidence in this cause that James Burr and Alanson Work, did steal, take and carry away the slaves as charged in the Indictment or any one of them, and that George Thompson as charged in the Indictment was in any way aiding and abetting, then they must find them all guilty as charged in the second count of said Indictment.

"2nd That if they, the defendants Burr and Work, had the slaves, or any one of them, under their control or Government, and while so, caused the said slaves to move one step, then the taking and carrying away was completed,

"3rd That if the defendants fraudulently intended to deprive the owners of said slaves of the property and labour of said slaves, and to confer the same on them, the defendants, or on any third person or persons, other than the said owners—that is sufficient to make the stealing, taking and carrying away, Larceny,

"4th That if the jury believes there was a taking, it is no difference, whether the taking was effected by physical or moral force, if the force was sufficient to effect the object intended,

"6th That if they find from the evidence in this cause, that the defendants James Burr and Alanson Work, attempted to steal, take and carry away the slaves, or any of them as charged in the Indictment, and that George Thompson aided and abetted in such attempt, but failed in executing said attempt, then they must find them Burr and Work guilty of said attempt, and Thompson guilty as accessory before the fact of said attempt."

(Circuit Court Records of Marion County, Missouri.)

Announcement of Lectures by R. S. Finley

We are exceedingly gratified to be able to make this announcement. We have long desired to receive a visit from an agent of this institution; and we expect to derive much enjoyment, and much valuable information from the Lectures of Mr. Finley, who is not only an able man, but has devoted a great portion of his life to the investigation of the subject. We earnestly entreat our fellow-citizens to do themselves the benefit and Mr. Finley the honor, of being present during his Lectures.

In an intellectual point of view, there is no theme more attracting than the history of Africa, either ancient or modern; and certainly none is better calculated to awaken the sympathies of noble and generous natures. The American Colonization Society proposes to effect for Africa a stupendous charity; and this in a manner perfectly consistent with the constitution and laws, and all the private rights of citizens. Its operations are based upon the following propositions, which it concedes and inculcates:

1st. That slavery in the U. States is protected by the constitution and laws.

2nd. That no citizen ought, or can be deprived of his slave *without his consent*, without the violation both of the constitution and laws.

3rd. That the presence of free negroes in the country is hurtful alike to themselves, the slaves, and the masters; and that all such whether now free, or hereafter to become so, should be colonized in Africa, their fatherland.

"Colonization" is therefore antagonistical to "abolition," in its whole nature, spirit and intention. Abolition aims to liberate the slave, elevating him to an equality of condition with the master here in our midst. Colonization opposes this policy as unwise, unsafe, and in fact impossible; and ruinous, if possible, to all parties. Abolition claims the power, and asserts the propriety of passing laws for the universal and immediate emancipation of slaves. Colonization denies both; and spends its force upon the removal of such persons of color as are already free, or may be hereafter liberated, out of the country; leaving the question of emancipation where it ought to rest, in the free will and pleasure of the master, and in the control of the States alone in which it exists. Under these circumstances, it is not strange that the most deadly hostility exists between the advocates of the two systems. Poor, wandering, helpless and unfriended, the free negro population of this country compose a class of society whose condition is singularly deplorable.—Hard must be the heart that would refuse them an asylum.

With a few exceptions, the great body of this class are idle, lazy and unprincipled. They infect the slaves with their habits where their intercourse exists, and the tendency of their associations is to do harm to themselves, the slave, and the master. Their desperate condition here is believed to be the result of the degradation of their former slavery, and that prejudice against their race; which is equally destructive of all manly pride and energy.

Some twenty years ago, or more, some of our purest statesmen, foremost among whom was the great Finley, father of the present Mr. Finley, projected in their far-reaching humanity, the scheme of colonizing the free negroes of the U. States in Africa. The measure had then the combined support and favor of such men as Jefferson, Adams, Monroe, Madison,

Lowndes, Clay and Jackson, and Liberia was chosen as the site of the colony.

Since its establishment the colony has been growing; and the free negro population of the country have been slowly but surely awakening to the necessity of making their homes in Liberia, which is already merging into national importance, and is entitled to the consideration of a very respectable young nation. Its people enjoy the blessings of a well ordered and stable government, whose administration is more ably conducted by a negro population, than that of any republic in America out of these States. Agriculture, mechanism, commerce, all the branches of industry, are flourishing in Liberia. In its existence and continued success now for more than twenty years, a sublime moral spectacle is presented to the world, under whose influences the darkest prejudices is fleeing away. The happiest consequences have resulted, and are now resulting, from the efforts of the Colonization Society. The civilization of Africa, the melioration of the condition both of the free negro and the slave, by separating them from each other, and the peace of society in all slave communities, are within the scope of their influences. Above all, a means is now offered to any citizen who may desire voluntarily to emancipate his slave, to do so, in a manner that will benefit the slave, by placing him in a position where he may enjoy a real freedom in Liberia, which nothing can ever secure to him while remaining in any part of the U. States.

Mr. Finley is a man of talents, and an interesting speaker; besides, he is profoundly versed in all that concerns the movements and intentions of the society. We again earnestly request our citizens of the town and country, to come and hear him; and we assure them they will be more than delighted.

(*Palmyra Missouri Whig,* June 10, 1847.)

Dialect Stories

LIGHT FROM DARK PLACES.—"Sam Jonsing," said Pete Gumbo last night, as he met his old friend just before gun fire—"Sam Jonsing, I's mighty glad to sees you."

"You is, eh?" queried the philosophic Sam.

"Distinctly I is," retorted Pete "and I'll tell you why. It's because I wants de lucerdations ob your obserbations and 'sperience on a subjec dat's lost in de mazes ob doubt and deplexity to me. I axes you, now, wot are meant by de *dark ages* ob which we hears so much?"

"De dark ages ob de world, Pete?"

"Ezackly so, Sam."

"Wat you tinks ob dem yoursef, pete?"

"Wall, sometimes I tinks dey has deference to de times afore gas, and de roarin' borallis, and lard oil, and the oder new lights ob skyence was inwented, and den agin I's lost in de darkness wich de lights aforesaid has giben me.—But my 'pinion is notin; I axes *you* to 'spainify, Sam."

"Wall, Pete, accordin' to de lights afore me, I tinks dat de dark ages you delude to was de times wen dar wasn't no one but niggers in dis terrestshul spere ob ours—de times wen white folks wasn't no whar!"

"Dat's de trut, Sam, De trut' I knows it is. You's lit up de darkness heeah!" and Pete struck his forehead a heavy blow with his open hand, turned upon his heel, and marvelled.

(*Palmyra Missouri Whig,* February 2, 1845.)

"A Fix"—While passing through Wilson lane, a few days since, says the Albany Knickerbocker, we saw a large black turtle "dragging his slow length along" on the sidewalk, and quite a crowd had gathered to look at the "cre'tur."—Soon a danky little negro man, who had just then come along with a very small dog, looked at the turtle with apparent astonishment for a moment, and asked—

"Wha, what do you call dat ar' feller?"

"That's a turtle," answered a bystander.

"Gor-ry!—what dey do wid 'um?"

"Make soup of him."

"Soup?—yah-ha!—*what* a lookin' feller dat is to make soup ob!—Heah, Caesar, bite 'im'" said the negro to his dog, as he "stirred up" the turtle with his cane.

The dog, seeming to know a little more about "the natur of the baste" than did his master hung back a little, but finally he crawled up to get a smell of the stranger customer, when the turtle made a dive at his foot, and, seizing it in his mouth, squeezed it so unmercifully that the puppy got up some of the tallest kind of yelling, and the negro made no less noise than the dog.

"Ki-ki-ow-ow!" yelled the dog, while his master puffed like a locomotive, exclaiming—

"Gorry mighty!—you brack toad, why you not let go dat ar' dog foot!"

And, after thrashing him lustily over the shell with a sugar-cane stick, until he had broken his weapon to splinters, he seized the turtle by the head, and attempted to force him to release his hold of the dog. Unfortunately, Coffy got his thumb into the trap, with the dog's foot, and then there was music! Finally, the "bark slipped" from the negro's thumb, and he "extended his area of freedom" to such a distance that there was no immediate danger of his being harmed by the turtle, which, with "adhesiveness 17," still clung to the dog, and it was considerable diffuculty that his jaws could be opened sufficiently wide to "render Caesar that which was Caesar's." The puppy was no sooner at liberty than Cuffy sung out:—

"Heah, Caesar, come 'way from dar! An' if dat d—d 'basty plate ob soup' git our finger in him mouf agin, he may bite till him toof ache; dat's all I's got to say 'bout 'im."

The negro "put," and his dog hobbled after him, on three legs, leaving a crowd of spectators who were shaking their sides with laughter.

(*Hannibal Journal*, February 4, 1847.)

RANK IN THE ARMY, OR, A DARKIE'S DIGNITY.

After a portion of the troops had landed on the beach near Vera Cruz, on the night of the 9th of March, a body of the enemy commenced a brisk fire of small arms into the encampment. Of course, all hands were on the *qui vive*, expecting the Mexicans woud make some demonstration upon our lines during the night, and when the firing commenced, concluded there was about to be a general attack. The lines were soon formed, and not a word could be heard from the soldiery, but there was a negro who kept running from one little point of hill to another, apparently in a state of great excitement. He finally laid himself flat on his face, at full-length, and commenced working himself into the soft sand with a good deal of energy. On being asked what he was about; he replied, "I is 'fraid some ob dem 'ere copper balls will put a stop to me drawin' my rashuns." "Why, in the devil;" asked the party speaking to him, "don't you get up and fight them?" "No sir-ee!" he said, "dat's my massa's part ob de biziness; he been down to West-pint, where dey make fightin' people learn dat and yu don't ketch dis nigger medlin he-self wid odder peoples' biziness. My massa does de fightin' an' I waits on him an' nusses him. If he gets wounded we gets promoted." "You get promoted! What good will his promotion do you?" inquired the individual. "Oh, Lor' hab mercy! Dat question is been settled long time ago in dese parts down here; a colored gemman what waits on a kurnel always outranks one dat waits on a capten, an' de way we colored gemmen reg'lar makes dese volunteer niggers squat is a caution to whitefolks."

(*Palmyra Missouri Whig*, March 22, 1847.)

A RAY OF ASTRONOMY.—"Caesar," said a negro to a colored friend of his, "which dose you tink is de mose useful ob de comets, de sun or de moon?"

"Well, Caesar, I's speck de moon orte take de furst rank in dat particlar."

"Why so, nigger?"

"Becaze, de moon shines in de night, when we need the light, and de sun shines in de day time, when de light am ob no conskens."

"Well Clem, you is de most larned darkey I eber seed; I guess you us'ter sweep out a school-house for a libbin."

(*Palmyra Missouri Whig*, June 12, 1849.)

"Cuffee, what do you tink de most useful of de planets, de sun or de moon?" "Well, Sambo, I tink de moon orter take de fust rank in dat ar tickler." "Wha, wha, wha, why do you tink so, Cuffee?" "Well, I tell you, kase she shines by night, when we want light, and de sun shines by day when we do not!"—Well, Cuff, you is de greatest nigger I knose on—dat are a rale fac.

(*Palmyra Missouri Whig*, January 8, 1845.)

An Animal Upstart. A negro boy was driving a mule in Jamaica, when the animal suddenly stopped and refused to budge. "Wont go, ha?" said the boy. "Feel grand, do you? I s'pose you forgot your fader was a jack-ass?"

(*Missouri Courier*, October 18, 1849.)

"John, is my coffee hot?"

"Not yet, Massa, me spit in it, and he no fizzle."

A long ladder leaning against a house a nigger at the top, and hog rubbing himself against the foot of it—"G'way, g'way dare—you am makin' mischief."

(Both *Missouri Courier*, November 22, 1849.)

"Where's the hoe, Sambo?"

"Wid de rake, massa?"

"Well, where is the rake?"

"Wid de hoe."

"Well, well—where are they both?"

"Why, both together, massa—you 'pears to be very 'ticklar dis mornin!"

(*Missouri Courier*, May 9, 1850.)

ETHIOPIAN PHILOSOPHY.—"Mr. Crow, can you explain to de subscriber why dat 'licious wegitable called de nutmeg neber comes to maturity?"

"Neber comes to maturity?"

"Yes; why dey am always small potatoes?"

"Why dey always small 'taters?"

"Yes, Mr. Crow. Why dey neber get to be some punkins?"

"Why dey neber"—

"Yes, yes, Mr. Crow. "Why don't de nutmegs, as a class, grow large instead of always growin' small?"

"No, Julius Caesar, I don't know nuffin about it. You must ax some gardner man about wegitables."

"Well, Mr. Crow, I kin tell you why nutmegs, as a class, don't grow larger. It's because ebery indiwidual nutmeg knows dat de largest nutmeg in de world am liable to come across a grater!"

(*Hannibal Journal,* March 26, 1853.)

Sam Clemens's Article in the Philadelphia *American Courier*

DEAR COURIER-

The first house was built in this city about sixteen years ago. Then the wild war-whoop of the Indian resounded where now rise our stately buildings, and their bark canoes were moored where now land our noble steamers; here they traded their skins for guns, powder, &c. But where now are the children of the forest? Hushed is the war-cry—no more does the light canoe cut the crystal waters of the proud Mississippi; but the remnant of those once powerful tribes are torn asunder and scattered abroad, and they now wander far, far from the homes of their childhood and the graves of their fathers.

This town is situated on the Mississippi river, about one hundred and thirty miles above St. Louis, and contains a population of about three thousand. A charter has been granted by the State for a railroad, to commence at Hannibal, and terminate at St. Joseph, on the western border of Missouri. The State takes $1,500,000 of stock in the road; the counties along the route have also subscribed liberally, and already more than one-third the amount requisite for its construction has been subscribed. The manner in which the State takes stock is this: for every $50,000 that the company spends in the construction of the road, the State gives her bonds for that amount, until the $1,500,000 is paid.

Within this year a plank-road will be built from Hannibal to New London, a small town in the adjoining county of Ralls, and about twelve miles from here. Every dollar of stock in this improvement has already been subscribed.

Your Eastern people seem to think this country is a barren, uncultivated region, with a population consisting of heathens. A man came out here from your part of the world, and in writing home to his friends, made the following remark: — "This is the queerest country I ever saw; a little cloud will come up, about as big as your hat, and directly a clap of thunder will knock the bottom out of it, and, Jerusalem! how it 'ill rain!'"

Among the curiosities of this place we may mention the *Cave*, which is about three miles below the city. It is of unknown length; it has innumerable passages, which are not unlike the streets of a large city. The ceiling arches over, and from it hang beautiful stalactites, which sparkle in the light of the torches, and remind one of the fairy palaces spoken of in the Arabian Nights. There are several springs, rivers, and wells, some of which are of unknown depth. Directly over one of the narrow passages, and supported merely by two small pieces of stone, which jut out from the main walls on either side, hangs an immense rock, end down, which measures ten feet in length by three feet in diameter.

Yours, &c., S. L. C.

HANNIBAL, MO., March 25,1852.

Article on Rumored Abolitionist Activities

ABDUCTION OF SLAVES.—In last week's paper, we stated that a rumor existed of the abduction of slaves by the citizens of Iowa from their owners in Missouri, and a riot growing out of the affair. We then doubted the whole story. We knew than an abolition paper had been commenced in Fort Madison, the perusal of which kind of papers, is generally well calculated to arouse the misdirected sympathies of the credulous, but we did not for a moment imagine that with all the hot-headed zeal of the leaders of any portion of the citizens of Iowa could be induced to violate the rights of his neighbor. The Republican of the 10th nt. A correspondence from Alexandria announces that eight negroes had been stolen from that place by citizens of this State. We have no sympathies for violators of the law, and he who entices away or conceals a negro slave so that his master may not get him again, is as criminal as if he had stolen that man's horse and the law will hold the wrong doer responsible. Individual opinion in regard to certain laws, afford no excuse for a violation of those laws, and we have yet to see a single person who does not condemn the act as a shameless violation of private rights and with all engaged in the matter, speedy and ample justice.

(*Hannibal Journal*, June 29, 1848 [from the *Keokuk Register*].)

[*Comments Buchanan in the same issue:*]
Abduction of Slaves.

On our first page will be found an article from the Keokuk Register, in relation to the abduction of slaves. We also noticed a similar article a week or two since in the Telegraphic Dispatch, printed at the same place. There appears to be no doubt of the fact that slaves have been successfully abducted from this State, through the instrumentality referred to, and have been lost to their rightful owners.

These enthusiasts, these Fanatics, as they are called by some, but who deserve no softer appellation than Thieves, have commenced their opperations in a new quarter. Heretofore our only danger has been from Illinois, in which direction we had some safeguard in the fact that the Mississippi River intervened. Now a more dangerous outlet is opened in the North in the facilities of getting to Salem in Iowa, which is said to be the headquarters of these depredators and in which direction their is no similar barrier, the River Desmoin almost at all times being easily crossed by an individual without assistance from others.

Selected Bibliography

Newspapers

Cincinnati Daily Gazette
Cincinnati Enquirer
Hannibal Commercial Advertiser
Hannibal Daily Messenger
Hannibal Gazette
Hannibal Journal
Hannibal Journal and Western Union
Hannibal Missouri Courier
Hannibal Southern Sentinel
Hannibal Tri-Weekly Messenger
Hannibal Weekly Messenger
Hannibal Western Union
Hannibal Whig Messenger
Liberator
Memphis Eagle and Enquirer
New York World
Palmyra Missouri Whig
Palmyra Weekly Whig
Philadelphia American Courier

Collections

Historical Society of Quincy and Adams County, Illinois
Mark Twain Papers and Project, University of California, Berkeley
Roberta and Hurley Hagood Collection, Hannibal, Missouri
Rogers Papers, New-York Historical Society
State Historical Society of Missouri, Columbia

Public Documents

Kennedy, Jos. L. G. *Statistical View of the United States Embracing Its Territory, Population—White, Free Colored, and Slave—Moral and Social Condition, Industry, Property, and Revenue: The Detailed Statistics of Cities, Towns, and Counties; Being a Compendium of the Seventh Census.* Washington, D.C.: A. O. P. Nicholson, Public Printer, 1854.

Eighth Census of the United States, 1860. Washington, D.C.: Government Printing Office, 1866.

Laws of a Public and General Nature of the State of Missouri, Passed between 1824 and 1836. Jefferson City, Mo.: W. Lusk & Son, 1842.

Laws of the State of Missouri, 1836. St. Louis: Chambers & Knapp, 1841.

Laws of the State of Missouri, 1838. Jefferson City, Mo.: Calvin Gunn—Jeffersonian Office, 1838.

Laws of the State of Missouri, 1840. Jefferson City, Mo.: Calvin Gunn—Jeffersonian Office, 1841.

Laws of the State of Missouri, 1842–1843. Jefferson City, Mo.: Allen Hammond, 1843.

Laws of the State of Missouri, 1846–1847. Jefferson City, Mo.: James Lusk, Public Printer, 1847.

Laws of the State of Missouri, 1852. Jefferson City, Mo.: James Lusk, Public Printer, 1853.

Revised Statutes of the State of Missouri, 1855. Jefferson City, Mo.: James Lusk, Public Printer, 1855.

Laws of the State of Missouri, 1858. Jefferson City, Mo.: C. J. Corwin, Public Printer, 1859.

Laws of the State of Missouri, 1859. Jefferson City, Mo.: W. G. Cheeney, Public Printer, 1860.

Laws of the State of Missouri, February 27, 1860. Jefferson City, Mo.: W. G. Cheeney, Public Printer, 1860.

Laws of the State of Missouri, December 31, 1860. Jefferson City, Mo.: W. G. Cheeney, Public Printer, 1861.

Manuscript Census Schedules for the State of Missouri: Slaves. 1840, 1850, and 1860.

Manuscript Census Schedules for the State of Missouri: Population. 1840, 1850, and 1860.

Preliminary Report on the Eighth Census, 1860. Washington, D.C.: Government Printing Office, 1862.

Other Sources

Adams County Anti-Slavery Society. *Narrative of Facts Respecting Alanson Work, Jas. E. Burr and Geo. Thompson.* Quincy, Ill.: Quincy Whig Office, 1841.

Adamson, Hans Christian. *Rebellion in Missouri: 1861.* New York: Chilton Company, 1961.

Armon, Dahlia, ed. *Huck Finn and Tom Sawyer among the Indians and Other Unfinished Stories.* Berkeley: University of California, 1989.

Balme, J. R. *American States, Churches, and Slavery.* London: Hamilton, Adams, & Co., 1863.

Bellamy, Donnie Duglie. "Slavery, Emancipation, and Racism in Missouri, 1850–1865." Ph.D. diss., University of Missouri, 1971.

Bennett, Franklin Howard. *The Hannibal and St. Joseph Railroad and the Development of Northern Missouri, 1847–1870: A Study of Land and Colonization Policies.* Cambridge: Harvard University Press, 1950.

Benton, Thomas Hart. *Thirty Years' View; or, A History of the Working of the American Government for Thirty Years, from 1820 to 1850.* 2 vols. New York: D. Appleton & Co., 1856.

Berlin, Ira. *Many Thousands Gone: The First Two Centuries of Slavery in North America.* Cambridge: Harvard University Press, 1998.

Blassingame, John W., ed. *Slave Testimony: Two Centuries of Letters, Speeches, Interviews, and Autobiographies.* Baton Rouge: Louisiana State University Press, 1977.

Blathwait, Raymond, "Mark Twain on Humor . . . T. B. Aldrich the Wittiest Man." *New York World* (May 31, 1891): 26.

Branch, Edgar Marquess, and Robert H. Hirst, eds. *Early Tales and Sketches.* Vol. 1. Berkeley: University of California Press, 1979.

Branch, Edgar Marquess et al., eds. *Mark Twain's Letters, 1853–1866.* Berkeley: University of California 1988.

Brashear, M. M. *Mark Twain, Son of Missouri.* Durham: University of North Carolina Press, 1934.

Brown, William Wells. *Narrative of William W. Brown, a Fugitive Slave.* Boston: Antislavery Office, 1847.

Chesnut, Mary Boykin. *A Diary from Dixie,* edited by Ben Ames Williams. Boston: Houghton Mifflin Company, 1949.

Christensen, Lawrence O., William E. Foley, Gary R. Kremer, and Kenneth H. Winn, eds., *Dictionary of Missouri Biography.* Columbia: University of Missouri Press, 1999.

Cleveland, Henry, ed. *Alexander H. Stephens, in Public and Private.* Philadelphia: National, 1866.

Congressional Quarterly's *Guide to U.S. Elections.* Washington, D.C.: Congressional Quarterly, Inc., 1985.

Dabney, Robert L. *A Defense of Virginia.* New York: Negro Universities, 1969.

Dalcho, Frederick. *Practical Considerations Founded on the Scriptures.* Charleston, S.C.: A. E. Miller, 1823.

Dillon, Merton L. *Elijah P. Lovejoy, Abolitionist Editor.* Urbana: University of Illinois Press, 1961.

Dodds, Elreta. *What the Bible Really Says about Slavery: This and Other Information on the Issue Slavery as It Applies to History and Religion.* Detroit: Press toward the Mark Publications, 2000.

Douglass, Frederick. *Narrative of the Life of Frederick Douglass.* Boston: Bedford/St. Martins.

Escott, Paul D. *Slavery Remembered: A Record of Twentieth-Century Slave Narratives.* Chapel Hill: University of North Carolina Press, 1979.

Ewing, Raymond. *Mark Twain's Steamboat Years: The Years of Command.* Hannibal, Mo.: Raymond P. Ewing, 1981.

Federal Writers Project. *Slave Narratives, Texas Narratives, Part 1.* St. Clair Shores, Mich.: Scholarly Press, 1976.

Fishkin, Shelley Fisher. *Lighting out for the Territory.* New York: Oxford University Press, 1997.

Fogel, Robert W., and Stanley L. Engerman. *Time on the Cross: The Economics of American Negro Slavery.* Boston: Little, Brown, 1974.

Franklin, John Hope, and Loren Schweninger. *Runaway Slaves: Rebels on the Plantation.* New York: Oxford University Press, 1999.

Frazier, Harriet C. *Slavery and Crime in Missouri, 1773–1865.* Jefferson, N.C.: McFarland & Co., 2001.

Genovese, Eugene D. *The Political Economy of Slavery.* New York: Random House, 1965.

———. *The Slaveholders' Dilemma.* Columbia: University of South Carolina Press, 1992.

Grant, U. S. *Personal Memoirs of U. S. Grant.* 2 vols. New York: Charles L. Webster & Co., 1885.

Greene, Lorenzo J., Gary R. Kremer, and Antonio F. Holland. *Missouri's Black Heritage.* Rev. ed. Columbia: University of Missouri Press, 1993.

Grimes, Absalom. *Absalom Grimes: Confederate Mail Runner.* New Haven, Conn.: Yale University Press, 1926.

Hagood, J. Hurley, and Roberta Roland Hagood. *Hannibal, Too.* Marceline, Mo.: Walsworth Publishing Co., 1986.

———. *Hannibal Yesterdays.* Marceline, Mo.: Jostens, 1992.

———. *The Story of Hannibal.* Hannibal, Mo.: Standard Printing Co., 1976.

Haines, Harold. *The Callaghan Mail, 1821–1859.* Hannibal, Mo.: Harold Haines, 1946.

Hemesath, Sr. Caroline, O.S.F. *From Slave to Priest: A Biography of the Rev. Augustine Tolton.* Chicago: Franciscan Herald Press, 1973.

Hermann, Janet S., "The McIntosh Affair." *Missouri Historical Society Bulletin* 26 (January 1970): 123.

Heyrman, Christine Leigh. *Southern Cross.* New York: Alfred A. Knopf, 1997.

Holcombe, R. I. *History of Marion County, Missouri.* St. Louis: E. F. Perkins, 1884.

Howells, William Dean. *My Mark Twain.* Mineola, N.Y.: Dover Publications, 1997.

Hurt, R. Douglas. *Agriculture and Slavery in Missouri's Little Dixie.* Columbia: University of Missouri Press, 1992.

Jackson, Francis. *Account Book of Francis Jackson, Treasurer, the Vigilance Committee of Boston.* Boston: Bostonian Society, 1953.

Johnson, Walter. *Soul by Soul.* Cambridge: Harvard University Press, 1999.

Kirkpatrick, James C. *Official Manual, State of Missouri, 1973–1974.* Jefferson City, Mo.: Von Hoffman Press, 1973.

Kolchin, Peter. *American Slavery, 1619–1877.* New York: Hill & Wang, 1993.

Lee, George R. *Slavery North of St. Louis.* Canton, Mo.: Lewis County Historical Society, n.d.

Leigh, Edwin. *Bird's-eye Views of Slavery in Missouri.* St. Louis: Keith & Woods, C. C. Bailey, James M. Crawford, C. Witter, 1862.

Lord, Nathan. *A Northern Presbyter's Second Letter.* Boston: Little, Brown, 1855.

Lovejoy, Joseph, and Lovejoy, Owen, eds. *Memoir of the Rev. Elijah P. Lovejoy.* New York: John S. Taylor, 1838.

Marvin, E. M. *The Life of Rev. William Goff Caples, of the Missouri Conference of the Methodist Episcopal Church, South.* St. Louis: Southwestern Book & Publishing Co., 1870.

Masur, Louis P. *1831, Year of Eclipse.* New York: Hill & Wang, 2001.

Mayer, Henry. *All on Fire: William Lloyd Garrison and the Abolition of Slavery.* New York: St. Martin's Press, 1998.

McCaine, Alexander. *Slavery Defended from Scripture.* Baltimore: William Woddy, 1842.

McCandless, Perry. *A History of Missouri, Volume 2: 1820 to 1860.* Columbia: University of Missouri Press, 1972.

McCrary, George. *Sketches of War History, 1861–1865*. Vol. 1, *War Papers and Personal Reminiscences, 1861–1865*. St. Louis: Bechtold & Co., 1892.

McPherson, James M. *Battle Cry of Freedom: The Civil War Era*. New York: Ballantine Press, 1988.

Mell, Patrick H. *Slavery*. Penfield, Ga.: Benjamin Brantly, 1844.

Meltzer, Milton. *The Black Americans*. New York: HarperCollins, 1984.

Meyer, Duane. *The Heritage of Missouri: A History*. St. Louis: State Publishing Co., 1970.

Middleton, Stephen. *The Black Laws in the Old Northwest*. Westport, Conn.: Greenwood Press, 1993.

Monaghan, Jay. *Civil War on the Western Border, 1854–1865*. Lincoln: University of Nebraska Press, 1955.

Neider, Charles, ed. *The Autobiography of Mark Twain*. New York: Harper & Row, 1959.

Osofsky, Gilbert, ed. *Puttin' on Ole Massa*. New York: Harper Torchbooks, 1969.

Overton, Richard. *Burlington Route: A History of the Burlington Lines*. New York: Alfred A. Knopf, 1965.

Paine, Albert Bigelow. *Mark Twain: A Biography*. New York: Harper & Brothers, 1912.

Parrish, William E. *A History of Missouri, Volume 3: 1860 to 1875*. Columbia: University of Missouri Press, 1973.

Perkins, E. F. *History of Marion County, Missouri*. St. Louis: E. F. Perkins, 1884.

Perret, Geoffrey. *Ulysses S. Grant, Soldier and President*. New York: Random House, 1997.

Peterson, Thomas. *Ham and Japheth: The Mythic World of Whites in the Antebellum South*. Metuchen, N.J.: Scarecrow Press, 1978.

———. "The Myth of Ham among White, Antebellum Southerners." Ph.D. diss., Stanford University, 1975.

Pettit, Arthur G. *Mark Twain and the South*. Lexington: University Press of Kentucky, 1974.

Poole, Stafford. *Church and Slave in Perry County, Missouri, 1818–1865*. Lewiston, N.Y.: Edwin Mellen Press, 1986.

Powers, Ron. *Dangerous Water*. New York: Basic Books, 1999.

Rasmussen, R. Kent. *Mark Twain A to Z*. New York: Oxford University Press, 1995.

Rawick, George P., ed. *The American Slave: A Composite Autobiography*. Supplement, series 1, volume 2. Westport, Conn.: Greenwood Publishing Co., 1977.

Sattelmeyer, Robert, "Did Sam Clemens Take the Abolitionists for a Ride?" *New England Quarterly* (June 1995): 294–99.

Simms, William Gilmore. *The Morals of Slavery.* New York: Negro Universities, 1968.

Sloan, James A. *The Great Question Answered.* Memphis: Hutton, Ballaway, 1857.

Snead, Thomas L. *The Fight for Missouri.* New York: Charles Scribner's Sons, 1888.

The Southern States, Embracing a Series of Papers Condensed from the Earlier Volumes of De Bow's Review, upon Slavery and the Slave Institutions of the South. Washington D.C.: J. D. B. De Bow, 1856.

Stamp, Kenneth M. *America in 1857.* New York: Oxford University Press, 1990.

Sweets, Henry. *The Hannibal, Missouri, Presbyterian Church: A Sesquicentennial History.* Hannibal, Mo.: Hannibal Presbyterian Church, 1984.

Tadman, Michael. *Speculators and Slaves.* Madison: University of Wisconsin Press, 1996.

Taft, William H. *Missouri Newspapers.* Columbia: University of Missouri Press, 1964.

Thomas, Scott G. *The Pursuit of the White House: A Handbook of Presidential Statistics and History.* New York: Greenwood Press, 1987.

Thompson, George. *Prison Life and Reflections.* Hartford, Conn.: A. Work, 1853.

Trexler, Harrison. *Slavery in Missouri, 1804–1865.* Baltimore: Johns Hopkins Press, 1914.

Twain, Mark. *Adventures of Huckleberry Finn.* New York: Oxford University Press, 1996.

———. *The Adventures of Tom Sawyer.* New York: Oxford University Press, 1996.

———. "The Old-Fashioned Printer." In *Mark Twain Speaking,* edited by Paul Fatout, 200–206. Ames: University of Iowa Press, 1978.

———. *Pudd'nhead Wilson.* New York: Oxford University Press, 1996.

Wallace, David. *John Rogers: The People's Sculptor.* Middletown, Conn.: Wesleyan University Press, 1967.

Way, Frederick. *Way's Packet Directory 1848–1894: Passenger Steamboats of the Mississippi River System.* Athens: Ohio University Press, 1983.

Wecter, Dixon. *Sam Clemens of Hannibal.* Boston: Houghton Mifflin Co., 1961.

Weld, Theodore Dwight. *American Slavery as It Is: Testimony of a Thousand Witnesses.* New York: American Anti-Slavery Society, 1839.

Wellman, Paul I. *The House Divides.* Garden City, N.Y.: Doubleday, 1966.

Index

Pages in italics refer to illustrations.